ADOLESCENCE
IN A MOROCCAN TOWN

■ A volume in the series
Adolescents in a Changing World

EDITED BY BEATRICE B. WHITING AND
JOHN W.M. WHITING

Project advisors:

Irven DeVore
Carol Gilligan
George W. Goethals
Jerome Kagan
Robert A. LeVine

Adolescence in a Moroccan Town

Making Social Sense

Susan Schaefer Davis
and
Douglas A. Davis

RUTGERS UNIVERSITY PRESS

New Brunswick and London

Copyright © 1989 by Rutgers, The State University
All Rights Reserved
Manufactured in the United States of America

Library of Congress Cataloging-in-Publication Data
Davis, Susan Schaefer.
   Adolescence in a Moroccan town : making social sense / Susan Schaefer Davis and
Douglas A. Davis.
      p.   cm. — (Adolescents in a changing world)
   Bibliography: p.
   Includes index.
   ISBN 0-8135-1368-5
   1. Teenagers—Morocco—Zaouia—Social conditions.   2. Zaouia
(Morocco)—Social conditions.   3. Zaouia (Morocco)—Social life and
customs.   I. Davis, Douglas A., 1943–   .   II. Title.   III. Series.
HQ799.M82Z363 1989
305.2′35′09—dc19   88-16897
                                                                              CIP

British Cataloging-in-Publication information available

To the memory of
Hajj Mbarek Belasri

الله يرحمه

■ Contents

■ Foreword

to Adolescents in a Changing World series
BEATRICE B. WHITING
JOHN. W. M. WHITING

Few periods of the human life cycle have generated as much interest, or as much concern, as adolescence. The psychological, behavioral, and physical changes that occur at puberty are dramatic and have been the focus of much research by psychologists, educators, and sociologists. The study of adolescence has recently become a priority research topic among many private and government granting agencies, largely as a response to the increase in adjustment problems among American adolescents: alcohol and drug abuse, teenage suicide, juvenile delinquency, and teenage pregnancy. The study of adolescence is important not only because there is an urgent need to understand the socially destructive aspects of this life stage, but also because knowledge of this life stage can contribute greatly to a general understanding of the social, psychological, and physical aspects of human development in our own and other cultures.

Only recently have anthropologists turned their attention to the study of adolescence. Other than Margaret Mead's classic work *Coming of Age in Samoa*, few anthropologists have entered the field with the primary intention of conducting research on the adolescent experience in another society. While many ethnographies contain data on initiation rites, age grades, marriage practices, and premarital sexual behavior, all of which are important to the study of adolescence, the reporting of these topics has often been anecdotal in nature. For this reason we have organized and edited this series of volumes describing adolescence in seven different societies. These works are the product of years of fieldwork, data analysis, and writing by the staff and fellows of the Harvard Adolescence Project. These ethnographies will contribute to our knowledge of human development in other societies and perhaps stimulate similar research in other cultures on this fascinating stage of life.

Our interest in the cross-cultural study of adolescence is a natural outgrowth of our work on child development. Over the years we have had the opportunity to study the social behavior of children in a variety of cultures. Either individually or together, we have made field observations on American Indian children, the Kwoma of New Guinea, the Yoruba of Nigeria, the Kikuyu of Kenya, and preschool children in the United States. We have also directed several cross-cultural projects on child socialization, including the Six Cultures study and the socialization part of Florence and Clyde Kluckhohn's study of values in the American Southwest. Most recently, as directors of the Child Development Research Unit of the University of Nairobi, we have had the opportunity to explore the patterns of family life among nine different cultural groups in Kenya.

Our involvement in these studies has provided us with a rich, cross-cultural data base on child development. We have learned that although there are many dramatic differences in the behavior of children across cultures, the common features are also striking. Some of these commonalities are particularly relevant to the study of adolescence. For example, in none of the cultures we have studied were boys and girls adequately prepared for the sudden surge of sex hormones that announce the onset of puberty. We have discovered that, in many respects, the socialization of children is counterproductive preparation for this event. Presumably as a consequence of the incest taboo, free and frank talk about sex is inhibited between parents and children. In none of the societies we have studied, nor in any other that we know of, do adults copulate in public. As a result, the sex act, from the child's perspective, is shrouded in secrecy and mystery.

Although adolescence requires many changes in the life-styles of girls and boys, the cultural scripts for social and economic behavior are more clearly formulated and more easily transmitted than those for sexual behavior. Since in late childhood same-sex companions predominate, learning appropriate heterosexual behavior and finding an appropriate mate are important tasks of adolescents. The hormonal changes that take place also require significant adjustment in self-image and emotions. Our studies focus on the changes in friendship formation, peer group relations, parent-child interactions, school achievement, self-image, and cognitive development.

In 1978, working with Robert Levine at the Laboratory of Human Development at the Harvard Graduate School of Education, we sponsored a postdoctoral fellow, Carol Worthman, to initiate a study of Kikuyu adolescence. A biological anthropologist interested in human growth, Carol Worthman conducted her research in the community of Ngeca, Kenya, a site where we had previously done fieldwork on Kikuyu children. While Worthman's study concentrated primarily upon the biological parameters of adolescent growth, it also focused upon the relationship between physical development and cognitive/behavioral changes. The success of this research proved to us the feasibility of conducting a multifactorial study of adolescence, thus laying the foundation for a larger cross-cultural study of children convinced us that a similar design could be utilized for the study of adolescence.

In order to ensure the multidisciplinary nature of the project, we persuaded a group of our colleagues at Harvard to join us in planning the project. Clinical and personality psychology were represented by Carol Gilligan and George Goethals, child development by Jerome Kagan, biological anthropology by Peter Ellison and Irven DeVore, and psychological anthropology by Robert LeVine and the two of us. Irven DeVore agreed to accept the role of senior investigator.

We all agreed that the Harvard Adolescence Project should consist of field studies carried out in different regions of the world in cultures representing varying degrees of complexity. We also agreed that our sampling universe in each field site should consist of some bounded microcommunity, such as a band, a hamlet, or a neighborhood. We had used such a unit in our cross-cultural studies of child rearing, calling it a PSU (primary social unit). Briefly defined, a PSU is a small group of households (thirty to forty) which sets itself off from the larger society in such a way that it has some sort of group identification, shares frequent face-to-face interaction among its members, and possesses temporal and/or spatial stability. The PSU has the advantage of being the most appropriate social unit for using standard ethnographic research techniques, such as participant observation and informant interviewing.

Knowing that most ethnographic studies require a prolonged "settling-in" period during which the researcher learns the native language and becomes acquainted with the members of the community, we decided to select experienced field-workers who had already done extensive research in some other culture and who would be willing to return to that society to carry out a study of adolescence.

To implement the above plans, we applied for and received a post-doctoral training grant from the National Institute of Mental Health (grant number MH14066-06,07,08) that would support ten fellows for two years each. Additional support for data analysis was provided by the William T. Grant Foundation. The fellows chosen were Douglas D. and Wanni Wibulswasdi Anderson, Victoria K. Burbank, Richard G. Condon, Douglas A. and Susan Schaefer Davis, Marida C. Hollos, Philip E. Leis, Mitchell S. Ratner, and Carol Worthman. The field sites listed from east to west included: the Inuit (Copper Eskimo) of Holman located on Victoria Island in the Central Canadian Arctic; the Australian aborigines of Mangrove located in Arnhemland, Northern Australia; the Thai Muslims of Nipa Island located on the southwestern coast of Thailand; the Kikuyu of Ngeca located in the Central Province of Kenya, twenty miles north of Nairobi; the Ijo of Ebiama and Opuware located in the central part of the Niger Delta in southern Nigeria; the Romanians of Baisoara located in the foothills of the inner Carpathian mountains; and the Moroccan Muslims of Zawiya located in North Central Morocco.

During the initial training period, a series of seminars was held in which the project's staff members and postdoctoral fellows gave presentations on topics relating to adolescent development. These seminar presentations proved helpful not only in identifying important issues in the field of adolescent development, but in assisting the project directors and fellows in developing research methods with crosscultural applications. In addition, the information and insights provided by the research fellows on their particular field sites helped immensely in developing a research strategy that could be applied reasonably in all the research settings.

It was clear from the beginning of our discussions that no single definition of adolescence would serve all purposes. Since we were approaching adolescence from a multidisciplinary perspective, both the physiological and sociocultural definitions of adolescence were necessary to incorporate into the research methodology. Our basic assumption was that while the physiological changes that occur at adolescence are universal to all human populations, the social and cultural reactions to these physical maturational changes are not. Thus, while one culture may celebrate puberty publicly, subjecting individuals to a se-

ries of initiation rites and expecting a consequent change in the behavior of initiates, in other societies the physiological markers are a
private matter.

Physiological definitions of adolescence, such as the interval between the beginning of the growth spurt and the attainment of full
skeletal maturity or the interval between adrenarche and the attainment of full fecundity, could ideally be objectively measured through
hormone assays in all the field sites. Theoretically, such physiological
measures would provide the most valid comparison of adolescent maturation across cultures. Unfortunately, the logistical problems associated
with such data collection as well as the social constraints encountered
in most of the field sites prevented this type of data from being collected. (Only in Ngeca was the field-worker able to make such hormone assays.) As a result, we decided to concentrate upon the growth
spurt for our physiological measure. Thus, the children at each field
site were measured twice during the fieldwork period—once near the
beginning and a second time near the end of the study period. From
these measurements of height and weight the field-workers were able
to calculate a growth rate for each child and from this determine his or
her status with respect to physical maturation.

These measures of physical maturation were essential to obtain
since we hoped to examine the effect the maturation process had upon
such things as friendship formation, cognitive development, peer
group relations, self-image, gender identity, and so forth. For example,
does the young girl who has menstruated for the first time have a different self-image than the girl who is two to three years past menarche? Does the young boy who has just entered the growth spurt have
a different gender identity than a boy who has attained full skeletal
maturity? By combining our measures of physical maturation (as an
independent variable) with other types of social and psychological data
(as dependent variables) we hoped to address these questions for all
the societies under investigation.

It was much more difficult, however, to operationalize a sociocultural definition of adolescence. Since we assumed that societies utilized different strategies for identifying and managing adolescence, it
was not feasible to develop precise definitions that had any degree of
cross-cultural comparability. In the end, we decided upon a broad definition: the transitional period between the end of childhood and the
attainment of adult social status. This broad definition made it essential for our field-workers to examine local definitions of adolescence,

which we assumed would vary among the seven cultures in our study. Thus, where one culture might rely upon physical maturation to mark the individual's transition into adolescence, another culture might rely solely upon chronological age as the criterion for entry into this stage. It was also theoretically possible that a society might not even recognize or name a transitional period between childhood and adulthood. As a result, the challenge to our field-workers was to remain as sensitive as possible to indigenous "folk theories" of human maturation.

To solve the practical problem of choosing a sample of subjects to be studied at each field site, we decided to select a single physiological marker that was transculturally recognized. The mean age of menarche was chosen for this purpose. For many of our field sites, an estimate of the mean age of menarche was available from previously published demographic and/or growth studies. For those field sites lacking such published estimates, the field-workers would have to collect data from postmenarcheal girls and women, which could then be averaged to produce an estimate of the mean age of menarche. This estimate could then be used as the anchor point for the selection of a study population that would include a group of preadolescents as well as a group of adolescents. Previous research on adolescent growth indicates that a ten-year interval centered on the mean age of menarche will include both the beginning of physiological adolescence for most of the early-maturing females and the end of physiological adolescence for most late-maturing females. Thus, for middle-class American girls for whom the mean age of menarche is thirteen, the catchment period would run from eight to eighteen years of age. Although there is no equivalent marker of physical maturation for males, we took advantage of the fact that males mature about a year later than females, and added a year to the interval used for females.

Ideally, we believed the sample size should range from eighty to ninety individuals. All of these individuals would be subjected to our physical measures of height and weight, while smaller subsamples would be subjected to clinical interviews, cognitive testing, behavioral observations, and a number of other structured and unstructured interviews designed to examine the social and psychological aspects of adolescence. Sample and subsample sizes would, of course, vary from one field site to the next, depending upon such things as community size and accessibility of informants. (The actual problems encountered in sample selection and informant interviewing were unique to each setting and are discussed in each of the volumes in this series.)

At the end of the training period, the staff and fellows produced a detailed field guide for the cross-cultural study of adolescence. This field guide represented the consensus of the research group concerning types of data to be collected and the manner of their collection. The document was developed in order to ensure a maximum degree of comparability among the field sites included in the study. The manual also suggested specific hypotheses to be tested and the methods for doing so. In line with the multidisciplinary focus of the project, we decided to draw upon the theories and hypotheses of a number of disciplines. The field manual included detailed discussions of research methodology (site selection, sampling procedures, genealogical and demographic data collection, psychological testing procedures, and methods for making physical measurements) as well as discussions on the substantive topics to be covered (parent-child relations, peer group formation, friendship, games and play activities, sexual activity, cognitive development, schooling, religious activities, pair-bonding, rites of passage, work, daily activities, and deviance).

With the training sessions over and the field guide complete, the researchers departed for their respective field sites, where the average stay was from nine to twelve months. The project directors and researchers maintained as much contact with one another as was possible, given the isolation of some of the field sites. In some cases, letters took several months to go halfway around the world. Nevertheless, all of us felt it important for the researchers to stay in contact with one another in order to share problems encountered and modifications made in the research design.

By February of 1983, all of the researchers reconvened at Harvard to begin the task of comparing and analyzing the extensive data that had been collected. Again, a series of seminars were held in which information was exchanged among all the project's participants. This phase of the research proved to be most exciting and stimulating as we saw the ultimate goals of the research begin to fall in place. Our research fellows returned with interesting observations and innovative ideas which were freely shared.

In the process of analyzing this extensive cross-cultural data base, all of us agreed that the first order of business should be the writing of a series of ethnographies providing detailed descriptions of the adolescent experience in each of the cultures. These would provide the necessary framework upon which later theoretical and comparative papers could be built.

Given the rapid rate of social change occurring throughout the world in general and in the field sites of the Harvard Adolescence Project in particular, we have decided to call this series Adolescents in a Changing World. With the publication of these ethnographically rich volumes by the fellows of the Harvard Adolescence Project, we hope that our cross-cultural and multidisciplinary examination of adolescence will contribute a much needed perspective to this fascinating stage of human development.

■ Acknowledgments

This work on the youth of Zawiya reflects our interest in that community over a period of twenty years. Our study of local adolescence and the construction of this volume have occupied much of the past seven years. During such a long period many debts accumulate. We have been exceptionally fortunate in our friends and colleagues in Morocco, at Haverford, and at Harvard, and we want to thank at least a few of them publicly.

Our old friends Hamid Elasri and Aziza Belasri helped daily with the collection of data, the running of our Zawiya household, the interpretation of results, and the thousand other details friends share in each others' lives; to each of them our warmest *baraka llah ufik*. Mjid Elasri was a constant visitor, a tireless helper, and an ever-enthusiastic reporter on the adolescent experience; he has our warmest wishes for the future. Among many other Zawiyans Fatna Khazzariya, Izza Abdullah, Qasm Elasri, and Fatna mrt Qasm will always be treasured friends. Thanks too to Si Mohamed Belayachi for helping us with data collection and to Si Mohamed Benayyad. These friends and dozens of other Zawiya residents welcomed us to their community and allowed us to share their lives in the interest of understanding how children become adults; we hope we have done them justice. For many years Mohamed Najmi has been a treasured friend, cultural guide, and patient teacher about all matters Islamic and Arabic; his careful discussion of an earlier draft of the manuscript, as well as his genius for translation, were indispensible. We are also grateful to Mohamed Dounas for his perceptive translation of many taped interviews. Among a host of other

Moroccan friends we thank Fatima Mernissi for her interest in our work and for many helpful discussions and Ahmed and Kathy Morabet for their boundless hospitality and encouragement. Warm thanks too to Abdelatif Benabdeslam, Mustapha Benyaklef, Alison Geist, and Gary Gregg for advice and help. Abderrahman Elqasmi kindly assisted us in our reentry to Zawiya, and Ted Curran offered the perfect escape on hot summer weekends, as did Ruby Apsler.

Back in the United States, Elizabeth Fernea and Lila Abu-Lughod have read drafts and given good advice from which we hope we have benefited. Jennie Keith and Sid Perloe have helped over the years by giving us the friendly criticism and encouragement with which friends help friends complete ambitious projects. To each of them and a host of special people at Haverford, warm gratitude and a promise of *tajines* to come. Marlie Wasserman has been the perfect editor, supportive and incisive, and Kathryn Gohl's copyediting has improved almost every page of the manuscript.

The Harvard Adolescence Project put us in regular contact with an exceptional group of social scientists, and we thank each of them. Among the remarkable group of friends and colleagues who were the project fellows—Douglas and Wanni Anderson, Victoria Burbank, Richard Condon, Marida Hollos, Philip Leis, Mitchell Ratner, Carol Worthman—we must single out Rick Condon for the continuing stimulus of his warm and good-humored interest in our work. We have learned a great deal from a stellar group of Harvard faculty who contributed to the project—Irven DeVore, Carol Gilligan, George Goethals, Jerome Kagan, Robert LeVine, Beatrice and John Whiting. We especially thank Carol Gilligan for the stimulus of her example, and her friendship. Beatrice and John Whiting created, nurtured, taught, and in the best sense parented the core group of sometimes adolescent/rebellious post-docs. It has been an honor to work with them, and we treasure the example they provide of how to do social science.

We gratefully acknowledge support from the William T. Grant Foundation and the National Institute of Mental Health (No. MH 14066-06, 07, 08).

■ Note on Transliteration

The spoken Arabic of Morocco is quite distinctive in sound pattern and vocabulary from the written *'arabiya,* which Moroccans share with the rest of the Arab world. Colloquial words and phrases are included in the text only when they are of unusual importance, occurred repeatedly in conversations we report, or are likely to be of special interest to readers with Arabic fluency. We have adopted a simplified transliteration system which is fairly readable by Anglophones and which has the advantage of being accessible from a standard word-processor keyboard. Place names and other commonly printed words are given their usual newspaper spelling. Since we have used capital letters as equivalents of some Arabic letters, a word beginning with a capital is not necessarily a proper noun. Arabic plurals are often irregular, so rather than confusing readers with two forms we follow a word with a nonitalicized *s* to indicate a plural.

Arabic letters without an English equivalent are written and pronounced as follows:

D, H, S, T	pronounced like the lowercase letters, but further back in the mouth, producing a heavier or deeper sound
j	like the *s* in pleasure, a *zh* sound
sh	like the *sh* in sharp
kh	like the *ch* in the German *Bach*
gh	like the *r* in the French *Paris*
q	similar to *k,* but back further in the throat
'	the letter *ain,* a bit like *ai* but deep in the throat
'	a glottal stop, like the pause in *uh-oh*

ADOLESCENCE
IN A MOROCCAN TOWN

■ 1
Introduction

When Rashid was young he sometimes used to follow the route the older boys took past the edge of town to the hillside. If he climbed all the way to the top of the hill he could see many kilometers in all directions. Behind him to the west was the hilly land on which his father had spent his youth in a *douar*, a small village of adobe houses and tents belonging to the Oulad Tadla, his kin group. Usually, though, Rashid looked the other way, toward today's Zawiya. It was nice to be several hundred meters from the dust and noise of the neighborhood, and as he looked across town he could see the green roof of the mosque and the facing hills across the road. He had not been inside the mosque since the night before he was circumcised several years ago, but now that he was starting to fast Ramadan he imagined going to Friday prayers as well. Sometimes a train would come whistling out of the tunnel at Bab Tisra and move smoothly along the line beside the road a kilometer away, and he liked to imagine that he was on it, headed for Casablanca. He had heard his cousin say Casablanca was bigger than most of the cities in France. From there you could fly to Europe or America.

Usually, there were girls at the watertap at the foot of the hill, and he wondered what the young men who hung around nearby found so interesting about them. Groups of older boys often walked out toward the fields beyond town, smoking and talking. Once in a while toward evening he would see a young man and a girl in her late teens silently passing on the path at the bottom of the hill, and he had heard kids say they had seen a couple sitting and kissing just after dark.

His father did not like him wandering off alone, so Rashid kept a look-out when it got close to time for Qaddour to return from work. If Rashid got home just before dinner there would not be too many questions about his schoolwork, and he might get to follow Hafid, his teenage brother, into his room and hear some music on the cassette machine his father had brought back from his year working abroad. Hafid liked popular music and reggae and even understood some of the words about love; Rashid was beginning to think how nice to would be if Hafid moved out after high school and he got the room.

The afternoon breeze smelled so good coming up from the orchards. Someday he would have a house in the country with a balcony looking over an orange grove; someday when he was an engineer, or maybe a high school teacher.

Rashid was eighteen in 1982, no longer a boy but not quite a man, when he helped us understand the feelings and activities of young people in his neighborhood.[1] He liked to talk about how his feelings and his under-standing had grown from the time described, when he was just a kid. He recalled his dreams and plans in one of the hundreds of conversations we had about adolescence in this Moroccan town. His generation of youth in Zawiya,[2] on the western edge of North Africa, is the subject of this book.

THE PSYCHOLOGICAL AND ANTHROPOLOGICAL STUDY OF ADOLESCENCE

The term *adolescence* has come into widespread usage in the social sciences during the twentieth century, following the publication of G. Stanley Hall's two-volume *Adolescence: Its Psychology and Its Relations to Physiology, Anthropology, Sociology, Sex, Crime, Religion and Education* (1904). As the title suggests, Hall's perspective was both psychological and anthropological. We owe to Hall the notion of adolescence as a difficult period of "storm and stress" (although the term itself comes from a German Romantic literary genre). Hall also formulated the important concept that adolescence as a physical life-stage is essential to cultural development, because youth pro-vides novel and even revolutionary alternatives to the established social or-der. Hall's conviction that both individual and cultural development could be ranged along a single continuum, from childish and primitive to mature and civilized, seems archaic and even racist to the modern reader, but the fasci-nation of twentieth-century social science with adolescence cannot be un-derstood without some attention to Hall's assumptions.

The most influential theories of adolescence in American psychology have been those deriving from the Freudian tradition (S. Freud [1905] 1953; A. Freud 1958; Erikson 1950, 1968). Freud's account of the period he calls simply "puberty" represents adolescence as a time for necessary retesting of social behavior learned in childhood. In the years after puberty, according to Freud, we see the final maturing of styles of thinking and behavior developed years before when the child was working out his or her relationship to the parents' sexual and authoritarian roles (S. Freud [1905] 1953, chap. 3). The Freudian account describes adolescence as a time of inevitable replay of childhood issues; it emphasizes adolescent problems of emotional self-control and of finding an emotionally acceptable object for one's love.

In the work of Erikson (1950, 1968), adolescence is characterized as the critical period for the formation of the psychological self, the "identity." This identity formation is frequently conflictual, since the adolescent must learn a variety of new social roles appropriate to various settings and yet must maintain a sense of personal continuity and internal oneness across these. Erikson's theory remains influential, despite important criticisms of the extent to which his theory describes the experience of persons who are not male, middle-class Westerners.

Gilligan (1982, 1986) criticizes much of psychological theory on adolescence as placing too much emphasis on autonomy and independence. She argues that current theories of adolescence fail to represent the interdependence of healthy adult life and notes: "The equation of development with separation and of maturity with independence presumes a radical discontinuity of generations and encourages a vision of human experience that is essentially divorced from history or time" (Gilligan 1986, 6).

The non-Freudian psychodynamic theory of Sullivan (1953) assigns great importance to relationships, treating adolescence as a phase in which new emotional issues lead youth to develop strong emotional ties with a nonfamily friend of the same sex. Sharing personal feelings with the intimate friend provides a basis for later emotional closeness with a spouse. Reconciling powerful needs for sexual gratification and for emotional intimacy forces the individual to develop a revised sense of self.

The cognitive-maturational theory of Piaget (Inhelder and Piaget 1958) developed in parallel to the work of Freud and his followers. Piagetian theory ascribes to adolescence the last crucial phase of cognitive development, the establishment of "formal operations." In formal operational thought the individual comes to think about his or her own thought processes and to apply these effectively to both abstract problems and dilemmas growing out of mature social relationships. Piaget also concerned himself with the emergence of moral reasoning (Piaget 1932), and from this basis Kohlberg developed a highly influential (and increasingly controversial) theory of developmental stages of moral reasoning (Kohlberg 1964; Gilligan 1982).

Determining the validity of these and related theories of adolescent personality for non-Western cultures was beyond even so ambitious an undertaking as the Harvard Adolescence Project. We intend, nonetheless, to reconsider the core contentions of Hall, Freud, Sullivan, Erikson, Gilligan, and Piaget in light of our findings in Zawiya. The Western reader will wonder whether the adolescents of this traditional Muslim town inevitably experience adolescence as a stressful confrontation with adult authority, whether they display conflicts over emotional intimacy or Oedipal anxieties about new feelings toward their parents as the young people become sexually active, whether the process of identity formation is a striking feature of their personal experience of the teen years, and whether they move toward separation and individuation or toward interdependence as they grow up. We have found that none of these theories can be applied uncritically to the youth of Zawiya, but it is true that, with rapid introduction of mass schooling and increased exposure to new social roles, some Zawiya adolescents find themselves confronted with dilemmas similar to those described in the Western literature.

Anthropologists too have been concerned with the topic of adolescence, but to a lesser extent than psychologists. Probably the best known ethnographic description of adolescence in another culture is Margaret Mead's *Coming of Age in Samoa* (1928), despite the fact that it was published over sixty years ago.[3] In the introduction to her book, Mead summarizes the work of Hall (1904) and other psychologists who treated adolescence as the inevitable result of universal physical changes, and succinctly poses the cultural anthropologist's question:

> The anthropologist listened to the current comment upon adolescence. He heard attitudes which seemed to him dependent upon social environment—such as rebellion against authority, philosophical perplexities, the flowering of idealism, conflict and struggle—ascribed to a period of physical development. And on the basis of his knowledge of the determinism of culture, of the plasticity of human beings, he doubted. Were these difficulties due to being adolescent or to being adolescent in America? (Mead 1928, 5)

Despite recent criticism of this work (Freeman 1983), Mead's conclusion that the adolescent period was very different in Samoa is still generally accepted. She explained the smooth, untroubled character that she saw in Samoan adolescence as due to several aspects of their life-style, which differed from that of Americans. Centrally important was that younger generations would lead lives very similar to those of older generations in this uncomplicated island setting. Parental knowledge and experience thus had clear relevance to youth, and they had little reason to doubt or reject it. Sexual behavior was relaxed and usually not a basis of conflict; if there were a problem, children and young people could live with relatives or neighbors for a time. Mead felt American adolescents experienced stress in several of the above areas, in part because their futures were uncertain and they had to both decide on and follow through into new adult life-styles. Given Mead's thesis, we should find stress in the rapidly changing lives of Zawiya adolescents: their parents' experience and knowledge are very different from the practical skills they need in their future lives, and sexual values are rigidly defined despite real change in behavior.

Anthropologists have also studied adolescence by comparison of coded ethnographic data from different cultures (the holocultural tradition). The classic study *Child Training and Personality* (Whiting and Child 1953) examines the relationship of different child-rearing practices to adult personality characteristics. Careful coding of the cross-cultural literature shows that most societies recognize the physical maturation signaling puberty, but that the sociocultural treatment of the adolescent period is widely varied (Frayser 1985). In general, adolescent experience is seldom described in detail by ethnographers.[4] One of the motivations of the Harvard Adolescence Project was to produce comparable ethnographies of widely varying adolescent communities. All of the Harvard research teams looked for transitional rites or ceremonies, but none of the cultures currently had clear adolescent initiatation practices. While marriage was a ritual event that ended adolescence in most cultures, it was not strictly speaking an initiation rite.[5]

Like anthropologists in general, those studying the Middle East and North Africa have seldom focused specifically on adolescence. In fact, Williams's *The Youth of Haouch El Harimi, a Lebanese Village* (1968) is the only such ethnography in English to date. Her emphasis on change and on sex differences is mirrored in this volume. References to adolescence in the Middle East are also found in older works on childhood (Ammar [1954] 1973; Granqvist 1950), but they are not central in these books. The opening sentence of Ammar's chapter on adolescence may explain why: "Adolescence as a stage of development in the individual's life assumes but little importance, and is unmarked by a ceremony or any other means of social recognition" ([1954] 1973, 183). Granqvist mentions puberty rather than adolescence in her research on a Palestinian town in the 1930s. Residents considered it best that children be married before puberty, because they were concerned with the disruptive force of sexuality. They "consider the awakening sexual feelings a reality . . . which has the force of a strong natural power" (Granqvist 1950, 186).

THEMES

Several central themes recur in our description of the lives of Zawiya adolescents. The first involves increasing social expectations of *maturity,* one of the most important goals of adolescence in Zawiya. We are especially concerned with the Arabic term *'aql,* used to describe the behavior expected of mature adults and often lacking in adolescents. *'Aql* is a key concept in Moroccan culture (Eickelman 1976; Rosen 1984) as well as in other parts of the Middle East (Abu-Lughod 1986). While it has various meanings in literary Arabic, the closest to its use in Morocco are definitions of the noun form given as "sense," "reason," "understanding," "rationality," "mind," and "intellect" (Wehr 1966, 630). The term is used most commonly about Zawiya adolescents in phrases like *Daret 'aqlha* or *Baqi ma-darsh 'aqlu*: "She is behaving reasonably," "He has not yet developed sense." One who has 'aql will be expected to act in a responsible, mature way, proper to Moroccan culture. Abu-Lughod's translation of 'aql as "social sense" (1986, 90) is especially apt, and we have incorporated it into our title. The term as used in Zawiya also conveys the idea of "maturity." Children are expected to lack 'aql and to develop it gradually, and often girls in Zawiya are said to develop it more quickly than boys (see S. Davis 1983a). The concept of 'aql is central in adolescence both because as one attains it, one is expected to behave like a responsible adult, and because its possession implies that one has a sense of oneself and one's functioning in Moroccan society.

Another important theme is the *self* and *self-awareness.* When a Moroccan has developed the level of 'aql to master appropriate self-presentation in varies contexts, he or she is no longer an adolescent. The working title of this book was *Presenting the Self,* which expressed our interest in (*a*) the young Moroccans' self-presentation in their daily lives, (*b*) the special ways they presented themselves to us as male or female ethnographers, and (*c*) our own self-appointed task of presenting them to our readers. However, that title suggested an uncritical acceptance of Western writing about self as adequate to describe people in Zawiya, and we have come to feel uncomfortable with the adequacy of self theory for the Zawiya context. Self is a concept that has been widely and differently used, and it is thus especially important to clarify our use of it with regard to another culture. We do so briefly here and continue our discussion in chapter 8.

The average Westerner thinks of the self as an internal, individually created entity. Geertz summarizes and criticizes this position:

> The Western conception of the person as a bounded, unique, and more or less integrated motivational and cognitive universe, a dynamic center of awareness, emotion, judgment, and action organized into a distinctive whole and set contrastively both *against* other such wholes and *against* its social and natural background, is, however incorrigible it may seem to us, a rather peculiar idea within the context of the world's cultures. (1983, 59, emphasis added)

Western scholars view the self as having two aspects: one that is internally, individually defined and a second that is socially influenced. Sociologist Erving Goffman's (1959) analogy of the theater illustrates these: he describes the self as both the *performer* of a part and as the *character* this performer evokes through social interaction with the audience. Goffman discusses the self-as-performer practicing "impression management," sometimes presenting a picture of the self that is not really "true"; it is this latter aspect with which we disagree.

The importance of the social construction of self, as opposed to a solely internal and individualistic view, has appeared in recent work on several Middle Eastern Muslim cultures, including Afghanistan (Anderson 1985), Yemen (Caton 1985), and Egyptian Bedouin (Abu-Lughod 1985). Work on Morocco has also dealt with the concept of self, with emphasis on the socially defined aspect (see Geertz 1983; Rosen 1984).

The opposition of a socially defined self to a Western individually constructed and almost independently existing "essential" self is an important corrective—if not taken too far. Zawiya adolescents seem to us clearly to display both an individual (based of course on social values) and a more contextual socially constructed aspect of self, although their proportions may be inverse to what they are in the West. Western cultures stress individualism and autonomy, and a person's focus on an internal and individually formed "self" is an outgrowth of this. The social context is more important than individual autonomy for many more traditional cultures. Essential to balancing the two aspects of self in Morocco is the development of mature thinking or ʿaql—revealed by proper behavior in varied contexts—which we regard as among the most important tasks of adolescence in Zawiya.

Since age expectations for acquiring ʿaql, the manner of self-presentation, and many other characteristics differ widely for males and for females, we discuss issues of *gender* at several points. Another theme concerns the phenomenon of *change* as central to the study of adolescence in Zawiya: personal change in the teenagers involved, and community change from the parental to the current generation. One important aspect of this change is the greater opportunity for contact between the sexes in the younger generation. As part of the discussion of historical change in Zawiya we also attempt to assess the effects of mass education and of such signs of "modernization" as television and easy travel to urban settings. As we discuss the relations of Zawiya adolescents with others, especially elders, we raise the themes of *hierarchy* and *ambivalence*. In contrast, the themes of *reciprocity* and *trust* emerge as key goals and characteristic problems in adolescents' relations with each other in this Moroccan town.

THE FIELDWORK

The research on which we base our account of Zawiya was conducted as part of a cross-cultural and interdisciplinary study of adolescence in seven cultural settings. The general goals of the Harvard Adolescence Project were to examine adolescence in cultures representing varied levels of complexity, ecological setting, and ethnic/religious background; the cultures studied are described in the foreword. While the studies undertaken were methodologically complex, and while each has evolved partially independent of the others, certain questions as well as a set of core methods were shared.

Research Site and Methods

The focus of our ethnographic observation, interviewing, and testing was on roughly fifty families living in one neighborhood of Zawiya, and in particular on their 150 children between the ages of nine and twenty at the time of the study. This neighborhood sample was selected to include a group of people who had lived near each other and had shared social experience over at least a decade. During eleven months of fieldwork in 1982 we lived in the neighborhood and took part in public and semipublic activities such as weddings and circumcisions. We collected physical growth measurements, as well as background data on family, education, and travel, on over one hundred adolescents. During the latter half of the fieldwork period we administered psychological tests and structured problem-solving interviews to a subsample of sixty-five young people (S. Davis 1983b; D. Davis

1989). We also interviewed two dozen teenagers and young adults at length about their experiences and feelings toward family, friends, and self. Finally, we continued a close personal association with many friends in the neighborhood whom we have known over a twenty year period of fieldwork and frequent short visits.

The Neighborhood

The corner of town where we conducted our research in 1982 is a thin slice of the western edge of Zawiya, perhaps three hundred meters in length by one hundred in width. It shares the steep slope up which the older sections of town have been extending themselves for decades and borders the open area reserved for the annual fall festival (*moussem*) of the local saint.

Our own neighborhood of Zawiya is a mixture of the house types and economic levels of the whole, containing examples of both the imposing multistory houses of the local middle class and the small mud dwellings of the very poor. We divided the families in town into three economic levels or "classes," basing both the number of these groups and the ranking of each family on the opinions of informed local people as well as on our own observations. About 5 to 10 percent of the population could be called well-off; this includes people with capital holdings such as large shops or cars as well as families with more than one salaried member, or a wage earner in France or Libya who sends substantial funds home. Roughly half the population is of the middle level, in the sense of owning or renting a comfortable house and having enough to eat and a regular source of income. The last third are poor, living in small mud-brick houses and having irregular and/or minimal incomes; this group includes many of the in-migrants during the 1981 drought, who sell donkey-loads of river water for 25¢ each, and agricultural day laborers. Among the families we studied, 14 percent were well-off, 48 percent middle class, and 38 percent poor by these standards. This fairly well represents the town, with a slight excess in our sample of those who are moderately well-off.

Zawiya and Morocco

Zawiya is unique, as are all Moroccan towns with a history; nonetheless it illustrates in important respects the contrasts or contradictions within larger Moroccan society. These contrasts, between the growing urban and traditional rural sectors, between mostly illiterate adults and their schooled children, have been constantly apparent in our dealings with old friends in Zawiya and figure prominently in the following chapters. However, as we describe the setting and local life in more detail, we caution the reader that these adolescents and their families do not typify Morocco in general; indeed, during our work many Moroccans said just that, and we agree. The Moroccan nation today includes the huge metropolis of Casablanca (pop. over 3 million) and the French-style "new towns" (*villes nouvelles*) of the major cities, yet much of the country remains a collection of *douars*, relatively isolated traditional villages of agriculturalists. The Zawiya we know is an often contradictory mixture of urban and rural elements, and this is nowhere more apparent than in the lives of the older children and young adults we came to study. Thus Zohra, an older resident who grew up in a nearby village comprised mainly of tents, has a husband who seven years ago boarded a 747 for the pilgrimage to Mecca, a daughter who can find her way alone about the avenues of Rabat, and a son who has lived in several cities of France. Upper-class youth in the large cities like Casablanca may live lives similar to urban Americans, with dating and discos a regular part of their experience. In more isolated rural villages, on the other hand, young people may attend only primary school, leaving early to help with the family land or herds. Such villagers would have only occasional access to the Egyptian, French, and American television shows their relatives in Zawiya watch so devotedly.

The adolescents of Zawiya know a mixed, transitional setting, neither isolated nor urban. Like theirs, most Moroccan towns have recently grown rapidly. People have come in from the countryside because land parcels are divided as they are inherited, and thus get smaller with each generation in which there is more than one child. A serious drought in 1981, the year before this research, brought many families to town as crops and animals died and people looked for new work. Many have stayed, and by the 1982 census the population of Zawiya had passed eleven thousand, while in 1960 it was about 4 thousand (Royaume du Maroc 1962, 666–667; 1984, 122–123). Thus many Moroccans live today in small- or medium-sized towns like Zawiya, towns where they have access to a high school education, easy travel to larger cities, electricity with which to study and watch television, and a variety of paying jobs. These changes are quite recent, and whole families are learning to deal with them all across Morocco. What follows, then, is based on work with only one group of adolescents in a particular place, but their situation is not strikingly different from that of many townspeople who live in neither large urban centers nor isolated mountain hamlets.

The Field-workers

While anthropologists have often written about a culture as if they were merely objective observers of it, in recent decades the ethnographer's own experiences in and of a culture have increasingly been seen as an essential part of the ethnography.[6] The situation of the researcher plays a central role in the kinds of work that person can do and in what she or he can discover. We feel that important factors influencing our research on adolescence included our long residence in and familiarity with Zawiya, our expressed admiration for many aspects of the culture, our special closeness to certain neighborhood families, our status as a married couple with a child, and the fact that our "team" included a researcher of each sex.

In describing life in today's Zawiya we often refer to changes we have seen. Susan first lived in Zawiya as a Peace Corps volunteer from 1965 to 1967, teaching home economics skills to women and older girls and helping to establish a kindergarten. Some of those kindergarteners were older adolescents in this study. We both lived in Zawiya for more than a year during 1970–1971, preparing doctoral dissertations (D. Davis 1974; S. Davis 1978). Susan's book *Patience and Power: Women's Lives in a Moroccan Village* (1983a) is based on this fieldwork. We returned to Zawiya for brief visits in 1977 and 1980, and continue to visit regularly. The Adolescence Project took us back to Zawiya from February 1982 to January 1983, during which time we lived just a block from our old house on the Zenkat Nasser (though streets bore no names in 1971).

Each time we have lived in Zawiya, we have had especially close ties to some individuals who explained Zawiya to us—and us to Zawiya. In the Peace Corps, Susan's first ties were to her colleagues who taught at the women's center and their families, and later to another family that "adopted" her. Beginning with our dissertation research in 1970 we have been treated as relatives by two Zawiya families: we eat together often, share holidays, and travel together. Young people in each family were especially helpful with our work on adolescence, including serving as research assistants. That these two families are generally respected in town has helped others to accept us. The ongoing relationship itself demonstrates that we are respectable—and in addition, people can ask questions about us and our activities that, out of a sense of decorum, they would not ordinarily ask us directly. Our kinlike ties also give people a niche in which to place us in the community.

Our close interaction with these families and our participation in neighborhood events have also helped demonstrate our appreciation of Moroccan culture. This has been important because of the French colonial past, when Moroccan traditions and people were often openly disdained. We had a clue to this when people looked surprised that we liked Moroccan food and ate, like them, with our fingers; one day in 1970 it was made overt when Douglas took a picture of children playing in the street. Several neighbor women came out and complained, saying that we wanted to show Americans how dirty and unkempt the children were; they could imagine no other reason for such a picture. That the photo would be used to denigrate them, instead of showing children's games, for example, illustrates an expectation of negative attitudes from foreigners. When we explained the purpose of the informal picture (photographs in Morocco are usually posed in a studio) and emphasized that we liked Morocco and wanted to write about it so others would understand it better too, people were more at ease with us.

Being a married couple with a child also helped make us comprehensible to local people, to whom marriage and children are both "normal" and very important. It also meant Susan could discuss sexual matters more freely than if she were single and thus assumed to be naïve. In other ways gender was important for both of us, even though our roles sometimes did not conform to Zawiya standards. We made some accommodations to Moroccan gender roles (more than Susan liked, at times)—Douglas never compromised his male status washing dishes in front of guests, for example —but we maintained a less-gendered division of labor than most Moroccan households. Thus Douglas sometimes cooked (his curry was a favorite), we usually entertained as a couple, and Susan was more outspoken with Douglas than were many women her age with their husbands.

It was important that both a male and a female researcher were interviewing Zawiya teenagers because some material could not have been discussed except with a person of the same sex. While a few young men discussed sexuality quite openly with Susan (surprising her), such discussions were rare. Young women were more circumspect with her and would not have spoken with Douglas on that topic at all. Comparison of what even our closest friends were willing to share with each of us also provides important information on an aspect of self-presentation which we now see as central: as they described themselves to a male or a female researcher, many Zawiya young people presented a different picture of themselves and of the behavior or feeling being described. Such differences were especially important in the areas of religion and emotion.

Our long friendship with many neighborhood residents and our long perspective on the town itself allow us to describe change in detail and to make longitudinal comparisons of living styles and individual or family characteristics, in spite of the different goals of our earlier work in Zawiya. Our relationship of trust and mutual respect with friends in Zawiya produced a very high level of cooperation with us and our work. It is highly unlikely that an entire Moroccan neighborhood would have opened its doors to foreign researchers who were not well known, and persons perceived as outsiders probably could not have persuaded teenagers to spend long hours discussing personal (and even intimate) matters. It was essential to have both male and female researchers to put adolescents at ease in general and to discuss these more intimate matters.

In what follows, we examine the themes highlighted above, by both presenting a general picture of the lives of Zawiya adolescents and discussing key aspects in more detail. The next chapter sketches Zawiya and some individual residents in an attempt to give the reader a feeling for life there today. We then devote a chapter to the concept of adolescence. The remaining chapters examine the important domains of adolescent interaction with family, friends, and potential spouses. Finally, we move to the individual level and discuss psychological aspects of adolescence in Zawiya.

■ 2
Daily Life in Zawiya

The period of life between childhood and adulthood is marked in Zawiya by substantial individual differences in the daily routine of behavior: it is very different for boys and girls, and it varies profoundly as a function of whether the young person is in school or not. The portraits in this chapter describe the social roles and relationships as well as the daily activities of a young woman and young man. We call the reader's attention to family and friendship relations, since it is in the context of relationships formed in the family and in school that much of the characteristic "adolescent" experience of young Moroccans occurs. Since rapid social change is such a significant theme of the book, we also present part of a vivid account by a lifelong resident of the area of how different things were in her youth. The remainder of the chapter describes the physical setting, history, socioeconomic situation, and religious values of Zawiya.

A FIRST GLIMPSE OF ZAWIYA

The visitor's first view of Zawiya is likely to be from the edge of nearby Kabar. Having driven north and east from Rabat, Morocco's modern capital on the Atlantic coast, on a springlike morning in early March, let us imagine, the visitor passes cork forests and then turns inland through eucalyptus woods. After an hour the woods give way to broad fields of wheat and irrigated citrus, with orange groves on both sides of the road, and the first foothills of the Middle Atlas Mountains rise slowly on the south. Finally, after some two hours' comfortable drive from Rabat, a large and newly painted billboard welcomes the visitor, in three languages, to Kabar, the "City of Petroleum." The journey is not, however, quite over.

Kabar, site of a modest petroleum refinery, is a former French colonial town. Stripped of its colonial associations after Moroccan independence in 1956 by being renamed for a popular saint whose tomb and associated religious brotherhood (*zawiya*) are located two kilometers away, it is known simply as Kabar by the residents of the original Zawiya it has overshadowed. The highway now passes up the broad central avenue of Kabar and divides to allow a double sidewalk and ornamental bitter orange trees along its center. The ambience suggests some wealth and leisure, with large shops bearing advertisements for the cosmetics and soft drinks of the multinationals, a movie theater displaying a French-language poster for *The Blues Brothers*, and dozens of young men in European dress seated outside several large cafés. At the head of the avenue the road splits to surround the imposing new three-story structure housing the provincial and municipal governments of Kabar, and in two more short blocks the visitor emerges from Kabar to face an intersecting road and an open field bounded by wooded hills. In the foreground are several large school buildings under construction, and toward the right, across two kilometers of fields and gardens, crouched at the base of a larger hill, is Zawiya.

The visitor now turns right and follows the highway for two hundred meters; the main road branches off to the left at an intersection where there are, during most daylight hours, several small blue taxis. After entering one of these and waiting for the other two seats to be let, a ride of five minutes leads to a right-hand turnoff, where a weather-beaten sign announces that one has reached Zawiya. The taxi pauses to allow passengers for Douar Doum, the smaller and newer village at the left-hand side of the road, to descend, crosses the tracks of the railway connecting the coastal cities of Morocco with those inland, passes down a 150-meter slope, and arrives at the gardens bordering the foot of the town. The taxi crosses the narrow bridge over the Rdoum River and stops in an open dirt turnaround. While the driver collects a price of 1.20 dirhams or DH (roughly 20¢ at 1982 rates) from the other passengers, there is time to notice a variety of bystanders. Several, including two young men dressed like those in the cafés of Kabar, an adult woman of indeterminate age covered from head to foot by a combination street-length *jellaba*, forehead-covering hood, and over-the-nose veil, and a young woman in tight Western clothes, are even now pushing their way into the taxi. Half a dozen teen-aged boys are lounging on the bridge, several older men in *jellabas* of heavy wool are standing in the shade of a large fig tree at the left, waiting for other forms of transport, and four persons seated ahead on the left are chanting and asking alms with palms extended. After paying the cabdriver and passing the beggars, the way angles left onto a kind of thoroughfare. Kabar's broad avenue is forgotten in a mixed throng of people of all ages, both sexes, and varied styles of dress on the ascending street. This is the *Suiqa* (the "little market"), Main Street for Zawiya.

The Red Crescent office on the left is the first landmark, facing a large coffeeshop on the right where cardplayers and tea drinkers are ensconced in semidarkness. The visitor continues past a barber shop, a general store, three butchers' stalls, several vegetable stalls, a cluttered radio-television repair shop, a spice seller, and a live-chicken shop. The street is full of people: older men squatting against the walls; young men leaning against the entrances to shops; a few girls and women negotiating over purchases at the grocers; small children of both sexes dashing about among pedestrians; mule-drawn wagons; heavily loaded donkeys being driven to market or hauling drums of water; and the occasional car inching its way toward the head of the Suiqa, where the road forks. Turning right, the visitor faces an open area where a small replica of the weekly market outside Kabar has been set up: merchants, most of them male, have claimed a few square feet each for the display of fruits and vegetables. This area is as crowded as the Suiqa, but as evocative of the countryside as the last block was of the town. The road nearly disappears at this point, but then continues straight ahead, past the bustle of activity at two water spigots on the right, where girls and women are jostling each other for a turn; past the crowd of children beyond awaiting the midmorning shift change at the elementary school; and past a low, peeling building across from the school, where a variety of preschoolers and teenaged girls attend a government-sponsored kindergarten and women's center.

Keeping to the left wall, the visitor makes slow progress past the vegetable sellers and their customers, then turns right at the first opportunity, entering a deeply gullied dirt street just wide enough to allow the passage of two cars. This street, identified in Arabic by a hand-painted sign on the wall of the corner house as the Zenkat Razi, is more obviously residential, although children are buying snacks of roast chickpeas and sunflower seeds from a small shop at the right, and there is a miniscule radio repair shop at the left, from which heavily amplified popular music (the style equally likely to be Middle Eastern or Western) is heard. The journey is nearly over, as the visitor passes down a lane of two-story brick houses, each having a closed door of painted metal facing the street and an overhanging second floor. A large grocery shop is passed on the left, and the proprietors of two much smaller establishments eye each other, and the visitor, from opposite sides of the street a few feet farther on. The Zenkat Jamal Abdul Nasser joins from the left at this point, and in one more short block Z. Razi abruptly emerges into an open space perhaps a hundred meters square. A footpath replaces the street at this point and continues out of town past scattered refuse on the left and an energetic soccer game on the right. Beyond are low hills verdant with young wheat, sprinkled with flame-red poppies and white narcissus. The visitor turns sharply left, continues a few more meters past an empty lot where small children are playing hopscotch, glances at a well-stocked one-room grocery shop where the proprietor is joking with two elderly men, and reaches a blue-painted door above which is the number 16. Farther up the hill the street assumes a proper appearance, as houses again join it on the right. This is the Zenkat Filistin, Palestine Street, comprising, with the adjoining Zenkats Razi and Nasser, the bulk of the neighborhood, the "Primary Sampling Unit," under study. The house is ours, where we spent 1982 with our five-year-old daughter, Laila.

DAILY ROUTINES

Detailed accounts of fairly typical days for two members of the neighborhood, Hakima and Abdelaziz, illustrate the lives of teenagers in school, as over half (55 percent) are. Naturally, no pair of individuals can adequately represent the diversity of personal behavior and psychological characteristics of the 150 young Zawiyans whom we interviewed and tested.

Hakima

Hakima is a slender, lively girl of fourteen with sparkling brown eyes and an interest in everything going on around her. She awakens early on this Saturday morning, because for her it is a school day; the primary schools have Friday, the Muslim holy day, and Sunday off.[1] Sleeping with her in the room are five of her seven brothers and sisters. Her oldest sister, twenty-two, and her seventeen- and twelve-year-old brothers sleep on the narrow couches that are arranged around the walls of the room and serve as seats during meals or for watching television in the evenings. Hakima and her ten-year-old brother and six-year-old sister sleep on blankets spread over the reed mats on the floor, while her two eldest brothers share a room of their own, a luxury many older boys desire but few families can afford.

Although her siblings are still asleep, Hakima hears her mother stirring in the other large room in the house, where her parents sleep.

After she awakens (she is used to the school routine and needs no encouragement to get up), Hakima washes her face, hands, and feet and combs her hair. The other children are stirring, and as soon as they are up she begins to fold the bedding and stack it at the end of the room. She hurries, because it is nearly seven and time for her to be at school. Because there are so many children in town, the school operates on double split shifts and Hakima attends from 7:00 to 10:00 A.M. and 1:00 to 4:00 P.M.

On her way out the door she snatches a piece of bread; she will not have her coffee and milk until after ten. If she is late, the teacher will strike her on the palm with a stick, so she hurries. She finds her neighbor and friend Khadija just leaving, and they walk the three blocks together, joining the throngs of children, who are among the first ones up in the still chilly November morning. Hakima is wearing a Western-style dress, as girls her age do, and a sweater for warmth. She arrives at school on time and takes her seat at a table with another girl (Hakima, like other girls her age, does not like to sit with boys) in her fifth grade class of thirty-six students. This is the last year of primary school and Hakima is repeating it, which is not at all unusual.

This morning's classes are history and the Qur'an, which is studied for both its religious and its literary value. The room is quiet as the teacher writes the next day's lesson on the board, although Hakima is passed a note by a girlfriend who wants to borrow a book later because she cannot afford to buy it. During recitation, the teacher (a woman, as are about half of the primary school teachers in Zawiya) calls on students who raise their hands, and each stands to recite. Hakima is relieved that many hands are raised because she did not study last night and does not want to be called on. After this lesson she goes into the schoolyard for a ten-minute recess, where she sits with four girls from her class. They discuss whether or not there will be an exam, fearing they may be punished if they do not know the lesson. In fact, just before coming outside a lazy classmate had made several errors and been struck by the teacher, and they laugh about that; they feel she deserved it for not studying harder. After recess they work on reading and Arabic dictation, and are ready to leave a little before ten so the next shift can enter.

Most of her school friends live in other parts of town, and Khadija has to run an errand for her father, so Hakima walks home alone. Her mother has saved some bread and milky coffee for her, so she has a proper breakfast before she starts her chores. Sometimes she buys the vegetables for the main meal at noon, but ten o'clock is too late to start cooking (she smelled stews browning in olive oil as she walked home from school), so that has been done by her older sister. Hakima's main morning task is to get the family's water supply from one of the town's seven water sources with the help of her two younger brothers. She prefers the tap near the school, because the one nearer her house often has little water pressure and is also known for the frequent fights that occur there; Hakima is assertive, but not quite up to that level. Her little brothers go ahead to "get in line"; actually, there is no line, but they serve as evidence that they have been waiting awhile when Hakima forges ahead to claim her turn.

Although she knows she is likely to get wet and possibly dirty, Hakima wears her good school clothes to get water; she is just at the age when girls start to care more about their appearance in general and has noticed that teenage boys often lounge against the buildings near the water taps, watching and sometimes flirting with the girls. As she arrives, she greets several of the girls she knows. Most of the people waiting for water from one of three spigots are girls between twelve and twenty-two, although there are a few boys from families that do not have girls in this age range. When older teenage boys show up, they usually push everyone out of the way and get an immediate turn. Hakima waits about five minutes, working her way into the crowd near the tap that has the strongest flow. Another tap is just trickling, and the less aggressive girls are waiting for that one; they seldom speak a harsh word. The tap Hakima has chosen has attracted a different crowd, in which girls are pushing and shoving and insulting each others' ancestors in a part laughing, part serious way. Just last week, Hakima and Khadija stopped speaking to each other because of a fight over turns at the tap, but a third friend patched things up and they are best friends again.

Hakima gauges the situation and decides to make her move, butting ahead of several girls she knows will not seriously oppose her. She and her brothers have brought almost all of the family's supply of five-liter water bottles and have forty of the plastic bottles lined up and waiting. As one girl finishes her turn, Hakima shoves aside the girl who thought she was next and jams a bottle against the tap. However, she finds she has misjudged the other girl, who hefts a bottle and knocks Hakima's away, spraying everyone nearby with cold water. Although slight, Hakima is strong and wiry, and uses her body to dislodge the other girl, jabbing with her elbows to discourage those behind her from moving in. She has clearly claimed her turn and is allowed to fill several bottles before another girl asks to fill "just two," and Hakima lets her. She has been passing the filled bottles to her brothers, and they carry them home four (roughly five gallons each) at a time. After a brief break Hakima resumes her turn, with reduced opposition. By the time she has enough water for the day's cooking and cleaning needs, she is thoroughly drenched and a little cold, but if she has lunch on the roof in the sun, she will be dried out for school.

After carrying the last of the water home, Hakima sets out two low round tables for lunch, while one of her brothers goes to the public oven to get the family's freshly baked loaves of bread. Her mother and oldest sister have cooked a stew of lamb and artichoke hearts for lunch. The family gathers for lunch, awaiting the father's arrival from work. After he comes in and is greeted by each child kissing his hand, he sits down. Hakima carries in a teakettle, basin, and towel and pours water over the hands of each in turn. Next Hakima carries in the main dish, with a little in a smaller plate for her two younger brothers, who eat separately because the table is crowded. She also brings a salad of green peppers, tomatoes, and spices, and everyone has lunch—except S'aida, her youngest sister, who has the other school shift and will eat later. There is not much talk over lunch, both because everyone is busy eating and because the children show their respect for their father by not speaking unnecessarily. At the end of the meal, Hakima's little brother asks for money for a notebook and Hakima says she needs a pencil case. Their father gives both what they need, but says an angry no to her oldest sister's request for money to buy a scarf. He feels school supplies are necessary but a scarf is frivolous, so Kebira will have to convince her mother to find the money in her household funds.

After lunch Hakima helps wash hands again and clears away the dishes. She usually helps wash them, but today she expects a French quiz, so she studies for fifteen minutes before returning to school. Her mother is understanding and allows her to skip chores when she has pressing schoolwork.

She walks to school alone, taking off her sweater because the midday sun is quite warm, even in November. Again she arrives on time and sits down to begin her mathematics lesson. French is the second class, and she is relieved there is no quiz, even though she had studied; she has found French difficult ever since she began it in the third grade. This afternoon there is another recess, and Hakima gathers with the same group of girls, talking again about schoolwork and classmates. In addition, they go over the plot of an Egyptian film most of them saw on television last night, wondering if the crippled girl will win her doctor's love in the next week's episode. After recess, they study French verb conjugation and then Hakima heads home.

She finds her mother has gone to Kabar and left Kebira in charge of the house. Her older sister has just finished a thorough housecleaning, sweeping cobwebs off the ceiling and moving furniture to clean under it. She tells Hakima to finish up by mopping the tile floors of the two large rooms, and also the kitchen and the courtyard. Hakima complains that she had planned to go out with a girlfriend, but sees from her sister's stern face that she cannot easily escape; she fetches a bucket of water from the large oil drum and begins. Apparently effortlessly, she bends neatly in half from the hips, so the damp cloth in her hands just reaches to wipe the dusty floor. Many families mop only once a day, but Hakima's mother prefers twice and can manage it with two daughters to help her.

Finally, Hakima has a little free time to spend with her friend Khadija. This is not one of the girls she spends school recess with; those girls live a few blocks away and it would be inconvenient to run over to see if they were busy or not. Khadija lives one door away and is ready to go out when Hakima knocks. Since the weather is neither hot nor rainy, they decide to walk out to the field on the west side of town, where grass is just sprouting, relieving the dusty color of the landscape since the June harvest. They sit among groups of other girls, women, and children; on the packed dirt beside the field, several groups of boys play soccer. Three girls sitting nearby watch the game of some older boys, whispering and giggling the while, especially when a tall, curly haired boy glances in their direction. Hakima and Khadija watch this interchange out of the corners of their eyes; sometimes they talk about which boys in their class are handsome, but only at home. They would not dare discuss it in public, even in whispers, and certainly would not actually show their interest by staring and giggling. Some other girls from their street walk over and sit down, and they begin to talk about their families' plans for an upcoming holiday. Hakima would like to go to the city of Meknes, where two uncles live, but her older sister will probably get to go instead.

Her mother has promised to buy her a new dress, but Hakima does not mention that now because the other girls are just acquaintances and might gossip about it; she will tell Khadija later when they are alone. As the sun starts to go down around six, the air gets chilly, and the two girls decide to walk to the main street where snacks of roasted sunflower seeds and chickpeas are sold. Hakima has about ten cents to spend because her father gives her and her siblings each a few coins every night, so she decides to treat her friend. The two girls stand at the shop awhile, listening to the loud music from the cassette store across the way, then head home in the twilight, passing groups of young men gathered in the pools of light from storefronts. Hakima and Khadija are too young and shy to be flirting with boys, but in two or three years the boys will be calling out compliments as they pass, and if one interests them, this time near nightfall is when they might arrange to meet and talk quietly in a dark corner of the neighborhood.

Back home, Hakima finds her family having sweet mint tea and joins them before beginning on her homework for the evening. She and her oldest sister, Kebira (who dropped out of school after the fourth grade but can read a little), answer the questions of the three youngest children about their schoolwork; the older brothers are not home yet. Since their mother is still visiting a sick relative in Kabar, Kebira has made dinner.

Their mother and father arrive home together about eight, and Hakima gives her father water to wash with so he can say his evening prayers before dinner. During dinner, Hakima helps again with the hand washing, sets out the dishes of thin macaroni with milk and butter, and clears away. They turn on the television and find that the new show they all like, "Le Hulk incroyable" ("The Incredible Hulk"), is on. Hakima is glad, because she only likes "foreign" shows if there is a lot of action, preferably violent. The Western shows are usually dubbed in French, which she finds hard to follow, but car chases and fistfights do not strain her vocabulary.

After "The Hulk," a serial Egyptian film comes on about ten o'clock, and the parents retire to their room. Hakima and Kebira spread out the bedding, and all the children settle down to watch; although the dialect of Arabic is different, they understand much of it. There are no regular bedtimes at Hakima's house—children fall asleep one by one when they are tired and would be allowed to do so even if this were a schoolnight. Hakima stays awake to the end, and she and Kebira talk a little about their disappointment that the heroine ended up in jail, even if she did kill her lover. Then they fall asleep.

Other Girls

Other girls' daily routines vary from that of Hakima, mainly because of differences in the girls' age and educational status. Overall, about half of the group of girls between ten and twenty was in school, while the other half had dropped out. These latter girls did more of the household chores, although the chores were of the same type as those Hakima did; in addition the girls cared for children and washed clothes. Hakima's youngest sister did not need to be watched, but many girls (students or not) take along a two- or three-year-old when whey go out with friends. With large families and no running water, laundry is a huge job; girls help their mothers with it about once a week. Although relatively few girls go past primary school, those who do still help with household chores; their special status as high school students does not exempt them. Girls who were not in school usually did chores all morning and then had an afternoon break to visit with friends, a break that was an hour or two longer than Hakima's.

The work a girl is expected to do increases in amount and complexity with her age and abilities. Even at five or six, girls help their mothers by watching younger siblings and running simple errands—usually carrying messages instead of buying things. By age ten they can do most of the daily household cleaning, including mopping, tidying up, and washing dishes, and also are sent to buy vegetables, which they help clean. A sixteen-year-old has all the basic skills necessary to run a household and is able to buy meat without getting too much fat, cook it up into a correctly spiced stew, and prepare the bread to go with it. Older girls hope to add to their repertoires of main dishes and desserts, and spend much of their spare time embroidering sheets for their trousseaus, but most girls have the skills they need for marriage by sixteen.

There are variations in the way girls spend their leisure time. Girls of ten or eleven are more likely to engage in active games like hopscotch or jumprope, occasionally in mixed groups of boys and girls, but as they get to Hakima's age they prefer to be with girls and pass time by talking. Older girls sun themsleves and visit in the field in good weather, or go to a friend's home and embroider in bad weather. If they were interested in a boy, they might make up an errand after sunset and talk to him in a dark side street near the shops. A daring girl near twenty might even agree to meet in the town of Meknes on Sunday, if she could manufacture an excuse to go there; it is always helpful to have relatives to visit. Once there, the couple would stroll and windowshop and perhaps go to a movie, and try to arrange a chance to meet again.

A few of the girls we knew spent their days in neither housework nor schoolwork. Some attended the town's women's center and learned to sew or embroider; their hours away from home about equaled those of the schoolgirls. Another couple of older girls worked full time, teaching others to embroider or doing agricultural day labor. Teaching sewing or embroidery is a traditional and respected job, and rather pleasant because a girl can work in the home and visit as she works. Field labor, on the other hand, is unpleasant; girls and women work from sunrise to sunset weeding fields or picking grapes or oranges. The work is hard, and, further, girls who work risk damaging their reputations, since they can easily talk to the few men who work with them. Only families who desperately need the money let their women work in agriculture for wages. Traditionally, families worked their fields, so the other workers were relatives, but in town that has changed. In spite of the problems with this sort of work, one often sees girls cheerily singing and clapping time in the backs of the trucks that bring them home near sunset.

Thus while older girls may have a more complete repertoire of household or cooking skills, and girls who have left school will spend more time on chores and sometimes work for cash while schoolgirls study, there was much overlap in the activities of girls we knew. In general, they spent much more time than their brothers helping to run the household.

Abdelaziz

Nineteen-year-old Abdelaziz awakens to a cold room that is still half dark. It is 6:30 A.M., a Friday late in November.[2] Everyone else is still asleep, his two brothers curled under covers on other parts of the couchlike cushions that line the room; he removes the long nightshirt he pulled over his underclothes the night before and steps into trousers. Abdelaziz leaves the room and washes in the courtyard of the house, pouring cold water from a clay jug kept beside the room where his mother will later cook. In the morning she is often awake before him and is the person with whom he usually talks first after waking. Filling an aluminum kettle, he turns on the buta-gas bottle under the counter, lights a burner, and places the water to heat for coffee. When the coffee is ready he adds an equal part of milk from the half-liter carton left from yesterday and mixes in several teaspoons of sugar. He quickly looks over the French homework for this morning's class as he drinks coffee and eats a bit of yesterday's bread, then leaves the house at seven o'clock.

When their schedules coincide, Abdelaziz often meets his sixteen-year-old friend Abdelaziz Kabiri (they became friends several years ago, in part because of the coincidence of identical first names) for the kilometer-long walk to their junior high school,[3] but Kabiri has this morning off, and Abdelaziz makes his way alone through the twisting streets of Zawiya. The seasonal rains have begun during the past week, and the steeply inclined dirt streets of his neighborhood are still rather slippery. He hates to wear the heavy boots made necessary when the streets are at their muddiest, and he has decided this morning to risk his new shoes. Several men and boys are also making their way along the street, those without boots walking gingerly along the dry edge under the overhang of houses' second stories while the boot-clad walk boldly in the gullies at street centers. As he nears the elementary school several blocks away he sees dozens of younger children gathering outside. He turns into Zawiya's main street, the Suiqa, at the head of which a pastry seller is deep-frying his doughnutlike wares. Most of the shops are not yet open, and Abdelaziz merely nods at several older boys waiting at the taxi stop at the foot of town for transport to jobs in Kabar, two kilometers away.

Crossing the bridge on the Wad Rdoum, Abdelaziz cuts behind the public bath and crosses a fallow wheat field, thankful that the rains have not yet been heavy enough to turn it to sticky muck and force him to follow the road. Stepping through an opening in the high hedge of yucca cactus that shields the railroad track from the field, he scrambles down the slippery bank and begins to walk quickly along from tie to tie. Fifty yards ahead of him are two girls he recognizes as a year below him in the *collège* (junior high school). By the time he has reached the small train station he has nearly caught up with them, but he maintains his distance some fifteen feet behind, enjoying the view. Were he with friends he might try a leading comment about one of the girls, a real beauty, but he is too shy to start a conversation on his own. He turns in behind them onto the road to the school, and by eight o'clock he is being told by a classmate that the principle's assistant has just announced a change of schedule: Abdelaziz's morning classes will not begin until ten o'clock.

Abdelaziz climbs the stairs to his empty classroom, takes his usual desk, and begins to review his morning lessons. At ten o'clock the French class begins, and the professor calls on him several times. After an hour of French he has a class of combined geography/history, and since the professor spends most of the hour talking, few students are called on. As a loud bell announces the end of class at noon, he quickly pushes his way out into the crowded corridor along with a male classmate, and they head home along a shorter route following the river, now that the morning sun has dried the path. This time he manages to greet several girls in what he hopes is a flirtatious way, and he and his friend discuss the science class they share as they work their way back up the now crowded streets of Zawiya. Ravenously hungry by this time, Abdelaziz makes his way straight home. As he reaches the head of the Suiqa he sees several old men dressed in long white woolen jellabas making their way toward the tomb of Zawiya's saint, which is also the largest of the five mosques. As he reaches the foot of Zenkat Razi he hears the call to prayer, first amplified from the saint's tomb behind him, then as if echoed by the *muaddin* of the mosque uphill from his house.

Abdelaziz's mother has lunch nearly ready when he arrives home, and he eats with his parents, his older and younger brothers, and the wife of his oldest brother. The brother is an elementary schoolteacher in a neaby town.

Since today is Friday, Abdelaziz has the afternoon free. He works at next week's homework, paying special attention to science, his best (and favorite) subject. He is lucky that his family's house is large enough to leave an empty room, so he usually has a quiet place to study. Were his married brother to move to a house of his own, Abdelaziz would try to secure the room the brother and his wife occupy. He could then, like a few lucky acquaintances, put up pictures from film magazines, listen to cassettes and radio without interruption, and know that his books were unlikely to be disturbed. At five o'clock he has had enough of study, and he leaves the house to see what his friends are up to, after asking his mother for half a dirham (eight cents) to buy a snack of roast chickpeas from the little shop around the corner. He walks two hundred meters to the foot of his street, where several young men are already gathered at the corner alongside Hammad's general provisions shop. He quickly gets into conversation with Kabiri, and they compare notes on the day's school experiences. Kabiri's crazy math teacher has spent the whole of today's class rambling off the topic, and they repeat the school joke that he's "body present, mind absent." They casually watch the steady trickle of customers approach Hammad's: young children of both sexes on simple errands for spices, dry grains, or dairy products; a couple of older boys bringing empty propane gas containers and staggering away with the replacements; pubescent girls rushing in for an item or two needed by their mothers in the preparation of tonight's dinner. They exchange glances and a self-conscious joke over a girl their age as she walks by with eyes lowered, then speculate on the truth of the rumors of her sexual escapades during the *mussem* (annual festival) of the local saint last month. Tomorrow's school is also a half day, and several of the boys plan to meet at the soccer field in the early afternoon.

At roughly seven o'clock Abdelaziz starts up the street with Kabiri, leaving him at his door and continuing to his own house. His older brother has returned for the evening, so the whole family is present, and there is some good-natured joking between Abdelaziz and his mother. His older brothers are more restrained with her, and she still treats his younger brother as a small child, even though he is twelve. Their father is a taciturn man of perhaps sixty-five, some twelve years older than their mother, whom he married after divorcing his first wife. He is treated with respect and reserve by each of his sons.

After dinner the males, leaving the two women to clear away dinner, make their way to the family's guest room, which also normally houses the television set. They are in time to watch both the French and the literary Arabic news broadcasts, neither of which their parents can understand. Tonight there is also a French-dubbed American family comedy and a Euro-vision crime mystery. By this time the women have joined the group, and the family remains at the set until 11:00 P.M. Finally Abdelaziz moves to the next room, furnished like the guest room with hard-stuffed cushions on wooden bases, along which large pillows are arranged as back rests. He moves these from a two-meter length of cushion, spreads a blanket, and lies down after pulling off his woolen sweater. His younger brother is already asleep at the opposite end of the room, and his older brother is making his bed on the cushion across the room as Abdelaziz falls asleep.

Other Boys

The previous account is typical of routines reported by other older male adolescents who were still in school. Although a much higher proportion of males (48 percent) than of females (23 percent) continues past elementary school, a minority of the older males in the study are still in school. Abdelaziz is perhaps somewhat more studious than average, but one is struck by the extent to which school dominates the waking activities of the male second-ary student. The working male adolescent's typical day also features several long walks; these usually take him into Kabar, where he may be either ap-prenticed to a skilled worker or employed in a shop. Other males of a variety of ages assist fathers at a variety of marketing or agricultural activities. Among the younger half of the teenage males, school can almost be taken for granted, although the seriousness with which studies are pursued varies. The reader has probably noticed how free of household chores Abdelaziz's day was, in contrast to that of Hakima. While some teenage boys run er-rands, fetching groceries from the store or bread from the oven, these duties tend to fall on older males only when no one else is available. Age and appar-ent physical maturation are important predictors of whether a boy will assist at household duties, and indeed of whether he will be visible to the observer at all. Older males in this setting have a knack for remaining out of view dur-ing most daylight hours, and it is doubtful that most could be pressed into household service even if glimpsed. They are perhaps walking on the hills and paths leading out of town, or hanging out at the large café in the Suiqa, watching the card games.

Leaving personality and physical growth aside for now, prediction of the whereabouts and activities of a male teenager in Zawiya requires at least knowing whether the boy in question is still in school; whether school is in session; and whether it is Ramadan. As the schoolday dominates the life of the schoolboy, so vacation time and Ramadan, the Muslim month of dawn-to-dusk fasting, are experienced as a profound change. For the older teenage male who is not in school, the major determiner of the daily schedule is whether he is employed in a regular job.

A GENERATION AGO

Our study concerns adolescents raised in one neighborhood, children of families who had lived in the neighborhood long enough to partake of its influences (a decade or more) and to give their own stamp to it; yet very few of the parents of the adolescents were born in the town of Zawiya. Most had lived in small settlements in the surrounding countryside where their families farmed and herded to make a living, as most rural people still do. Thus the history of our neighborhood took place not in Zawiya, but in much smaller settlements differing in many ways from the Zawiya of today. To give the reader a sense of the changes that have occurred in one generation, the differences in life-style between the adolescents just descibed and their parents, we present the reminiscences of Zohra, one of the mothers, tape-recorded ten years ago while Susan was studying the lives of women. The phrasing and style are those of a middle-aged woman, long resident in Zawiya and known locally as an interesting speaker. The village she describes was about six kilometers from Zawiya and included roughly fifty households.[4]

> Well . . . I'm going to tell you about when my father was alive—may God have mercy on his soul—when I was very small. The first thing I remember was when my father—God have mercy on him—was there, when I was seven years old [around 1930].
> There were houses in the village early on. My father didn't have a tent. The people who were well off had nice houses. The others had tents; they used them to move with the cows and the sheep. Now, when spring arrives, we move the tents from the place where we were living and go to land that has grass and flowers. We build the tents there and we bring our cows and stay with them until the springtime was past . . . only then did we return to the village. We stayed with the animals until they ate well, and we milked them there and we churned the milk there. . . .
> But my father wasn't like that; he used to have a house. They had big jars in which they used to churn buttermilk. Now, there were people who did the milking, six or eight women. Every evening they came to milk, but not for money like now. They took milk, or buttermilk, or butter, and that's all. They didn't live with us; each had her own house.

But when it's milking time, the neighbors would milk for you. Again, if it were the time of the wheat harvest coming up, they gave it to them first; when they threshed the wheat, they gave it to them. Those things were not like they are now. Now, if you want meat, you buy it with money. They won't give you even a chicken; you won't see even a chicken!

There was plenty of everything at that time; it was just fabric that wasn't plentiful. A woman used to wear just a robe [a rectangular piece of cloth wrapped around the body and fastened into a loose-fitting dress]. And the woman who was considered elegant, she would have two robes; that woman was good and important. But there was just the robe: no pantaloons, no nothing. People used to weave *haiks* [outer cloaks] of wool themselves. Well, now that fabric has become plentiful, they go around in the streets selling it; whoever wants buys fabric or sweaters or pants. Whoever used to wear sweaters or pants? No one!

There was plenty of wheat and plenty of milk and plenty of everything. A poor woman used to have six or seven hundred kilos of wheat in her house. A person never used to buy grain at the *suq* [the weekly market]. Now all the people only buy grain at the suq; it's gotten so that everything is at the suq. There are only a few who have things at home. Now that the Christians have come and there are machines and tractors, and there's all this . . . it's not like that time anymore.

The coming of the French or "Christians" (in Arabic, *nSara*, from "Nazarenes") to the area soon after they took control of Morocco in 1912 directly affected this woman's life, as it did many of the families in agricultural Morocco:

> My father had a lot of land. He had farmland, and he had sheep and cattle. . . . He had land near the Sebou River, and he had land here. Then my father sold the land near the river to a Christian. And when he gave him the deed to that land, he also gave him the deed to this land. He only sold one piece of land, but he gave him the papers for the two pieces of land [her father was illiterate]. And when he asked the Christian to give him back his papers, he said "You sold me everything."
>
> But that Christian didn't throw us off the land; he left us the land. He stayed on one piece of land and we stayed on the other. We grazed our animals and we farmed and we ate and we drank; he didn't say a word about it.

While many people lost their land through legal or illegal bargains with Christians, they did not react with a bitterness that precluded any further dealing with them. Rather, they were pragmatic, finding that contacts with these outsiders were sometimes very useful. For example, when Zohra was an adolescent, her mother arranged her marriage to a man she did not like. After she objected and ran away once, her family put manacles on her feet to keep her close to home. But as she describes it:

> A girlfriend helped me take the irons off one leg and I ran away from the village until I got to the farm. It was the farm on which that Christian lived, the one who took my father's land. When that Christian saw the iron on my leg, he took it off. He telephoned the city and took me away from that man . . . and that was that. From that time, I never went near that man [the fiancé] again.

In another instance, when Zohra was married and had a sick child, the Frenchman's wife helped her get medical treatment.

As Zohra recalls, the separation of the sexes both before and after marriage was quite strict, and men controlled women's activities to a large extent:

> When a woman was still young, it was shameful for her to go to the suq. Her father-in-law or mother-in-law went; I never saw the suq until I moved into town. Honest to God, I never ever saw what the suq looked like. It used to be that only the men shopped. They brought you potatoes or meat or soup or whatever, and you had to cook it—it was your business.
>
> And also at that time, if I wanted to visit someone, I couldn't go unless my father-in-law gave me permission or someone came with me. After I was married we lived in a tent, and my boundary was the edge of the tent. We couldn't visit each other, even if I knew you very well. If there was a party or a wedding or if someone was sick, it would be okay, but you couldn't just go to visit. The old people were with us, so we couldn't just leave.
>
> And if you asked and if he feels like it or it pleases him, he'll let you go. And if he doesn't want to, he won't. Even if you're helping him harvest the wheat and you talk to a woman, he'd say "Why are you talking to her?" even though it's only a woman, not a man. Well, that's what the old people used to do. Old people used to be naïve, not like us.
>
> It used to be that even if you had sugar in the house, you couldn't make tea or coffee . . . you couldn't make anything at all if the man didn't make it. And if he didn't give you any, you didn't drink any. And you wouldn't complain loudly and say, "I didn't get any at all," or make tea yourself; that was shameful. Now, everything is topsy-turvy [laughing].
>
> Once I was grinding flour with my sister-in-law when she was still a virgin [unmarried]; we had a stone mill and ground by hand. Every day we had to grind whatever we were going to eat. We were grinding

flour and singing and my brother-in-law came and chased us away. He chased us maybe six kilometers, and he was catching up and we were going, running away. He wanted to beat us, and said, "Do I have dancing girls [prostitutes], that you're singing in the house? You're singing and people are passing next to the tent! Goddamn your father!" Now, that's all over with. Now that's finished.

As Zohra's account illustrates vividly, much has changed in Zawiya in the lifetime of its older residents. The economy has been transformed from subsistence to cash, a population of peasant farmers has become one of wage laborers (or unemployed) living in much larger settlements, and technology and public transportation have brought the world to Zawiya. Gender relations and male authority, though still quite distinct from U.S. norms, have also changed significantly since Zohra's youth. On the other hand, the pragmatic reaction of Zohra's generation to the profound changes brought by dealings with the French indicates that this is a population with great resilience and readiness to accommodate to new circumstances; these qualities are still noticeable in the adolescents of today's Zawiya.

THE SETTING

Various characteristics of Zawiya influence daily life and expand or constrain the options of adolescents. For example, its Islamic character and rural surroundings give adolescents a firm grounding in Morocco's traditions. Its colonial history deprived many families of land and livelihood, and introduced wage labor as a widespread alternative. Today this means adolescents expect to be less economically dependent on parents in adulthood, which has many implications. They also see education as a prerequisite for many new jobs. A fuller description of the setting elaborates the context in which adolescents function and characterizes its influence on their lives.

Physical Setting

The town of Zawiya is in the more fertile northern section of Morocco, on the southeastern edge of the rich agricultural plain called the Gharb. Nestled against the first foothills of the Middle Atlas mountain range, it is on the edge of Berber-speaking territory. A small river flows along the eastern side of town. While snow falls in the mountains, the climate on the plains is warm temperate (much like California), with wet winters and warm dry summers. Winter temperatures often fall into the forties (Fahrenheit), which is surprisingly cold without central heating. In the summer months temperatures can exceed 115 degrees, usually cooling sharply at evening.

Although there are about eleven thousand inhabitants in the densely settled town, in some ways it resembles a village in its lack of amenities. Only the one market street (the Suiqa) is paved, and few are wide enough to accommodate cars or trucks. Most are clay and mud and become impassable during winter rains. Only one home (that of the leader of the founding saint's descendants) has running water; eight public taps supply the remainder of the community's drinking and cooking water, while water for washing floors or clothing is carried from the river on donkeyback and sold door to door. Most houses have their own cesspools, but used dishwater and such is poured out into the streets, and at all seasons there is a trickle of muddy water running toward the base of the hill. In the last few years some of the houses have been connected to a central sewer system, providing an example of the questionable value of "progress": the modern system dumps raw sewage into the river, near the major point where water sellers draw wash water.

While many physical aspects of Zawiya still give it a rural appearance, there is evidence of change toward a more urban character. Ten years ago there were no local government offices such as a post office, bank, or police station. Now there is a small postal service, where one can buy stamps, make phone calls, and receive money orders (often from relatives abroad), as well as offices of the new mayor, the police, and other government functionaries. Many government services are still obtained in the market town of Kabar two kilometers away, and a much wider selection of goods is also available there. Zawiya has electricity in most neighborhoods and an elementary school,[5] and there are a few telephones in shops and in the most prosperous homes. The town's most imposing feature is the tomb of the saint who founded it three hundred years ago and the attached mosque, located at the center of the original settlement. In the last ten years, several new mosques have been built in other neighborhoods. There are three public baths, and several butchers, vegetable sellers, and public ovens, providing a range of services and products usually unavailable to residents of smaller, more isolated villages.

The streets are narrow and often winding, lined with the facades of attached houses, broken up only by heavy wooden or metal doors. To ensure privacy, no windows face the street; light comes into the two or three rooms of each house through windows opening onto its interior courtyard. The poorest homes are built of sun-baked mud and straw bricks, and usually have just one small room and a small courtyard. Most of the more prosperous homes are built of fired, hollow bricks, now available in two local shops. The bricks are smoothed over with cement, and the surface may be decorated by texturing the cement or forming designs of stars, flowers, or flags before being painted white, blue, gold, or pink. These more substantial houses have two or three stories and tend to be found in the more prosperous of the new neighborhoods.

The town has seven or eight neighborhoods, each of which has a general socioeconomic status and considerable internal variation; ours was mainly middle level. Zawiya is close to Kabar, and they are connected by an all-weather road on which local taxis operate a shuttle service. The walk between the two towns is a daily experience for many of the adolescents and provides an important chance for contact with the ideas and temptations of the larger world. There are, in addition, excellent road and train connections from Kabar to the.rest of Morocco, and in the last ten years a train stop has been added only one kilometer from Zawiya. Thus a local teenager can leave town at 11:00 A.M. and be in Rabat, the capital, by 1:00 P.M. or in Casablanca, the second largest city in Africa, by 2:30. Many do travel, usually to visit relatives during summer vacation. These adolescents thus live in a semirural setting, within easy reach of what is going on in more urban parts of Morocco.

Historical Background

Morocco has a long recorded history, the last millennium of it as a Muslim country. Contacts with the Romans and Phoenicians were common before the time of Christ, and Volubilis, capital of the Roman province Mauritania Tingitana, lies thirty kilometers east of Zawiya. The town lies in an area that has been populated by herders and farmers for a long time, although the town site became permanent only three hundred years ago when the local saint lived here. The town is considered to have been founded by this saint, and his descendants remain important today; they live at the other edge of town from our own. The descendants of the saint formed a brotherhood, a *zawiya*, to follow and teach the way the saint had set out for them; this organization still exists and has branches in Fes, Meknes, Rabat, and Sale. It has also given its name to the town.

During most of its history, Morocco was divided politically into two parts, *bled al-mukhsen* and *bled es-siba*, roughly translated as "land of the government" and "land of anarchy." These were not static entities: government was the land that the sultan could control with his troops and whose residents paid taxes, while the majority, who could escape for the time being, were *siba*. Geertz (1968) notes the importance, in this unsettled context, of charismatic individuals who became warrior saints. One could argue further that the history of fluid control which allowed the rise of charismatic individuals also set the stage for the important role of self-presentation in Morocco to this day.

In prior times, a tribe called the Gharbawa inhabited the Zawiya region, the neighboring Beni Hsen were their traditional enemies, and both tribes and the Berber Zemmour used to raid passing caravans. Descendants from both government and dissident or revolting groups live in Zawiya today, but in general tribal ties are unimportant now. An exception is membership in a government-supported tribe, the Sherarda, because the members are granted the use of land which is inherited by sons but may not be sold.[6]

The Gharb area underwent rapid and lasting transformation during French colonization, from 1912 to 1956. Because of the flatness of the terrain and the superior weaponry and tactics of the French, the plains were relatively quickly "pacified" (Le Coz 1964; Porch 1983). Their agricultural potential was exploited almost immediately, and land was both legally bought from Moroccans and expropriated for large-scale mechanized agriculture. Partly to transport the products, the French built a railway and road system, with important intersections in Kabar. They also built an oil refinery there, although Morocco must import its petroleum. These factors increased contact with the outside world and combined first to bring the town of Kabar into existence and then to increase its size, until today it is much larger than the older, original town. The new town was made the seat of the local government under the French and has remained so, becoming a provincial capital in 1982. Since independence in 1956, Zawiya has nearly tripled in size, because of both a high national birth rate and in-migration from more rural areas. Most of the parents of the adolescents studied grew up under colonial rule. Their lives have been in important ways more traditional than those of their children, but the parents' exposure to rapid change in the colonial period has also encouraged in many a flexibility that affects their responses to their children's changing circumstances.

Social Groups

Ethnographers working in Morocco usually specify whether the group studied was Arab or Berber, and some feel this distinction is important in understanding social behavior. The great majority of Zawiya residents speak Moroccan colloquial Arabic as their mother tongue, and on this basis we refer to them as Arabs. To label the population as ethnically Arabs or Berbers is, we believe, of questionable value; noting linguistic ties is more relevant. Ethnologically, there is some difference between Arab and Berber custom. However, there is also variation within the customs of each group, depending on its geographic location, and there has been much borrowing and mixture over the years (Gellner and Micaud 1972; S. Davis 1983a). Less than 10 percent of Zawiya's population speak Berber as their first language: these people speak either the southern or the Middle Atlas dialect. The former is spoken by the families of some of the shopkeepers, who have been present for at least a generation, some of whom are quite well-off. The other dialect is spoken by more recent in-migrants, many of whom moved into town during the 1981 drought. In both cases, most family members also speak Moroccan Arabic, while very few of the majority who have Arabic as their mother tongue can speak or understand Berber. Thus Zawiya is mainly an Arabic-speaking community, and people identify themselves as Arabs.

The patrilineal descendants of the local saint form a small but important social group in Zawiya. The extended family of the saint are *shorfa*, tracing their lineage back to Ali, the husband of Fatima, and thence to the Prophet Mohammed. There were said to be 334 living descendants of the saint in 1971, most still residing in town. Several members of the immediate family of the head of the zawiya (the *mizwar*) held important government jobs in the capital city. While in number this group constitutes only about 3 percent of the population, their influence in the town is considerable. Associated with them are the Buakher, the descendants of the slaves originally sent to guard the saint and his followers. The Buakher have gradually intermarried with local families, and some of these families have been important in local government, with a few also holding office in the capital.

The majority of the population are people who have moved into the town from the surrounding countryside during the last thirty years; a few come from as far away as the Rif Mountains in the north or the Sahara in the south. The physical variety is striking: a group of local schoolgirls, for example, may contain what looks like a Scandinavian, with blond hair and blue eyes, walking with a girl with creamy complexion, brown hair, and hazel eyes, a more stereotypically Arab-looking young woman with coffee-colored skin and dark eyes and hair, and a Negroid girl with dark brown skin and very curly black hair.

Social Organization

Morocco is a Muslim country, and the residents of Zawiya follow Islamic family law concerning marriage, divorce, and inheritance, as well as the custom of patrilineal descent. Briefly, this means that marriage is traditionally arranged by the couple's parents, and a man may have up to four wives. Both partners can request a divorce, but this is easier for the male. Both sexes inherit, but a son inherits two shares to the daughter's one. One's family line is traced through males, and after marriage the young couple ideally lives with the groom's parents in what soon becomes a three-generation extended family. These are the general rules, but, as with many things in Morocco, knowing only the rules gives one a very incomplete picture.

Traditionally, marriage should occur between patrilateral parallel cousins (*awlad l-'amm*), which means that the children of two brothers should marry. In fact, an earlier survey of households in our neighborhood showed that only 13 percent of the marriages were to any close relative, whether on the father's or mother's side, first or third cousin, or in-law.

Economy

The town's economy is based on agriculture, trade, and the provision of services. Unlike earlier generations who lived on family farms, today's adolescents need not expect to be economically dependent in adulthood on their parents because of the availability of a variety of jobs. In this new (and highly competitive) economic situation public education is valued as preparation for many jobs.

Zawiya's agriculture is not the traditional subsistence form, in which each family lives on what it grows and trades the surplus for items like tea, sugar, and manufactured cloth. Because land plots have shrunk with inheritance, most can no longer support a family, and most persons involved in agriculture now work as day laborers on a few very large farms in the area. The descendants of the saints or of their previous slaves are the only local owners of large tracts of land; it was reputedly given to them by Sultan Moulay Ismail around 1680 when he built the saint's tomb. Rather than working their own land, the owners hire local people to work it for them. The crops grown are typical of this area, a kind of "Imperial Valley" to Morocco. The irrigable land is devoted to vegetable and herb gardens, often grown under trees bearing almonds, figs, pomegranates, lemons, oranges, and olives, while the hills are planted with wheat, lentils, barley, chickpeas, and sugar beets. A few people have small landholdings, held either privately or as members of the Sherarda descent group who have the use of eight to seventeen acres of land. Both traditional and modern methods are used; wheat is harvested by both scythe and combine, and threshed by mules as well as by tractors.

Most of the flat land around town is owned in large parcels by Moroccan individuals (absentee landlords) or by the Moroccan government. It is on these large tracts that the majority of the day laborers work, being transported at dawn by truck up to sixty kilometers away and returning at sunset. In 1982 the minimum agricultural wage was 14 dirhams (roughly US $2.25) a day, and some nongovernment farms paid less. Most of the workers are women and girls (including a few in our study); this is a low-status job, and men do it only if they are desperate for money. While the job is not permanent, one can live by day labor nearly all year round by following the cycles of the various crops.

An important part of the local population works in nearby Kabar; most are employed by either the oil refinery or the government. These people are important not in absolute numbers but in their influence; their situation is one to be emulated. They are almost the only people receiving a fixed monthly income and are among the most secure in the town, and many adolescents aspire to such employment.

Many Zawiya people are merchants and craftsmen. There are a few large grocery shops and many tiny ones selling basic staples. Several butcher shops sell freshly slaughtered lamb and beef, and other shops sell live chickens. Fresh vegetables are sold from tents. Men in shops weave woolen fabric and sew women's and men's dressy clothing, while women sew everyday women's and children's clothing, working out of their homes. Two electric mills grind wheat for flour, and several public ovens bake the bread each family prepares daily. Several local men work in transportation, either as drivers of transport trucks or of the taxis that operate between the town and Kabar or Kabar and neighboring towns. Other jobs for men include carpentry and construction work. A few local men have migrated to France to work in construction, in factories, or in agriculture, and they send money back to their families and visit every year.[7]

There are several religious schools, in which a man who has memorized the Qur'an teaches it to young children for a small fee. He may supplement his scant income with traditional curing and magic. The elementary school has a principal, his assistant, and about fifty teachers, male and female. Among these jobs the authority and status of the teachers and the income of the emigrants are particularly appealing to adolescents.

This economy is clearly cash based, even though people do each other favors and may barter at times. They are dependent on industrial products from the city or abroad, including much clothing, radios, televisions and tape recorders, motorbikes and cars, and soft drinks. Most food is purchased fresh. Even one hundred years ago people depended on imported tea and sugar to make the traditional mint tea, but recently their dependence on outside sources has grown, including greatly increased grain imports as a result of inadequate harvests. Many families also depend on money sent by relatives working in the cities or abroad. There are government programs to aid those in need, like the blind or poor widows, but these affect relatively few people; there are no large welfare programs. Medical care is available at low cost to anyone who can demonstrate poverty; there is a first aid clinic in Zawiya, and several clinics, private doctors, and a government hospital in nearby Kabar.

The people of Zawiya are well acquainted with modern technology, and most of our neighbors wished they had more access to it. The majority of families we studied had a radio–tape recorder and a television set. When Susan first lived here in 1965, the only televisions were in a few large cafés. By 1970 many well-off families had them; by 1982 most of the families in our neighborhood had sets, some, according to gossip, managing the cost by scrimping on meals. There was a new village down the road that did not yet have electricity, but many families there had sets that ran off car batteries. One of television's main effects has been to put people into closer touch with the outside world. In 1965, for example, only a few local women had seen snow, and they were intrigued by Susan's descriptions of it. In 1970, when we mentioned there had been a blizzard in our home country, many said "Oh, yes, we saw it on television; they have those big machines that move the snow and all." There is only one Moroccan channel, operated by a government agency, with programs in Arabic and French. These include a variety of American programs dubbed into French; "Dallas" and "The Incredible Hulk" were among the most popular broadcasts in 1982, along with Egyptian soap opera–type films. Television would have a much greater impact if it were broadcast in the Moroccan dialect, but so far only some news and occasional dramas are.[8] Another sign of the times is the popularity of the Tangier-based radio station Medi Une. They play Arabic, French, and U.S. music intermingled and move among all three languages for announcements. One may well hear Oum Kulthoum followed by Bob Dylan, Mozart, Bob Marley, and Jacques Brel. Older male adolescents love it, although their sisters tend to prefer the all-Arabic stations with their Moroccan popular music.

Political System

Morocco is a constitutional monarchy headed by King Hassan II. Much of the nation's present formal political structure has been carried over from the French colonial period, incorporating some traditional roles but placing them in a broader and more hierarchical system than before. Before independence in 1956 many officials were French, but now all are Moroccan; the government is the largest employer of white-collar workers.

The French-introduced system now in operation is very bureaucratic, and no individual is expected to act without the approval of his or her superior, who is ultimately the king. Briefly, the king appoints several ministers, each of whom has a subordinate organization. Most important is the minister of the interior, since under him are the provincial governors and mayors of large cities, and beyond them all local political officials. Each large town has a *qa'id*, somewhat like our mayor and county commissioner combined; Zawiya recently acquired its own qa'id. This man's local assistants are the *shikh* and the *moqqadam*, who carry messages and issue some official papers. There is also a council of respected elders, both elected and appointed, from several nearby settlements; their power is limited to quite minor local affairs. There are now police located in the town, and they are sometimes called in the event of disputes. Adolescents have relatively little contact with these political officials, but some aspire to the power upper-level bureaucratic positions provide.

There is also an informal power structure, involving people who are respected locally for their wisdom, their wealth, their connections, or some combination of these. The head of the saint's lineage often has a formal position as a member of the local council. However, his influence goes far beyond that office, and he is always consulted by town officials on any important matter; local people also often directly ask for his advice or mediation. One of the former slave families used to have several members involved in local government; although they no longer are, they are still influential in Zawiya. Various individuals may have influence by virtue of their access to information (cf. S. Davis 1983a). Taxi drivers, for example, are sometimes a locus of informal power because they are always on the road and know the movements of both locals and outsiders; they can use this information to their benefit. They are also acquainted with local police and can serve as a contact or intermediary for townspeople.

Religion

No discussion of Moroccan culture can be complete without emphasis on the central role of religion in the lives of both young people and adults. Islam has guided the thought and actions of most Moroccans for a thousand years, and the Qur'an and Traditions (*Hadith*) of the Prophet Mohammed continue to be the basis for thinking about moral action and family relations. Islam is seen as a complete system for living by most Muslims, and its concepts of growth and maturity form part of the discussion of adolescence as a stage of life (see chap. 3).

All of the permanent residents of Zawiya are Sunni Muslims. Orthodox (Sunni) Islam favors a direct relation between the individual and God, and does not foster the development of powerful religious officials. There is an *imam* who speaks in the mosque at the Friday group service; he may alternate with others and derives no great status from this role. There are several local *fqis* who teach religious school and who may cure or do magic; again, they are not pivotal figures.

Islam prescribes five essential practices. They are (1) the declaration of faith, saying "There is no God but God and Mohammed is His Prophet" (which is all one need do to convert to Islam); (2) praying at five designated times a day; (3) giving alms to the poor; (4) fasting from before sunrise until sunset during the month of Ramadan; and (5) making the pilgrimage to Mecca, if one can afford it.

All townspeople subscribe to these tenets of the faith, but many admit that it is difficult to find the time to pray, especially women with small children. Older people are most likely to pray regularly, but older adolescents today are more likely to pray than in the past. Only a few people have been able to afford the pilgrimage, but almost all give some alms. For outsiders, the most conspicuous aspect of Muslim practice is the annual Ramadan fast; it is also the one most directly affecting the lives of adolescents. Fasting is taken very seriously by Moroccans generally. All Muslims are supposed to fast after puberty, and in Zawiya most do; those children nearing puberty practice fasting a few days each year. In big cities some young people rebel by not observing the fast; while there were a few local rebels, no one violated the fast openly.

In addition to orthodox Islam, Morocco has a strong tradition of local saints and spirits and shrines. These popular aspects are especially apparent near a zawiya, with its saint's tomb and annual festival (*moussem*). The rural-urban split has always been essential in understanding Moroccan Islam (Eickelman 1976). Popular Islam in Morocco has long venerated local *siyyids*, persons (usually men) believed to be possessed of an unusual degree of *baraka*, or spiritual power (see Geertz 1968). Popular shrines sprang up on the site where a saintly figure had performed miraculous acts or perhaps prayed. These had become common by the seventeenth century, and the zawiya at such a site became the focus for a great deal of popular religious activity. Like most Moroccan towns, Zawiya is also the scene of many heterodox practices involved in magic and in countering the influence of *jnun* (spiritual beings); some of these practices affect adolescents as students or prospective marriage partners.

The town, then, has existed for over three hundred years, but grew rapidly during and after the colonial period in this century. Grandparents described French soldiers maneuvering on mules; the father of one woman was said to have carried the then sultan's brother sixty kilometers from Fez to Meknes on his back because the horse's pace jostled him. Now there are easy road and train connections to Fez, Meknes, and other cities, and one can write or telephone relatives there as well. Radio, telephone, and tape recorders mean that Moroccans share more of a common, and sometimes more Western-influenced, culture that they did in the past. Free universal education means that most of those under sixteen have a basic level of literacy, while almost none of their parents can read or write. School also gives boys and girls a legitimate excuse to meet and talk, so the traditional segregation of the sexes is breaking down. All these factors are important in the rapidly changing lives of the young people of Zawiya.

■ 3
Defining Adolescence in Zawiya

There are several parts to the problem of defining adolescence: determining whether a clear concept of adolescence exists in Zawiya, deciding who—if anyone—is "adolescent" according to local people, and setting our own working definition of adolescence so we can decide whom to include in the study. As the local references of the concept became clearer we concerned ourselves with a variety of physiological, sociocultural, and behavioral aspects of the adolescent experience in Zawiya.

As with so many things in Morocco, there is no unequivocal answer to the question "Is there a Moroccan life stage corresponding to our *adolescence*?" Finding out whether so-and-so should be considered adolescent was difficult. Indeed, there was no traditional colloquial word clearly translating *adolescent*, so the question could not be directly posed to parents and other uneducated residents.

We used several strategies to discover which, if any, local concepts might be related to the idea of a life stage and certain behaviors that we associate with adolescence. We asked young people how they knew they were grown up, and we asked people of various ages to describe the stages in the life cycle. We asked both mothers and youth if they expected different behavior as children got older, and what this behavior might be.

As the various field research teams of the Harvard Adolescence Project returned to Cambridge and began to compare notes, we were struck by several remarkable similarities among the daily experiences of the young people in the widely different settings. Perhaps the most pervasive of these was the involvement of the majority of the young residents of each community with public education, something that usually had not been true for their parents. In the case of Zawiya, the increase in the proportion of neighborhood girls who were attending school is one of the most striking changes to occur in the twenty years since Susan first lived there. Increased participation in formal education (by both males and females) has affected every aspect of adolescent life.

At a cultural and institutional as well as an individual level, therefore, we looked at the influence of education on adolescence in Zawiya. Education is important in that young people have more opportunity for what have been considered adolescent activities if they attend secondary school. They learn there a term for adolescence and are taught stages in the life cycle, as a result of which many come to think of themselves as adolescents.

Religion provides another frame of reference for issues of physical and moral development by Moroccans. Among religious practices in Zawiya the observance of the Ramadan fast demonstrates moral responsibility; we describe the importance of this observance in the teenage years.

PHYSIOLOGICAL ADOLESCENCE

We began our research using a physiological definition of adolescence because we wanted to have a maturational base for comparing the seven communities in the Harvard Adolescence Project. As we planned the study with our colleagues at Harvard, we decided to include girls from the age of five years before the average girl began to menstruate until five years after; and a group of boys whose range of ages began and ended a year later than girls, to adjust for the somewhat later development of males (Marshall and Tanner 1970). However, the age of physical puberty could not be specified until near the end of the study, after repeated measures of height and weight had been collected and sensitive questions about sexual development could reasonably be asked. Thus we began by using age, selecting children from a sample of families meeting the criteria for long-term residence in the neighborhood. Susan visited each of these households and asked an older person the ages of all household members. All those reported as between the ages of nine and twenty constituted the initial sample on whom other data were collected. Calendar ages are much less salient in Morocco than in the United States, however, and more detailed questioning and comparing of ages resulted in our changing many of these initial estimates as the year wore on.

Physical Growth

Physical growth was a developmental measure used at all settings in the Adolescence Project, since it did not require laboratory facilities and touched fewer personal and cultural sensitivities than an alternative method, the measurement of secondary sexual characteristics (Tanner 1960). One can estimate the age of menarche, as well as adrenarche (the period when the adrenal hormones begin the changes of puberty), by finding the age of the growth spurt, when a child grows four to six centimeters (approximately 1½"–2¼") a year instead of the usual two or three. One can then infer that adrenarche occurs about six years earlier than the spurt for girls and seven for boys, and that menarche will follow in nine to twelve months for girls in Western populations. Repeated measures of height and weight were collected from 103 young people in Zawiya.

These data suggest that for females in Zawiya, maximum height velocity, the peak of the "adolescent growth spurt," occurred at about twelve years of age, while for males the peak velocity was between ages fourteen and fifteen; this is similar to the two-year gap found in the West (Marshall and Tanner 1970). Most individuals experienced rapid growth within a two-year period centered on the collective peak for each sex. Almost no girls gain significantly in height after age fifteen, while for males the end of the rapid-growth range appears to be between ages sixteen and seventeen. The three years between the growth spurt and menarche for Zawiya females is longer than the approximately one year for Western populations, but there is some evidence of longer gaps in other groups, such as that reported by Worthman in Kenya (1987, 29).

Puberty

Later in the year, after we knew people better and could pose potentially embarrassing questions, we were able to get data on age of menarche for the girls. This was done in two ways: by direct questioning of a group of girls who were relatively comfortable talking with Susan about such matters, and by adding questions regarding the number of Ramadans fasted to our standard interview forms.

Adult Muslims are obliged to fast (to abstain from food, drink, and sexual activity) from first light to sunset during the lunar month of Ramadan, and it is usually assumed in Zawiya that it is shameful for a child who has visibly matured sexually not to fast. For boys this judgment of maturity is loosely linked to beard development and change in body shape, but for girls in appears to be quite specifically related to the onset of menstruation. Hence we asked how many days each each young person has fasted during the past Ramadan and how many prior Ramadans they had fasted. If a girl had fasted for two full Ramadans, it usually meant she had begun menstruating between two and three years before.

The mean age of menarche estimated from observance of the Ramadan fast was roughly fifteen, using both retrospective (recall) and status quo (current menstrual status) approaches, as well as a probit analysis portraying the cumulative percentages claiming to fast at successive ages. The probit showed fifteen to be a sharp demarcation point for these girls, with only 1 of 31 girls below that age reporting complete observance of the fast and 25 of 26 girls over sixteen saying they had fulfilled the complete fast. Onset of menstruation in Zawiya appears to occur at a somewhat later age than it does in Tunisia, the nearest African site for which there are published data. In Tunisia it was found that girls from upper socioeconomic groups in urban Tunis menstruated at 13.4 years and those from lower groups at 14.0 (Eveleth and Tanner 1977, 245). Several persons in Morocco, including a physician who had researched the topic and a local midwife, estimated the age of menarche at thirteen, but our data suggest that fifteen is more accurate for our semirural sample.[1]

The use of Ramadan as an indicator of puberty is more difficult in the context of male physical development. Direct questioning of boys about the beginning of seminal emissions was felt to be too sensitive for general use, so the Ramadan data cannot be compared with this physical marker. Fifty neighborhood males responded to the question regarding observance of the last Ramadan fast. Since most of these interviews were completed after the beginning of Ramadan in 1982, recall is probably quite accurate. Among the 50 males who responded to the question about the most recent Ramadan fast, 16 (32 percent) claimed to have fasted the whole month. These included 1 very pious thirteen-year-old, 2 of 5 fifteen-year-olds, 2 of 8 sixteen-year-olds, and all 12 males over seventeen. Seventeen is thus a fairly clear age for undertaking the full fast among males in Zawiya. Eleven of the males who said that they had fasted the most recent Ramadan claimed to have completed fasts in previous years: the number of years given indicate initial fasting ages ranging from twelve to eighteen.[2]

Several local males, asked to generalize about the typical age for fasting among their peers, indicated that such clear signs of physical maturation as beard growth and an adult physique were the important indicators. While a boy of fifteen with only the beginnings of beard growth may fast scrupulously (and will be respected for doing so), local opinion is clearly offended by a mature-looking eighteen-year-old who does not fast. Since these clearly visible indicators of adulthood typically follow by several years the point at which most males probably experienced their first seminal emission, there is considerable scope for males' individual decision about beginning the fast. The occasion of Ramadan also provided examples of older adolescent and adult informants criticizing the low level of fast observance by others in the neighborhood. These comments often included an observation that people were in general growing less faithful, and that young men in particular were more likely to cheat than in their parents' generation.[3]

The Ramadan fast has a sexual dimension as well: for a day's fast to be valid, one must be in a state of ritual purity throughout. Sexual intercourse or a seminal emission during sleep, like female menstrual blood, renders one impure until one has ritually bathed. Hence sexual activity is forbidden during the day in Ramadan, and several older males observed that even lustful thoughts during the day are a form of fast breaking.

YOUTH AND ADULTHOOD IN ISLAM

Religion is central to the life experience of most residents of Zawiya, and its importance grows during the years following puberty. Islam is a complete system of belief and practices expressing the relationship of the believer to God, a system of legal and moral prescriptions for Muslims as well as a set of spiritual beliefs. The fundamental content of Islam is expressed in the revealed word of God (the Qur'an), the authenticated sayings and religious practices of the Prophet Mohammed (the Hadith), and the accumulated body of Muslim practice.

Three Arabic terms rooted in Islam have special implications for the discussion of adolescence in a community like Zawiya. These are *bulugh, 'aql,* and *rushd*. In the Sunni Islam of North Africa and most of the Middle East, each Muslim community follows one of the four "orthodox" schools of Muslim practice. Each of these makes presumptions about maturity, specifying the age at which children shall be considered mature enough to bear full legal responsibility for their actions, to inherit property, or (in the case of an heir to the throne) to rule.

Bulugh

Physical puberty, particularly in the male, is referred to by the literary Arabic term *bulugh* (Wehr 1966, 73–74). The term also conveys the sense of arrival, attainment, and sufficiency; it has connotations of the intensity and potential disruptiveness of the experience. The Malikite school of Muslim jurisprudence is that officially recognized in Morocco. It treats puberty (bulugh) as knowable from a variety of signs, including, (1) the production of sperm by the male, both in sleep and waking; (2) female menustruation and/or pregnancy; (3) growth of "rough" (as distinct from soft) pubic hair; a moustache or beard alone is not taken as conclusive in the male; (4) the smell of the armpit; and (5) deepened voice.

Bulugh was used by a minority of local informants in discussions of adolescence.[4] A related literary term, *Hulum* (from *Halama*, "to dream"), which can mean forbearance or emotional maturity but which also connotes the reflective and "dreamy" side of puberty (see Lane 1865), was not used in conversation by local informants. However, the expression *Hlimt* ("I dreamed") was mentioned by male informants as a euphemism for having a wet dream.

Bulugh is primarily a physical marker, but like the other developmental terms discussed here, it may carry connotations of responsibility: "For a Muslim to reach puberty is to enter the age of responsibilities. *Bulugh* is the end of childhood, but it transforms the child into a *mukallaf*, a responsible being" (Bouhdiba 1985, 168).

ʿAql

One of the most subtle and important concepts in Moroccan discourse, and a theme of our treatment of adolescence in Zawiya (see chap. 1), is that of *ʿaql*. The term itself, which has in literary Arabic connotations of reasonableness and intelligence, suggests variously mind, responsibility, memory, and thoughtfulness. The altered functioning of one who is intoxicated or possessed by spirits (*jnun*) may evoke the comment *"kherj l-ʿaql dyalu,"* "He's out of his mind" (more literally, "His reason has left him"). Generally, ʿaql involves a readiness to consider all the consequences of one's actions and to behave like a responsible person, to exhibit "social sense" (Abu-Lughod 1986).

We see more explicitly how ʿaql is used in the advice of an elderly Moroccan woman to her niece:[5] "Don't get yourself totally drawn into the *qadiya* [event, problem, affair]; try to look constantly at what is there under, above the *qadiya;* try to remember what was there before; and try to train yourself to guess what is likely to happen. All the possibilities, dear Fatima, all of them" (Mernissi 1987, xii–xiii).

Moroccans who have developed ʿaql are able to discern, and react responsibly to, the variety of social possibilities in any situation.

The demonstration of ʿaql as social sense is closely connected, as Abu-

Lughod shows, with the concept of *Hasham*, a key term in Moroccan discourse as well. Often translated simply as shame or modesty, Hasham in fact suggests, in Zawiya as among the Awlad 'Ali community in Egypt described by Abu-Lughod, a display of behavior that is appropriately deferent for the situation, showing regard for propriety (Abu-Lughod 1986, 105). Hasham as voluntary deference is thus closely linked to 'aql: "Just as the possession of 'aql enables persons to control their needs and passions in recognition of the ideals of honor, so it allows them to perceive the social order and their place in it" (Abu-Lughod 1986, 108).

Sensible behavior can be problematic for any person, since all are also endowed with natural essence or desire, *nafs* (Wehr 1966, 985). Rosen describes a Muslim and characteristically Moroccan notion of a basic tension between the passionate, animal side of one's nature and the gradually acquired restraining force of reason, and he refers to this as the *"nafs-'aqel* paradigm" (Rosen 1984, 30–34; cf. Eickelman 1976, 130–138). Children are conceived as virtually all nafs, capable through instruction and effort of gradually acquiring 'aql and thereby achieving the balance on which both salvation and earthly happiness depend. Women are typically viewed as having stronger passions, and therefore have more need of (and less ability to acquire) 'aql (Rosen 1984, 32). Although the term *nafs* was seldom used by Zawiya residents in conversations with us, the tension between desire and reason is implicit in many interviews. Rosen quotes an adult male informant who expresses the nature of this dialectic eloquently:

> We need desire, for example, in order to have children, but if it is not controlled by reason we would just be like animals. . . . We say that if a man "has *nafs*" he has "self-respect," but if he is "in love with his *nafs*" he is just an "egotist." What you call psychology we call *'ilm n-nafs*, "the study of *nafs*." Reason gives us the flexibility to handle our *nafs* and all the bad things it might lead us to do. Just as God put joints in our body so that we would be flexible enough to cope with a variety of physical situations, so too He gave us *'aqel* so we might also have flexibility of mind and know good from bad, right from wrong. (1984, 32)

The social sensibility denoted by 'aql is inherently contextual rather than involving absolute moral principles, as the reasonable person seeks "to discern accurately the contours of existing social and political realities and on this basis to calculate an effective course of action" (Eickelman 1985, 132).[6]

One is struck by the difference for males and females in the expectation of behavior that demonstrates 'aql or responsibility: while for males the ultimate expectations may be higher than those for females, males appear to be given at least an extra decade of life to achieve this mature behavior. The irresponsible or forgetful behavior of even a boy in his late teens will often be excused with the comment "He still has no 'sense'" (baqi ma'andu l'aql). For the girl, on the other hand, responsibility for a variety of shopping and housekeeping functions and for the welfare of younger siblings is usually expected during the elementary school years.

Rushd

The final literary term that is central to educated discussion of adolescence is *rushd*, which refers to the attainment of adult, reason-guided, maturity of thought and action, particularly in religious and moral matters (Wehr 1966, 341–342). As noted above, the concept of maturity is most likely to be discussed in Zawiya in terms of 'aql. The term *rushd* and the life-stage label "age of maturity" (*sinn ar-rushd*) were used only a few times by relatively educated local male informants, who spoke of this maturity as being attainable only after adolescence, beyond the age of twenty. In Islamic jurisprudence, a child cannot inherit property or assume other adult functions until *sinn ar-rushd* is attained, and this determination may require the physical and psychological examination of the young man or woman by religious scholars. While few residents of Zawiya know the details of these scholars' debates over concepts of maturation, the high tradition impinges in a variety of ways on local discourse. The most obvious influence is on the thinking of the approximately one-third of adolescents and young adults who have continued far enough in school to hear these matters discussed there. One required course in the secondary school curriculum is Islamic Education, in which proper behavior for the Muslim male and female is discussed, as well as some of the physiological changes of adolescence.

The impact of such instruction is evident in the response of one sixteen-year-old informant to questioning by Douglas about *bulugh*. We have known this boy, Sa'id, since he was a toddler.[7]

■ D: *Do you know what* bulugh *is?*
 S: *Yes.*
 D: *How does a boy know he's reached* bulugh?
 S: *A teacher was talking about it. One gets a moustache, and—wait, I'm thinking. Do you know what* manay *is, that yellow stuff?*
 D: *You mean, that comes out of the penis?*
 S: *Yes, and the same from a woman. Do you know when it happens?*

Douglas mentioned differences between various countries, noted that the age has fallen in some parts of Europe, and asked when it usually happened in Zawiya.

> ■ s: *About fifteen or sixteen. The teacher in Islamic Education says there's nothing to be ashamed of, and he also mentioned hair growing in the armpits as a sign of* bulugh. *This begins at sixteen.*
> d: *Has it happened to you yet?*
> s: *Yes, some [touches armpit].*
> d: *Sometimes that* manay *comes out at night, and kids feel embarrassed, so it's important for teachers to explain things. . . . Do you remember when it first happened to you?*
> s: *No, it's never happened yet.*
> d: *Oh? Well, it will,* insha'llah *[God willing]. Do kids talk about this when it happens?*
> s: *Some do. I've heard it a lot.*
> d: *Does life change then?*
> s: *Yes, they say, "He starts to live in his imagination"* [khayal].

THE LIFE COURSE IN ZAWIYA

It seems clear to us that while adolescence may be a problematic concept for Zawiya, puberty is recognized and quite readily associated with important behavioral as well as physical changes. To identify locally recognized developmental categories and to relate these to individual young people we solicited lists of terms for life stages, asked young people to give us their criteria for deciding they had grown up, and interviewed members of the neighborhood about the characteristics of people in transition from childhood to adulthood.

Terms for Life Stages

It was clear from the first that no widely used Moroccan term conveys the sense of our "adolescence." We had found the dictionary term *as-sinn al-murahaqa* as a literary Arabic rendering of "adolescence," and this term seemed well understood by a certain group of people, including government officials, educated persons, and adolescents in secondary school. The classical Arabic root of the term (the verb *rahiqa*) conveys both the idea of attaining physical puberty and of being oppressed or overburdened.

The dictionary term does not appear spontaneously in the conversation of most people in Zawiya, however. As Susan was doing the household census and explaining our work, she had no way to say "We want to study adolescents" or "This is a study of teenagers." Instead, she had to say "We want to ask about your children who are not really small and not really big." No one responded at this point, "Oh, you mean the ———s," which suggested there was no obvious and universal colloquial term for the concept. Later, in a further attempt to discover a local term, we asked several of the boys and girls, as well as some older people, to name the stages people go through in their development. These are listed in table 3.1.

While all of these terms were mentioned by at least two people, by no means did all people give every one. Everyone asked did mention some form of *baby*, as well as *boy* and *girl* and grown or married *man* and *woman*, but other terms varied. Only a quarter gave the terms *shabb* and *shabba*, and only half mentioned the stages of *'azri* and *'azba*, all of which fall between childhood and adulthood. We also asked for examples of local youth in these categories so we could see what the relevant characteristics were. Girls gave mainly boys in their early or mid twenties as examples of an *'azri*, while boys of sixteen and eighteen were said by some to fit and by others to be too young. The girls they listed as *'azba* were fourteen and over, while those they described as too young were fourteen or younger. About a third said being an *'azba* is related to getting your period, but two-thirds said it was not. Boys tended to give *shab* and *shabba* as the terms corresponding to the just-preadult years, if they did not produce the classical terms *murahiq* or *baligh*. Some informants used the term *shab* to refer to unmarried males in their twenties, and several were careful to dissociate the term from the formal *murahaqa*. Generally, *shab* seems both a more commonly used and a more

TABLE 3.1
Life-Stage Terminology

Term		Translation
Male	Female	
tifl	tifla	baby, infant
Sabiy	Sabiya	baby, infant
weliyd	bniya	little boy, little girl (about 2–5 years old)
weld	bent	boy, girl
'azri	'azba	bachelor, virgin (literally)
shabb	shabba	youth
rajel	mra	grown man or woman
shayb	kebira	old man or woman

inclusive term than does *murahiq*.[8] The terms *'azri* and *'azba* appear less commonly used by boys than girls. Several older males who had some college education provided an extended list of very precise terms for life stages from birth to death, but these again seem to be the memorized translations of perhaps imported concepts, particularly from textbooks. From the overlapping of these categories, and the failure of many people to mention some of them at all, we concluded there is not a clearly defined social phase of adolescence among most of the people in this setting, nor a term clearly refering to an adolescent as an individual.

A recent study of male high school students in Casablanca by a Moroccan psychologist also notes the absence of a colloquial Arabic term for adolescence (Ouzzi 1986). Ouzzi's discussion of terms for youth in Morocco draws attention to the negative connotations of many expressions. Moroccan adults perceive and describe the physical changes of puberty, but they tend not to label youth as distinct from childhood and adulthood unless moved to criticize adolescent misbehavior (Ouzzi 1986, 31–34). The study of adolescence is primarily a result of changes in industrial and urbanizing societies, and these changes have only recently become widespread in Morocco (p. 32).

"How Do You Know You're Grown Up?"

Since we could not identify a generally understood local term for adolescence, we added to our basic interview the question, "How do you know you're grown up?" Responses frequently gave us criteria by which individual young people assumed one had made the transition from childhood to adulthood.[9] The most salient distinction among the answers seemed to be between those persons who mentioned only physical growth or chronological age itself in response to the question and those who referred to some behavioral or moral criterion. Among the girls, a majority (24, or 62 percent of the responses) emphasized physical changes or chronological age itself as the criterion by which the girl would know she was "grown up."[10] Only 12 girls (31 percent) mentioned behavioral, moral, or mental changes, either alone (nine responses) or in combination with physical factors (three responses). Five of these (none of whom had secondary education) explicitly used the term *'aql* (maturity or responsibility) to refer to a characteristic that develops as one becomes grown up. Age may be a factor in the nature of the answers given: the median age of those who mentioned nonphysical factors was 17.3, while the median age of those who mentioned only physical or chronological factors was 14.4. Interestingly, only one girl mentioned marrying as a basis for knowing that she had grown up.

The responses of the thirty-six males who answered the question were classified in the same way. Among the males, however, half (18) of the responses mentioned behavioral, moral, and mental factors either alone (39 percent) or in combination with physical factors (11 percent). Only 3 of these referred explicitly to "maturity" ('aql), however, and 2 of these had secondary education. Slightly over a third of the males (13, or 36 percent) referred only to physical factors or chronological age. As among females, the median age of those who mentioned nonphysical factors was greater (16.2 years) than that of those who mentioned only physical factors (14.1 years). Seven boys mentioned marriage as a factor.

Thus most of these Zawiya youth tended to emphasize physical maturation as the primary basis for judging that they had grown up, with older males and females likely to mention also psychological qualities. In general, ideas about the stage of life corresponding to our concept of adolescence suggest that physical puberty is clearly recognized as an event, while subsequent social and individual behavioral changes are less likely to be described.

Zawiya Perceptions of Adolescents

We found that local people used certain terms to describe behaviors that they said were most common during the years around puberty. One term used by local persons with varying levels of education to characterize the postpubescent individual is the adjective *Taysh*, a term that in literary Arabic can mean reckless or rash as well as frivolous, confused, or helpless (Wehr 1966, 579). Several informants mentioned that the stage of life we were asking about was the "age of Taysh" (behavior).[11] A related colloquial usage involves applying the terms "light" (*khfif*) and "heavy" (*tqil*) to refer to one's quality of mind or behavior. A Moroccan who is quick-witted will be spoken of as having a "light head," while the slow-witted dullard is characterized as having a "heavy head." Although the connotations of being "light" mentally are positive in Zawiya, we several times heard flighty or irresponsible young people characterized as "light" in their behavior in what was obviously a pejorative sense. Thus a girl who was seen as very frivolous might be described as *Taysha* or *khfifa*, and she would not be respected; the same concepts are applied to boys.

The use of these terms for adolescent behavior is nicely illustrated in an interview Susan conducted with Naima, a particularly articulate neighbor in her midthirties. She is atypical of parents in the community in that she completed elementary and part of secondary school. Both her daughter and son were in the neighborhood sample. We enter the interview as the mother is discussing brothers' attempts to keep their sisters from getting into trouble with boys.

■ N: *That is the cause. Usually the girl is still young and her mind is frivolous [*Taysh*].*

s: *What does this word* Taysh *mean?*

N: Taysh—*It starts at the age of fifteen, sixteen, seventeen, eighteen, nineteen until twenty. [It lasts] until she develops her responsibility [*'aql]. She is frivolous [*Taysha] for about four years: the age of adolescence [*sinn al-murahaqa]—you understand?*

s: *How about boys? Do they go through the same thing or is this reserved for girls?*

N: *Boys too. . . . A boy too goes through this "age of frivolity" from the age of eighteen to twenty-two or even twenty-five years of age at which he becomes responsible.*

. . .

s: *Now I want to ask you about "the age of frivolity" [*sinn Taysh] *of both boys and girls. How do you know they have reached that age? How would you know when Najet [age thirteen] gets there?*

. . .

N: *You can recognize it. The girl becomes frivolous. She adopts flighty [*khfifa] *behavior. She starts caring about her appearance, dressing well, wearing fancy clothes and showy things, you understand.*

s: *The meaning of "flighty" is "to dress in a fancy and showy manner"?*

N: *Yes. She pays attention to her appearance, wearing fancy clothes. She also messes up her school schedule. She either leaves too early or comes too late [i.e., she may be changing her schedule to meet boys]. You have to be watchful with her at that juncture. If you see she is on the right path, you leave her alone. If you notice that she is too late or far off the timing, then you have to set the record straight with her until the "age of adolescence" is over. When she is twenty years of age she recovers her ability to reason and be rational.*

s: *Is Najet now [at thirteen] a "reasonable" girl? Is she rational?*

N: *Najet is now rational. If she remains as she is I would assume she will be OK. She now criticizes situations where she notices that something bad is done. She says, "Mom, that's a wrong thing. It is a shame that it is done." Now she knows, she does know.*

s: *When your son Saleh [age fourteen] reaches the "age of adolescence," how would you know about it?*

N: *I will notice that he doesn't come home on time, he will start playing hookey. . . . He will start following girls. . . . Girls will start complaining, "Your son is following us." This is the first consequence. . . .*

s: *So it's similar to the girl—the girl will dress in a fancy way, while the boy will start getting interested in her.*
n: *That's it. You see.*
s: *Did you ever study the "age of adolescence" [sinn Taysh] in school?*
n: *Yes, we did study that—"adolescence" [sinn al-murahaqa] and Taysh is the same thing.*
s: *It is the same phenomenon.*
n: *Yes, the two things have no solution. Only parents can struggle against them. Parents, or even the girl or boy when they have a good mind, they don't succumb to the driving force of adolescence [Taysh].*
. . .
s: *When does the girl reach physical puberty?*
. . .
n: *When the girl reaches the age of fourteen or fifteen she reaches the age of puberty [katrshed]. [She also says the term katblegh means the same thing.]*
s: *Does that happen before the "age of adolescence" [Taysh] or after?*
n: *Before the "age of adolescence."*

We see in this woman's comments both a clear set of expectations re-garding the consequences and timing of physical puberty in both sexes and a ready transition between physical and interpersonal connotations of "adolescence."

While they do not usually talk about a named stage of adolescence, most mothers we asked about their children's behavior said they often changed in their midteens. We noted with interest that these changes were described calmly, without the strong negative or beleaguered tone often en-countered when discussing adolescents with Americans. Although Najet's mother had very specific ideas of what she expected, most mothers de-scribed more general changes. The most commonly mentioned change was that teenagers listened less to their parents, especially when told to do some-thing. This is supported in the responses of the young people, most of whom said that usually disagreements with their parents occurred because they re-fused to run an errand. However, neither parents nor children seemed to feel this was a serious problem. One mother described with a laugh how her sixteen-year-old daughter had become headstrong lately, while the daughter sat next to her looking amused. A girl of fourteen had a shouted, five-minute discussion with her very pregnant mother about buying some mint for tea, which finally ended when the mother said she would go herself. Neither one appeared upset nor did either harbor bad feelings as they drank the tea afterward, and in fact the mother discussed with her mother how girls cared more for their parents than boys did.

Susan interviewed the argumentative girl's mother at length on a later occasion (when the girl, Fatiha, her oldest, was fifteen, and Fatiha's brother, Sa'id, was eighteen) about the stages of life, marriage, and her children's relations to her. That interview provides another glimpse of the views of a Zawiya mother on the changes of adolescence; this woman mentions more physical changes and more conflict than did Naima. Mbarka was in her midthirties at the time of the interview, and she has an elementary education. We join the interview after she has described the shyness many girls feel about the onset of menstruation.

■ s: *So, when a girl reaches puberty* [belghet, *from* bulugh] *she has her periods, right?*

m: *When she reaches puberty, she has her periods, then if she gets married she can bear a child. . . .*

s: *Does she change in her behavior or personality after she becomes adult?*

m: *She changes. She becomes like a woman. When they change and have periods, when the girl reaches adulthood, she needs a husband. . . . It is said that many fathers stand in the way of their daughter's getting married. If a girl is asked for in marriage, her father should give her away right away. In the past a girl used to be given away at the age of twelve.*

. . .

s: *With regard to puberty, do you say that a boy has "reached puberty"* [belegh] *also?*

m: *These days Sa'id also has reached puberty. . . . His voice has become like that of a man, hair has grown on his face [shows]. Pimples grew here also [shows]. . . . They call it "youth pimples." Fatiha also has gotten "youth pimples." . . . When those pimples grow, the boy reaches adulthood. Again, if that guy gets married he will get the woman pregnant the first night. So many boys get married at that age and get women pregnant.*

s: *That young!*

m: *The one whose father is wealthy. So many whose parents are well to do get them married. . . .*

s: *Do they also change in their behavior?*

m: *Yes, they change their behavior as well. They start saying "We are men." Now Sa'id says, "I am a man, not a kid." If you talk to him now he will shrug his shoulders at your words; or give him a small portion of something, he won't accept it. He takes himself seriously. . . . Nor would he accept the amount of .50 DH [5 cents]. He feels ashamed [kayHeshim]; he says, "I am a man." . . . He says, "I have a beard and you are fooling me with .50 DH or 1 DH; I need 5 or 10 DH [one dollar]." He doesn't even allow you to address him. If you talk to him he says, "You mean to show me?—I am a man." . . . The girl changes too. . . . Nowadays Fatiha also says, "Don't show me anything."*

s: *She means she knows everthing.*

m: *She says she isn't a little kid, she knows everything. Even when she does something the wrong way and I tell her, "That is not right," she says she knows how to do it.*

s: *Do they fight with you more when they reach puberty, while before puberty you get along well? Or are they the same before [puberty] as after, with regard to conflicts?*

m: *No, when they are little they are not like when they grow up. When they grow up, then they increase in that stuff. When Fatiha was still little, . . . if I sent her to run an errand, she would go. She was different than today. Now she is much more difficult. Sa'id too is not considerate toward me. If you do his laundry and he finds a stain, he won't shut up as he used to do when he was little. . . . When he was little he didn't pay attention to how he looked as he is doing now. With regard to food, he doesn't tolerate having just a little of something. . . . That is the way also with Fatiha nowadays. . . . How can this be compared to childhood? When they reach puberty, when they grow up, they start looking only upward [i.e., they start having great expectations]. They want to dress well, they want to eat well, they want to have lots of money. Only the person who has a big salary could afford a good life to children. But anybody who just has our income, if he can keep them alive will do a great job.*

s: *You said they start to look upward—Didn't you "look up" when you were young, when you reached puberty? That didn't happen to you?*

m: *No way. I never "looked up." When I reached puberty, even if I did not get any new clothes, it didn't matter.*

Social customs also have an influence on adolescents. Parents realize that after their midteens girls may become the object of gossip or get pregnant, so their movement outside the house is monitored more closely. They are still allowed to go out with friends or on errands, but parents try to know where they are and will send younger children on errands if they are available. This restriction seems motivated mostly by concern for family status: the less an older girl is seen in the street, the better her reputation and supposedly her chances of a good marriage. Although older girls may run fewer errands, they take on more of the adult chores in the house like cooking and washing clothes.

Boys, on the other hand, experience an increase in freedom of movement and a decrease in the number of household chores they are expected to do during the teen years. Whether continuing in school or not, most males in Zawiya move around a great deal outside the neighborhood by the time they are in their early teens. This movement may take them several kilometers from the neighborhood; in any case a sizable percentage of the teenage males in Zawiya are away from home much of the time during the day. Indeed, one could traverse each of the streets in the neighborhood on a typical afternoon and see only a couple of older teenage males.

A conversation with a half dozen males ranging from fifteen to nineteen in age, all of them educated to at least the junior high school (*collège*) level, yielded a variety of physical, behavioral, and social "signs" of male adolescence (*murahaqa*, in their words). These included changes in facial hair, voice level, and strength, and the development of the nipple (referred to as the *Hamamsa*, from the diminutive for chickpea). Male nipple development was also mentioned on a different occasion by a thirteen-year-old informant, but he associated it with physical puberty (*bulugh*). At the behavioral level, these young men agreed that increasing interest in girls is a major social indicator, evidenced by time spent near the water taps and shops frequented by teenage girls. They recalled great excitment over conversations with girls at and enroute to school, the exchange of letters, the attempt to persuade girls to listen to one's radio, and a variety of other signs of a rather romanticized fascination with the opposite sex. Taste in music was thought to change as a result of adolescence, with educated boys turning to the romantic music of the West, while more traditional and less educated boys tended to be devoted to Moroccan popular groups.

A vignette that revealed these young men's perception of male adolescence occurred at the end of this conversation. The eighteen-year-old brother of one of the most vocal older informants had listened in silence to most of the discussion of adolescent markers, finally leaving and walking back alone across the fields to town. As the rest of the group returned later, one young man said, "Look there, on the roof of Hafid's house!" We followed his gaze and saw Rashid, the brother, standing alone staring into the hills outside town beyond where we had been sitting. One of the young men said, "That's what adolescence is all about, Douglas," and the rest agreed. Rashid's strong desire to be alone with his thoughts is particularly striking in view of the general rarity of opportunities (or apparent desire) to be alone

among Zawiyans generally. The picture that emerges from the self-descrip-
tion of the adolescence of the more voluble males (who are also likely to be
among the most educated in the neighborhood) is of a set of romantic fantasies of courtship reminiscent of the American generation of the 1950s, and
strikingly at variance with the actual prospects of most rural Moroccans.

EDUCATION AND THE CONCEPT OF ADOLESCENCE

The concept of adolescence is related to education in two ways. The first is
that before widespread public education was introduced after independence
in 1956, most young people in Zawiya married soon after they reached physical puberty; after marriage, one is considered an adult. Thus in the past, one
moved from childhood to adulthood more quickly (Whiting, Burbank, and
Ratner 1986). The second influence of education on adolescence is that students in secondary school learn about a life stage called adolescence, so for
some school has "created" the concept as well as the expectation of behaviors associated with it.[12] Our data indicate how recently schooling has become the norm in Zawiya, and interviews confirm that education has been a
major influence on how individuals think about adolescence.

Generational Change

The rapid increase in educational facilities after 1956 created important
differences between the experiences of Zawiya adolescents and their parents. The perception of today's parents that children need a rather long period of schooling and the parents' willingness to support their children's
continued study have helped create the potential for an "adolescent" period
in Zawiya. The contrasts between the generations are vividly illustrated in
the interview with Naima, whose description of the behaviors of adolescents
has already been quoted. She is describing here how different things are in
town now from what her mother remembers from the countryside.

■ N: *So when they brought us here we grew up here. This is what my
mother tells me. They didn't have beds, covers, medicine, doctors, good
food. She said they would eat low-quality food, yet they had good
health. She said they only slept on mats or carpets and they woke up
in good shape—Now we have become addicted to sweaters, beds, covers, this and that, and even then our health is not that great. . . . Our
time is different than theirs. . . . We had schooling but they had no*

education, they were like savages. You know what juhala *means? . . .*
Excuse the expression, they are like animals. But we did have educa-
tion. We know our ways in and out. If we take a trip to some city we
can find an address just by looking. When we go some place, we know
on our own, we need no assistance from anybody. It is not like when
my mother goes to Rabat, she has to ask for help to get where she wants
to go. . . . Our era is a modern one, an advanced one. The era of our par-
ents was backward. You understand. . . . This is the difference that ex-
ists between our parents and us and our children and us. . . . You got
back from school, threw your bag in the corner and nobody bothered
whether you studied or not. She won't say a single word. That's it. Now
there is also a gap between ourselves and our children. We educate our
kids, explain things to them, help them learn things, tell them about ev-
erything and advise them to study, to work hard, to do their best. . . . I
tell them to look up to their teachers and work hard to become like them
so that their future becomes bright. Not like mine, staying home: "You
will be educated and earning good money to be able to dress well and all
the rest."
s: *Do you think it is better to be a teacher than to stay home?*
n: *I think a woman with a job is better. A career woman makes money,*
you see. The essential is that she can come back home. There is time for
home and time for work.

This woman vividly conveys the idea of social change—illiterate
mother, to literate wife, to career-woman daughter—which impressed our
teams all around the world as we collected the data of the Adolescence Project. The role of education in this change is central.

By delaying the age of marriage, the availability of education has made
the life stage we call adolescence both more common and in some ways
more problematic. In the past, Zawiya's young people married in their mid to
late teens, only waiting until they had skills necessary to run a household
and to support a family, skills learned readily from parents. No extended education was necessary to make one's living, and there existed little or no gap
in which young people were physically able to marry but were delaying in
order to finish an education or to find a job. Mbarka, the other neighborhood
mother quoted above, contrasts the present with the past when she notes
that girls sometimes married at the age of twelve.

■ s: *Before they reach puberty?*
m: *[At] twelve, thirteen—she stayed only one year with her husband*
and she started bearing children. But nowadays we don't do it that

*way. The girl has her periods for ever and ever. For example, Fatiha, it
has been over a year now and she'll wait another four or five years before she gets married. . . . Khadija [her daughter of fourteen] is the
same. Before, people in the countryside married their daughters quite
young.*
s: *In your opinion, would you approve of Khadija starting to have
kids?*
m: *I find her still too young.*
s: *Do you think she'd know how to take care of a house?*
m: *You see, in the countryside it is different than here. In the countryside she doesn't go to school. She knows how to cook, how to sweep the
floor, how to make bread, and when she married, her husband's mother
showed her how to do more things. They marry them just at the size of
Khadija [fourteen] and they know everything. We have been to so
many weddings, and I swear to God they were just Khadija's size when
they went to their husbands. They keep learning . . . and become a
woman knowing all. But we here in town, we don't do that.*

As Mbarka notes, Zawiya marriages are now delayed years after physical puberty. Increasing numbers of both sexes are recognized as no longer
children, but not married and parents, and therefore not full adults.[13] The
development of universal education in Europe and the United States during
the past century has been, together with postindustrial changes in the structure of the family, an essential aspect of the "adolescent" experience in the
West. Morocco is now experiencing a similar development, and one way in
which an extended education and delayed marriage can cause problems is
that it provides a context in which the sexes can mix; such mixing chal-
lenges Moroccan norms of propriety as it does those of other traditional societies. Burbank's volume in this series notes that Aboriginal Australians
traditionally had no period of maidenhood between sexual maturity and
marriage. The existence of such a period today has led to conflict between
adult expectations and adolescent behavior, and these are an important focus of Burbank's discussion (Burbank 1988, 5).

The Prevalence of Education

Nearly all Zawiya youth have attended school. Of 146 young people between the ages of nine and twenty-one surveyed in our neighborhood, 92
percent had attended school at some time and 55 percent were currently attending. The national average was 47.5 percent in 1980 (United Nations

1983, 50). Among the parents of these Zawiya youth, however, only three had attended public school.[14] Table 3.2 shows school attendance by age and sex.

There is a sharp drop in school attendance for both sexes at the secondary level. This is partly because many students do not pass the nationally standardized exam at the end of primary school, even after two or three years of attempting it.[15] Many Zawiya students said they felt the best teachers got jobs in the cities, so pupils in smaller towns and rural areas received lower quality instruction and found it more difficult to pass. Another reason fewer students attend secondary school is the cost. Although education is provided free by the government, students must buy or rent books and feel they need decent clothing to attend. The family also loses any income students might earn if they were not in school. The principal of the junior high school estimated that it cost each student about 400 dirhams ($66) each year to attend school, which is about what a woman would earn working as a field laborer every day for a whole month. Many families have more than one child of secondary school age, so the cost can become a burden.

Fewer girls than boys attend school at either level. One reason there are fewer girls in secondary school is that, with the coeducational setting, families worry about them getting involved with boys. Another reason for lower female school attendance at all levels is that girls' labor is much more important in the household. Finally, if a family can only afford to educate one child, they will usually choose a boy in the expectation that he will more easily get a job later and contribute to the family's future income.

In general, parents now send all children to primary school and encourage them to finish, unless they are especially poor students or the family really needs the money they can earn. Although 27 percent of primary age children in our sample were out of school, there were very few (8 percent) who had never attended. This represents a large shift in opinion and practice since 1965, when education was seen as less important, fewer children at-

TABLE 3.2
School Attendance for Adolescents Ages Nine to Twenty-one

	Females	Males	Total
Primary school age (age 15 or younger)	63%	82%	73%
Secondary school age (ages 16 to 21)	23	48	36
Total percentage in school	43	65	55

tended school, and girls were likely to leave after a few years' attendance. Of the twelve young people we knew who had never attended school, all but one were females (the one boy appeared to have mild brain damage), and all but one were sixteen or older. Based on these figures, we calculate that by 1973 parents began to send all children of both sexes to school. It is now recognized that education is necessary for white-collar jobs and that both sexes can have access to these jobs. Or more correctly, they have had access—there is currently a dearth of such jobs, and students especially realize this and are concerned about their futures.

Education is important even to those who are not currently in school. Susan saw this when she asked key informants what had made them happiest in the last year. Of twelve girls, half mentioned passing in school. Interestingly, it was not just their own passing; four of the six said that their siblings' passing was the best thing. An educated sibling with a good job would be expected to help the family out, even as an adult.

Education also reinforces hierarchical values learned at home. As a social arena outside the family, classroom education is more structured than friendship, and this corresponds to the rather rigid structure of many of the other social institutions with which an adult Moroccan will have to deal. The youth who attends school is learning to function in ways that will be useful in later life. Relationships in the classroom are hierarchical, and the teacher's lessons are to be learned and repeated, not discussed or debated; this corresponds to the usual situation in government and business settings. Deference to authority and following directions to the letter are good preparation for successfully dealing with bureaucracies, whether to register a child's birth, transfer a deed, or carry out any other transaction.

Schooling and Friendship

In contrast to its conservative function in preparing young people to interact with bureaucracy, education also plays an almost revolutionary role in Zawiya in that it has led to many social changes, some of which are just beginning to be seen. A child's friends are now either neighbors or schoolmates. In the past, parents could monitor their children's neighborhood friends more closely and were apt to know the parents, but this is less true when friends are schoolmates, who may live in another neighborhood. Visiting school friends means greater mobility, as does the walk to secondary school in Kabar, especially for girls. This mobility gives some girls the opportunity to meet with boys, as do coed classes. Jobs requiring education delay marriage. There is thus an increasing time span in which boys and girls may meet as couples outside marriage, although dating and premarital sex are still condemned in Zawiya (see chap. 6).

School and Aspirations

Another aspect of mobility affected by education is that both sexes now have new aspirations for white-collar jobs, jobs that are usually located in a larger town or a city. Young people are thus drawn away from their families; also the option of a separate household for young couples becomes more possible, to the dismay of the groom's mother and the delight of the bride. These raised aspirations are likely to be met by only a few, however, and many will be disappointed by their inability to complete school or to obtain a higher level job than their parents have. The fact that in one generation virtually all children have begun attending school means that these changes are widespread. However, these changes have not had a major disrupting effect on the society. Both parents and children value education highly and expend much effort to see that youth are educated.

■ 4
The Family

In the U.S. literature on adolescence, two topics mentioned frequently with regard to parent-child relations are autonomy and conflict. The American stress on the individual means that often adolescents assert their independence and individuality by claiming their autonomy, or ability to act without parental direction. This tendency is one of the bases of the conflict between parents and their teenage children that is popularly believed to be characteristic of adolescence in American society.[1] Relations among family members in Zawiya during the years after puberty focus more on two themes that are important in many areas of their lives: hierarchy and ambivalence. Most social relations in Zawiya contain an element of hierarchy; within the family these differences are based on age and sex.[2] While family relations that are positive and supportive are the cultural norm, there are also ambivalent feelings among family members, which often come from unmet expectations of financial or emotional support. Even with widespread change, conflict is less characteristic of adolescent-parent relations in Zawiya than one might expect. Some conflict does occur, under circumstances we examine after presenting data on the composition and structure of neighborhood families.

FAMILY STRUCTURE IN ZAWIYA

The family is the basic social institution in most Muslim cultures,[3] and this is certainly true for Zawiya. While in the West the important social unit is the individual, in Zawiya it is the family. This is exemplified in the different kinds of questions people ask when first meeting in the two settings. Americans are likely to ask, "What do you do? Where are you from?" While a new Zawiya acquaintance may also ask these questions, more important is, "What family are you from?" Family is not the only important factor,[1] but it is a much more central concern than in the United States.

Writing about contemporary Egypt, Rugh (1984) stresses a point that is central for Westerners trying to understand Arab (including Moroccan) society. Misunderstanding occurs, Rugh argues, because isolated facts are evaluated in terms of Western-derived, questionably relevant, theories. A central fallacy is the assumption that "all societies fundamentally believe in and derive their social behaviors as we do from a deep-seated faith in the individual and individualism. This is such a natural belief to Americans that they find it difficult to conceive of another world view that places corporateness of certain kinds ahead of individual interests and rights . . . a social system based on fundamentally different values than our own" (1984, *vii*).

Americans are struck, for example, by the contrast between individual choice of marriage partners and the central role played by the family in Arab (and many non-Western) cultures. "How can they do that?" American students demand. Despite the value placed on individual choice in American culture, however, the family typically plays an important role in mate selection here as well. For example, Americans send their children to schools and colleges where they will meet potential spouses of the "correct" social class; they often discourage proposed marriage partners on the basis of religious, ethnic, or personality considerations. This is not to suggest that Arab and American families are the same. In Arab society, the stress is on the corporate unit of the family.

Several of the themes we found important in Zawiya are revealed in obligations to and expectations of one's family. The hierarchical relationships dictating respect for elders, especially males, are first experienced within the family. Differential treatment of and expectations for each sex are learned there as well, and it is in the family setting that adolescents often try new ways of "presenting themselves." The issues of honor and shame are crucial for the individual and the family, since both are dishonored by a shameful act (S. Davis 1983a; Abu-Lughod 1986). The family is thus a strong and central institution, and the rights and duties individuals experience in relation to their families are sometimes the source of ambivalence and tension.

Nuclear Families

The largest percentage of the adolescents in our neighborhood lived in a nuclear family household. While many readers may have expected to find three-generation extended family households dominant in a Muslim culture, this is not the case in Zawiya. We do not have complete information concerning the proportion of our parental sample who grew up in extended family households. However, we did see a change in the terms used for family, and this may reflect an actual change in form. In the past, 'a'ila was used to mean "family," both nuclear and extended. Now, some people are reserving that term for the larger extended family, or to refer to both parents' siblings and parents, and call the two-generation group residing in one household the usra.[5]

Of the forty-nine neighborhood families for whom we have data, almost all had monogamous marriages and relatively few of the households contained extended families. The largest number of families were nuclear, composed of parents and their unmarried children (47 percent). A nuclear family was often augmented by a widowed grandmother, or a cousin or an uncle who wanted to live in town because of the better schools and job opportunities (20 percent). Families were also large, with an average of 5.8 surviving children (an average of 3 had died). Table 4.1 shows the frequency of the different types of households in our neighborhood sample of forty-nine families.

Extended Families

As shown in Table 4.1, relatively few families were of the "extended" type, which included parents, their married children (usually only sons), and their grandchildren. Most of these apparently extended families were in a "transitional" phase (Goody 1958): often a young couple would live with

TABLE 4.1
Household Types of Zawiya Adolescents

	Number	Percentage
Nuclear family households	23	47
Nuclear family plus another person	10	20
Extended family (3 generations)	9	18
Widows	5	10
Divorcées	1	2
Polygynous households	1	2

the groom's parents for a few years after marriage, until they could afford to rent or buy a place of their own. Seven of the nine extended families in our neighborhood contained newlyweds or a couple with a baby less than a year old, thus fitting Goody's model. Young women often do not want to live with their mothers-in-law and will press for a separate household if it is at all financially possible. This is due partially to the strong emotional tie between a man and his mother, and partially to the fact that the bride is a newcomer to the household and thus must learn to interact with a whole new set of people and to meet their standards in her behavior, housekeeping, and cooking. The groom's mother has someone whom she can freely command, and her orders are not limited by the sympathy she might feel for an overworked daughter; rather, they are magnified because of rivalry for the loyalty of the young man (see S. Davis 1983a; Mernissi 1975). In the past, many brides could not escape this phase of their lives, since they and their husbands lived on his father's land. They were dependent on his family for their economic survival until the father died and his sons inherited the land; at this point many extended families split up. Since sons can now find work on their own, they can split off much sooner, and most do.

Foster Children

One type of addition to a nuclear household is a child who is "fostered." We do not use the term "adopted" because there is rarely a legal procedure, and the child recognizes and feels close to its biological parents. If a married woman is childless, she may ask a sister or brother with several children if she may raise one as her own. She is usually given a girl, who will help the wife to be accepted as a full adult by having a child to care for and will also assist with housework. Zawiya families having their own children will still often bring in a country cousin, usually female, to live with them and help with chores. The country family benefits by having one less child to feed and clothe, and those in town have extra help. Although she is usually expected to work hard, the girl is treated more like a daughter than a servant, and her relatives may even help her find a husband and pay for her wedding when the time comes.

Five families (10 percent) in our neighborhood contained fostered children, but only one of the couples was childless. This couple was given the wife's brother's daughter when she was about two, and she called her aunt and uncle "mother" and "father" and felt very close to them. However, her biological father and siblings (her mother had died) lived just a block up the street, and they visited back and forth several times each day, so she was not lonely for them. Nor was she at all concerned about having been "given away"; she loved both families. In the four other families, girls were brought in to help because the children of the household were too young or too old to run errands for their parents. One of these families also had two boys with them for part of the year; one was a distant cousin attending the town's school rather than his rural one, and the other was a grandson being raised by his grandparents. That this family, with two extra boys in the household, still needed to bring in a girl to help with chores demonstrates vividly the disparate roles and the very different utility of boys and girls in running a home. All these young people were in contact with their biological parents, but this sort of living arrangement was useful for all the families involved. Thus the pattern of fostering children seems partly utilitarian, partly a duty to help relatives, and partly an outgrowth of people's pleasure in children.

Polygyny

Islam allows men to have up to four wives simultaneously, provided they are all treated equally and justly (Qur'an, *Surat Al-Nisa*, 4). Muslim feminists sometimes argue that equal treatment is impossible and thus that men should be allowed only one wife, just as women may have only one husband (al-Hibri 1982).[6] Polygynous marriages are rare in Morocco in general and comprise only about 2 to 3 percent of the total (Royaume du Maroc n.d., 51; Maher 1974, 223). This is because they are both expensive and stressful, and because young people see them as old-fashioned. While three of the neighborhood's marriages were legally polygynous, with the husband married to two women simultaneously, in only one case did the wives live in the same household. This family used to be prosperous, but has had harder times recently. However, their economic problems have indirectly led to less stress within the household, since one wife runs the house and the other has an outside job to supplement their income. In the other two families, one of the wives preferred to live with her grown daughter and her family, although she was still just a block away from her husband and his third wife and children. Although she was in her sixties and had not lived with her husband for a long time, her cutting comments about the "new" wife betrayed her jealousy. The third woman lived like a divorcée; her husband took his new family to France with him and seldom sent money. Polygyny will probably become even rarer in the future. Muslim marriages have always involved a contract, and today many young women insist on a clause specifying that if their husband takes a second wife, they will receive an automatic divorce.

Widowhood, Divorce, and Step Parenting

Six households were headed by single parents, all of them women. Five were widows (10 percent of the families) and one was a divorcée. We have marital histories for thirty-nine (80 percent) of the families we worked most closely with, and in half (48.7 percent) of these families the parents were both in their first marriage. In the other half at least one parent had been married more than once, and such remarriages were considerably more common for fathers (46.2 percent) than for mothers (23.1 percent). These figures are strikingly close to those of 51 percent for men and 24 percent for women that Maher (1974, 198) found in the early seventies for a town in southeastern Morocco. Since half the marriages involved a divorced parent, it appears that many of the adolescents may live with stepparents, but on careful examination we find this is not true. Only two of the households (containing five adolescents) contained stepparents, in both cases women whom the father had married after his wife died. In nineteen of the households, parents had children (a total of about thirty) from previous marriages, but these had been left with other relatives when the current marriage began. It is interesting that while Moroccan family law traces descent through the father and gives him the primary right to the children after divorce, eighteen of the children were left with their mothers' relatives and only twelve with their fathers' families. It seems that mother's role counts as much as father's rights in determining children's residence after divorce in Zawiya.

The six divorced or widowed neighborhood women with children had not remarried and were raising the children as single parents. There is no cultural rule preventing a woman with children from remarrying, but it is somewhat difficult. The pattern is for men to marry younger women, so a widower can look for a young single wife. A woman with children needs a husband the same age or older, and most of these men are already married. Unmarried men usually prefer to take on just a wife and not several extra mouths to feed, so women who must care for children seldom remarry. One of the two stepmothers we knew was a widow with children, and she left these children with her relatives in the country when she remarried. The family had a meager income, and it was all they could do to support the husband's three children and their own three. We did not hear that single mothers had special problems with their children, but only one of those households had boys between fifteen and twenty, the age when mothers might expect difficulties.

Five adolescents had what we call stepparents; the Moroccan terms used are "father's wife" or "mother's husband" rather than "mother" or "father." The relationship is different from that with biological parents. It is expected that the stepmother especially will favor her own children over those of her husband, giving them better food and less difficult chores to do. While we did not see blatant examples of this in these two families, and the children did not complain openly of their unequal treatment by their fathers' wives, they did not feel as close as they would have to their own mothers. In fact, an older brother in one of the two families (age approximately twenty) had moved in with his father's brother in the larger town because he did not get on with his father's wife.

Absent Fathers

In addition to the 12 percent of households that had no father (there was none without a mother or stepmother because widowers remarry as soon as possible), in another 20 percent of families the mother virtually raised the children alone because the husband worked in another city or abroad. The fathers working abroad would usually visit for one month a year, and those who were elsewhere in Morocco visited every month or so. Thus about a third of these families lack a father in residence, which can be a source of adolescent stress (see chap. 7). Several of those women said it was very hard for them to be responsible for all the child-rearing, especially as the boys got older.

FAMILY RELATIONS

Relations between parents and children in Zawiya are strongly influenced by the sex of the actors and by the cultural norm of respect for one's elders. Since there are several differences in the way girls and boys interact with parents, depending on sex, they will be treated separately. In general, however, there is great respect for age, which results in an age hierarchy reflected in many aspects of the society. There are no formal age grades, but the person who is older is entitled to respect and obedience from those who are younger. The key influence of age on social relationships is readily apparent in the family setting. Although there is a great deal of affection expressed between children in the same household, younger siblings are expected to show respect for older brothers and sisters, particularly those who are nearing adulthood.

The fact that a generation of unschooled adults are raising the current literate generation of youth is a striking feature of life in Zawiya. We were prepared to find educated youths refusing parental advice or instructions on the grounds that their uneducated parents did not understand the modern world (see Mead 1928), but this was generally not true.[7] Today's parents in Zawiya display great respect for education and a hope that schooling will open new opportunities for their children, and children remain respectful of parents.

Zawiya families are large, and almost all parts of the house are used by all family members. Except perhaps for the bedroom of an older son, there is little sense of private space. The crowdedness and flexibility of these family settings must be understood as a feature of relationships within the Zawiya family.

Space in the Household

The typical home in our neighborhood has a ground floor, with the front door opening from the street onto a central courtyard. The courtyard is hidden from view by a baffle of extended wall or a stairway, so passersby cannot glimpse family members or possessions accidentally. The home is a private space, and no windows face the street. Around the courtyard are usually two long rooms, and a smaller kitchen and toilet. Often the courtyard is roofed over, and the roof is used as a sunny extra workroom in good weather, a place to hang laundry, and an area for storage and domestic animals. As families accumulate money, they often use it to build more rooms on the roof. However, most families of eight or nine people live in three large rooms on the ground floor. The roofed-over courtyard is a sort of family room, where people may eat and watch television in the evenings. One of the side rooms will be the parents' bedroom, furnished with a double bed, a wardrobe closet to store clothes, and low couches around the other walls for seating. Since this room is used less heavily than the others, the decoration is often more extravagant: the parents' bed may have a red satin spread and the couches be covered in plush fabric with arabesque designs. The other room will serve as a family room or parlor in the day and a bedroom at night and will have low couches, covered with a show-no-dirt washable print, around all the walls. The toilet is usually a small room with a hole in the floor which leads to a cesspool under the house. One pours water to flush after each use, and a water trap in the pipe prevents odors. Since none of the households has running water, family members use a ewer and basin in the courtyard to wash hands, face, and feet and visit the public baths for more extensive washing. Kitchens usually have a countertop bottled gas stove for cooking, although charcoal braziers are still sometimes used. Only the best-off families have refrigerators or stoves with ovens, although nearly all have electricity.

All of the rooms are available to all family members during the day (with the exception noted below) and can easily alternate functions. The covered courtyard is a cooler place to watch television in the summer, but a family will watch in one of the long rooms for more warmth in the winter. At night, the division of space is more marked, especially with regard to the parents' bedroom. Parents are very modest about their sexual activity and nearly always have a room to themselves. A baby will sleep with the parents (there are no cribs or baby beds) so it can be nursed on demand, but is put into another room "when it is old enough to open its eyes," as a neighbor said, usually about three or four years of age. Thus children of both sexes and a wide range of ages usually sleep in the same room. Siblings are modest about their bodies with the opposite sex, but these sleeping arrangements did not pose a problem because most people sleep in their clothing. Some older young men mentioned to Douglas that they felt uncomfortable sleeping in the same room with their pubescent sisters, but no girls ever mentioned any embarrassment to Susan. The older siblings get the choicer places on the couches, and the younger will sleep on blankets over mats on the floor. In the morning the bedclothes are folded up and the room again becomes a family room.

A Room of One's Own

The large nuclear families and relatively crowded houses seldom allow adolescents their own room for sleeping, studying, or storage of their possessions. If anyone in a household achieves a single room, however, it is likely to be the oldest son. The claim on a room is particularly strong if the oldest adolescent male is working or has continued in school. Parents usually still control the disposition of space. Themselves illiterate, they often strongly value the academic success of their son and see the private room as a necessary accommodation to his need to study. In the case of the older boy who is bringing in additional income, a desire to keep him pleased and in the home as well as perhaps to minimize the disturbance caused by his schedule is often reason enough for allowing his claim on a room. In some cases a young man's room will be held for him even though he is working in another city or abroad, and it is striking to see the care with which these rooms are kept safe from the normal flow of household activity, even though the rest of the family is crowded.

The decoration of the adolescent male's room is often striking in houses having little decor. Rock musicians' pictures, illustrations from magazines, and posters may paper the walls. A radio or cassette player, if owned by the family, is likely to be appropriated for the private room, and it is in this room that the books in the household will be found.

We have seen several cases in which the room established by the oldest son has passed on to his younger brothers in succession, despite the presence of one or more sisters between them in age. None of the sisters in these cases was in school, and we wondered if they would have been given the room if they had the excuse of needing a "quiet" place to study. In fact, the room seldom has a door to shut but uses a curtain for privacy from the rest of the household, so quiet is not really the issue. In a similar-sized Moroccan town Spratt (1985) found that high school girls she knew did their homework with the television blaring in the courtyard while their younger brothers had a separate room.

Morocco provides an interesting contrast to Condon's report on the Copper Eskimo (1987), where girls are as likely as boys to have their own rooms. The small number of Moroccan males with their own rooms also provides a contrast to the American adolescents of both sexes—described by Csikszentmihalyi and Larson—who spend 25 percent of their waking hours alone, about half in their bedrooms (1984, 59). The desire of young men in Morocco for a separate room is related to shyness associated with newly awakening sexuality as well as to studying. However, the majority of young men without a separate room must find other ways to deal with these problems. The town is surrounded by fields and gardens, and these are possible places (as opposed to the busy household) to achieve solitude.

Mothers and Daughters

A girl owes her mother respect both because she is older and because she carried and bore her; the latter social value is often mentioned in conversations concerning the duties of both sons and daughters. However, respect does not prevent a mother and daughter from having a warm, openly affectionate relationship. They are in constant contact, talking to each other as they go about their work. They may have their disagreements, but these do not interfere with their basic closeness. When Susan resided in town for two years in the 1960s without a visit home, the question local women most often asked about her adjustment was, "How can you bear to be away from your mother for so long?" In taped interviews Susan asked several girls how they were getting along with their mothers and whether the relationships had changed since the girls had gotten older. Kebira, and eldest daughter in her twenties and out of school, emphasized how her mother looks out for her interests:

> Our relations are good. My mother likes me. She sacrifices herself for my sake; she forgets about herself to buy me things. Even if there is only a small amount of something, she still saves a fraction of it for me. My mother wants me to go out, take walks, have good health.
> Our relations are still the same [since I've gotten older]. She knows my temper—when she knows I am upset she doesn't talk to me, she leaves me alone.

Another girl, also the eldest but in her late teens and still in school, also had a positive relationship, but illustrated it differently. Her closeness with her mother extends even to conversations about sexuality, usually a forbidden topic:

> The relations between us are like she is not my mother. I am not inhibited by her. . . . She is like my sister or friend. I tell her things. For example, I tell her what a guy says to me when I am on my way back [from school] and we laugh. Our relations have changed [since I've grown up]. In the beginning, when I was still young I used to be inhibited by her. I couldn't tell her a joke, for example. I couldn't tell her dirty jokes. . . . Now I can tell her.

Girls learn both their general comportment and their household skills from their mothers, and this is recognized when a girl marries. The groom's mother considers whether the prospective bride's mother is a good housekeeper and is known to be moral, that is, limits her interactions with unrelated men. If she falls short in either area, it is assumed the daughter will follow in her footsteps and she is rejected. Most of a girl's instruction is by example; very little is explicit. If she does not wash the dishes well, she is told to do them over and get them clean, and learns from the experience. She knows she should not joke with the boys at the well, but mainly from the gossip she hears about girls who do rather than by direct instruction.

Her mother's talk with friends is also the basis of a girl's somewhat indirect sex education. Women discuss sexual ailments and the sexual behavior of others (respect prevents description of their own activities) in front of small children of both sexes, and in front of girls of all ages. Boys are usually banished from such discussions by the time they are eleven or twelve. The girls remain and seldom interrupt, but listen intently, especially as they reach puberty.

None of the girls Susan asked had been told explicitly about menstruation by their mothers; most had heard about it from friends. One girl's reaction to her first menstrual period demonstrates well the relationship of children and parents with regard to sexual matters. When Kebira got her period in her midteens, she said nothing to her mother and just washed out her underwear. She knew from talking to her friends how to manage things. Her mother, seeing the wash when it was not a washday, surmised what had happened and mentioned it to her visiting sister in front of the girl. At first Kebira denied it, but then burst into tears, which her mother comforted by saying, "It's OK, it happens to all of us."

Another mother described how both her daughters (then fourteen and sixteen) had resisted reporting the onset of their periods.

> She [the sixteen-year-old] was hiding it from me. It was only when I found that piece of cloth that I asked her, "Did you start having your periods?" Then she replied, "Leave me alone! Leave me alone! Who told you to ask me, who told you I started having my periods?" I replied, "I found the piece of cloth." So she added, "It is none of your business! Periods—do I know anything about periods?" Then I started watching her. . . . Whenever we wanted to wash clothes she would tell me "You don't have to do the laundry." . . . But the truth of the matter is that she doesn't want me to see her stained clothes. . . .
>
> She feels embarrassed to have her periods, it kind of feels awkward. Khadija [the fourteen-year-old] also had her period, but she hides it from [us] her parents.

The close and normally supportive relationship between mothers and daughters is of course often also the setting for conflict. when Susan asked adolescent girls whether they ever disagreed with their mothers, those she knew less well often denied any conflict, probably because it is shameful to fight with parents in Moroccan culture. However, the girls she knew best admitted that sometimes they had conflicts with their mothers (see chap. 7), although most examples given were minor like refusing to run errands.

Mothers and Sons

The closeness of sons to mothers is an important positive feature of the lives of males growing up in Zawiya. However, this closeness and readiness to interest herself in her son's affairs may also be the source of conflict or embarrassment for the young man. A mother's influence over her son is lifelong. She has indulged and protected her son in infancy, comforted him and protected him from magical influences at the time of his circumcision in late childhood (Crapanzano 1980a; S. Davis 1983a), and sometimes intervened when he is threatened by other boys on the street. She has typically pressured his father and a variety of teachers and officials for favorable treatment of him as he has grown to a teenager, and kept a skeptical eye out for suitable girls for him to marry. Her influence over whom he will eventually marry is still often crucial, if only by opposing his relationship with a girl she deems unsuitable. Knowing the wiles of women as she does, she will warn him about entrapment by girls through either pregnancy or magic. On the eve of his wedding night she may provide him with charms to ward off evil influences and assure potency. After marriage she is a regular visitor to her son's household, if not an actual member of it, and in times of serious marital stress hers may be the only food her son will willingly eat, since he fears magical influence and/or poisoning by his wife. The tension between a man's feelings toward his "seductive" wife and his "protective" mother demonstrates a general ambivalence about females that is common in North African males (Bouhdiba 1975; Mernissi 1975).

Infants are treated indulgently, and male children in particular are seldom disciplined in early childhood.[8] Indeed, the difference in mothers' treatment of male and female children is a major lesson each Zawiya child learns about the role of the sexes in Moroccan society. The male's relationship with his mother is close since the son is likely to be seen as a fulfillment of her destiny as a mother, a powerful insurance against repudiation by her husband, and a hope for support in her old age. Mothers act to protect this special relationship with their sons by attempting to maintain a strong influence over grown sons' behavior. Sons' achievements are a great source of pride to their mothers. The relationship allows the mother to count on economic and emotional support from her sons, and to guide and sometimes to constrain their marriage. Mothers are eager for their sons to marry girls who have both an honorable background and skill as a homemaker, as well as docility; the reliance of a well-brought-up son on his mother's advice about how to handle his wife is often a source of tension between the mother and her daughter-in-law. Even fully grown sons are generally deferent toward their mothers, and they conceal from them their sexual behavior and violations of social norms. Nevertheless, the relationship between mothers and their older sons is often quite friendly and relaxed.

One source of intergenerational tension and misunderstanding that was repeatedly mentioned to Douglas by males of various ages was the unschooled mother's belief in traditional magical practices; these often offended her son's sense of what was compatible with orthodox Islam on the one hand and modern science on the other. The parents, although respected for their attempts to raise and care for the children under difficult economic circumstances, were often described as old-fashioned and superstitious in their attitudes. Traditional practices commonly involve attempts to counter magical influences or to prevent or remove possession by spirits, and women are the major seekers of such services for their afflicted sons.

For example, a highly motivated science student, aged eighteen, prided himself on his rational attitude toward the world and disdained the "women's world" of local saints and spirits. When he began to have nightmares that involved being chased and held by monstrous creatures (the *bughatat*), however, he had no compunction about asking his illiterate mother's help. At her suggestion that he keep iron nearby (because iron has power over spirits [*jnun*]) he began to sleep with a large knife concealed under his mattress, and the nightmares stopped. We collected many stories from male and female adolescents of fears associated with dreams and spiritual influences, and in the majority of these the mother had been consulted for help.

Even after marriage, young men expect to maintain a close relationship with their mothers. A young man in his midtwenties, an age when he could appropriately think about marrying, said that after marriage he would like to live near his family because "Your mother for instance may want to see you, or you may want to see her and if you have to travel a distance of 100 or 200 kilometers, it is bad. But if you are near Zawiya or at a distance of 4 or 5 kilometers it is better. I can go on foot, just walk over."

Fathers and Daughters

A girl's relation to her father is much more distant than that with her mother. When she was small, she was hugged and brought candies like her brothers, but after six or seven all children show more respect and share less intimacy with their fathers. Men spend most of their time outside the household and therefore interact with children much less than women do. The father's main roles are provider and disciplinarian. Especially with daughters, the father is concerned about maintaining the family's honor. One young woman who talked to many young men and was known to have affairs ruined not only her own reputation, but that of her entire family. Her father was condemned for letting her behave in this way. While tradition states that a father (and brothers) should kill or at least publicly beat a girl who loses her virginity before marriage, we know of no recent examples of this and believe it is more a dramatic threat than a reality. Most fathers care too much for their daughters to do them physical injury. This contention is supported by the fact that in the past in several local cases of premarital pregnancy, girls were punished by banishment from the household at worst, or simply by verbal scolding.

The contrast a girl finds in dealing with her mother as opposed to her father is clear from a statement by Kebira (in her twenties). Her father is an uneducated and traditional man who (it seems to us) hides his affection for his family behind a brusque exterior.

> My father is too tough. You know him: if I want to go to Kabar I have to plead for a week or a month before I can go. He doesn't let me go. If I want to buy things, he says he is broke. Only my poor mother buys what I need. My father doesn't care too much about kids. . . . I am the one he cares least about because I neither go to school nor work. I am constantly forgotten.

In their daily interactions, girls show respect for their fathers in many ways: by waiting to be spoken to first and responding with deference, by being ready to pour water for them to wash, and by serving them meals and waiting on them without being asked. While on the surface this appears as a distant kind of respect, many girls also care a great deal about their fathers. The young woman quoted above had earlier described how she and her older brother had discussed their relationship with their father, both wishing it could be more affectionate. The father worked long hours and just came home to eat and sleep, while they wished he would talk more to them about his day or family affairs so that they would have more contact with him. Another young woman, whose father had divorced her mother and remarried abroad, felt sad that she had no father (her mother had not remarried). When her father visited town he did not even stop to say hello, which greatly upset her. So although girls spend less time with their fathers than with their mothers, and interact with them more formally when they are present, they still feel a deep affection and respect for them.

Fathers and Sons

The father's role in his son's socialization is distant and reticent by comparison with the mother's. He will have dandled and indulged the boy infant, but he will usually have become less ready for either physical or verbal closeness by the time the boy is circumcised between the ages of three and seven. He will perhaps occasionally beat the boy for major infractions of rules, sometimes acting on the mother's complaint. The father will be treated, if present, as the final arbiter of family disputes and resources; he is likely to be either taciturn or brusque with a son beyond elementary school age.[9]

The emotional distance maintained between fathers and their sons from the time of the boy's adolescence on is the result of both the hierarchical relations based on age and reticence over the communication of sexual information. A Zawiya father would find it acutely embarrassing to directly counsel or educate his son about sexual matters.

In a small community his son's misdemeanors or experimentation with sexual activity may reach the father by hearsay. He will probably ignore this, unless public knowledge of the son's wrong-doing threatens to bring shame on the family. His role in the marriage of his son is similarly circumspect, although he may be required to raise with difficulty the large sum required as bride-price. If forced to recognize signs of severe sexual problems such as impotence in his son, he may take him to pray at a saint's tomb or to see a doctor in another city, but even here the mother is likely to play the more active role. The relationship unfolding between his wife and his daughter-in-law, whether conflict or alliance, will probably be viewed by him with either anxiety or cynicism. He is likely to find it difficult to express the sympathy he feels for a son caught between two powerful women. The son for his part will continue to show respect in the presence of his father throughout his life, extinguishing a cigarette before his father enters the room and speaking to him in a deferent manner.

The descriptions above are immediate, in the sense that they focus on the way adolescents interact with each parent. Our interview data give a more general picture of the place of the mother and father in the family. We asked a question phrased roughly "Everyone at home is dear ['aziz] to you, but whom do you especially prefer?" Mothers were by far the most commonly mentioned figures, and were preferred over fathers by an almost two to one margin by both sexes.[10]

Sibling Rivalry

The same respect for age that marks the relationship with parents is seen between siblings. Older siblings are to be obeyed, although there is some variation, depending on each sibling's sex. Sibling rivalry is recognized, however. When a woman becomes pregnant while still nursing the previous child, the fetus and the nursling are called by a specific term (1-awlad al-ghiyal), based on the verb for "to snatch away." The nursling is weaned immediately and after the birth is expected to be jealous. There is a general expectation that during childhood a sibling will fight with the next born, although we saw several examples of children who were adjacent in birth order yet were very close.

Sisters

Girls have strong ties to their sisters, and this carries over into adulthood when the contact is maintained. While in most families there is small-scale bickering over which sister does what chores, it is usually quickly forgotten. Sisters do not guard their behavior or their tongues (except concerning sexual matters) as they would if outsiders or men were present.

The relation between sisters is different from the relation between friends, although both are highly valued relationships. Sometimes girls would say "We're just like sisters" to stress how close they felt to a friend, but in fact in our neighborhood we found only one case of sisters being best friends. When asked if sisters could be friends, most girls said no, mainly because if sister-friends had a fight, each would tell their parents all the secrets (presumably about boys) of the other.

We also found exceptions to the general closeness between sisters. One case was a middle daughter who hated her eldest sister, saying the sister did such things as break a dish, claim the younger girl had done it, and then stand by as she was beaten. This girl's feelings were vividly revealed when she told with obvious relish a story she heard about a young woman who had been accidentally hung by her younger sister. Usually, however, such negative feelings were forgotten and adult sisters were close.

Sisters and Brothers

There is more variation expected, and found, in the relationship of sisters to their brothers. The ways they interact change with their positions in the life cycle. Their feelings for each other are often ambivalent: they may be positive or negative, and sometimes both emotions are experienced simultaneously.

During childhood, the hierarchical law of respect for greater age holds in a general sense, and girls expect to obey their older brothers and to have their younger brothers obey them. There is also warm affection, especially for oldest brothers or for those who are quite a bit younger, whose sisters become like a second mother. When Susan asked which of their siblings they were closest to (eliminating the choice of a parent), only one girl chose the eldest brother; the rest named a brother or sister under eight years old, reflecting their affection for the children they so often help to raise.

While boys should obey their older sisters, we sometimes saw them strike these sisters during temper tantrums. No retribution and little remonstration resulted from these assaults on siblings.[11] In allowing younger brothers to strike them during tantrums, girls learn a lesson about the gender hierarchy in Morocco, while boys develop a willfulness that remains characteristic of many males.

As they move into the adolescent years, girls' relationships to both their older brothers and those only a little younger change. These brothers are expected to monitor a sister's sexual behavior, to defend her from the attentions of flirtatious young men, and to punish any inpropriety on her part. While the father is nominally responsible, if a girl has older brothers it is they who are more likely to observe her chatting or walking with boys, since they are in many of the same settings. Several girls said their brothers had told boys to leave them alone. In some cases this intervention was welcome, but in others the girls resented it. Later, at home, the brothers would both report to the family and sometimes punish (strike) their sisters.

The following exerpt from an interview with a now-married woman shows some of her ambivalence about her relation to her older brother during adolescence:

■ M: *I told [my brother], "There is a guy who follows me [home from school in Kabar]." . . . When [my brother] walked behind me, he saw [the guy] blocking my way. So he asked him, "What's your problem with her? How do you know her? What do you want from her?" The guy answered, "She is my classmate." So [my brother] told him, "What do you want from her?" . . . That's how my brother got into a fight with him.*
S: *They had a fist fight?*
M: *Yes, a fist fight.*
S: *And what happened to you? Didn't you get scared watching?*
M: *I was just watching. He told him "If you keep on following her and she comes again to complain to me, I'll handle you worse than I did this time." And he did give me a break—he didn't follow me any more. . . . When I finished [school] that year, he [her brother] told me to stay home. . . . We heard about that girl who had that problem [she was pregnant] and he then said to me, "Stay home; no school." And he told my mother that I shouldn't go to school, otherwise he'll raise hell. You see. . . . My brother was older than me, and was responsible for me, you understand, so I quit [school].*

This young woman had hoped to continue her education. On the one hand she appreciated her brother's defense, but on the other hand she resented that he made her leave school.

The growing sexuality of siblings at this time is a source of ambivalence and discomfort in other ways. Males, whose access to girls is limited by those girls' brothers, often sleep in the same room with sisters whose bodies are changing—and they are expected to be sure these stimulating sisters remain pure. Any open discussion of sexuality between brother and sister is considered shameful, and thus one potential avenue of information about the opposite sex in this segregated society is off limits. This was demonstrated when one young man said he wanted to talk to Susan "like a sister" about a sexual question. When she asked, "Would you *really* discuss this with your sister?" he was horrified.

After marriage, the responsibility for a woman is transferred from her family to her husband, but if she were to be divorced or widowed, her father or brothers are again formally responsible. She also depends on them during her marriage to protect or support her interests in case of marital disputes. This is one reason girls prefer to live near their families after marriage, in addition to maintaining their contacts with mothers and sisters. In fact, adult males in our neighborhood seldom gave financial support to their widowed or divorced sisters; several such women we knew did agricultural day labor to support their children. Yet even though brothers may fail to provide the regular help expected of them, sisters feel they are available and will protect them from adversity or a major financial crisis.

Brothers

The bond among brothers is often the most lasting and important for males in Zawiya. On the other hand, the brother who competed for parental affection and limited family resources in childhood may also emerge as the major competitor in adulthood for control of land or economic resources. Older brothers were mentioned with some frequency by males of various ages as the person whose advice was most often sought. Older brothers seem to be especially important as models for males in the later adolescent years, particularly regarding continuation in school. Several of the most highly motivated neighborhood males in secondary school had older brothers who had continued their schooling into senior high school or beyond. These older brothers were often the first and last persons seen during the day, and they clearly served as important sources of information and opinion.

The topics discussed by brothers include studies, music, and sports. There is frequently considerable reticence about sexual and romantic matters in the company of one's older brother, and these topics are much more likely to be discussed with a similarly aged friend.

Brothers often share money, and an older brother who is employed is expected by the family to help purchase clothing for younger siblings of both sexes. In the case of a younger brother, this help often extends to taking him shopping and both selecting and purchasing such clothing items as shoes or trousers. The older brother may also be given money by the younger for the purchase of clothing in Kabar or a larger city. Not only may the older brother exercise his judgment about what to buy for the younger, but it sometimes happens that the older brother uses the ready cash to purchase something for himself, requiring the younger to wait on his later convenience. One of our neighbors, himself eighteen and quite experienced in purchasing his own clothing, entrusted the price of a good pair of sneakers to his twenty-four-year-old brother. Instead of purchasing the sneakers in the city the following weekend as agreed, the older brother bought himself shoes. The younger brother was still awaiting his sneakers when we left eight months later. Although disappointed, he was not bitter about the incident.

Kinship Networks

Moroccan families are closely tied into large networks of kin, and traditional Moroccan values stress the importance of kin. Moroccan society is partrilineal, patrilateral, and patrilocal; descent is traced through males, the preferred form of marriage is between the children of brothers, and preferred residence after marriage is in the household of or nearby the groom's family.

If women moved into their husbands' homes when they married, we would expect there to be more of the father's relatives in town. However, there were nearly the same number of mothers' relatives as fathers' relatives in Zawiya, and nearly twice as many mothers' as fathers' relatives in nearby Kabar. One explanation could be that since both husband and wife come from the same town, both have relatives nearby. However many of the parents of the adolescents were born in villages in the surrounding countryside and both moved to Zawiya—as did many of their families. We found no clear trend of following only the paternal side of the family in these movements.

We also asked adolescents if they traveled to cities and whom they visited; again, the mother's side of the family is important. Girls visited relatives on both sides about equally, but boys visited the mother's relatives three times as often as they did the father's. In addition to tracing descent through males, children of a divorced couple legally belong to the father. Yet when we looked at the location of children from previous marriages in our neighborhood, eighteen lived with the mother's side of the family and twelve with the father's side.

The general picture of kin network that emerges is that the mother and her side of the family are very important in the life of the adolescent. It is not that the father's relatives are unimportant, but they are not the only or even the primary focus of family relations, as has been reported for other areas in the Middle East. When we asked, "Whose advice do you seek at home?" a little over half the boys (in this male-oriented culture) and three-quarters of the girls said their mothers.

There is much visiting back and forth between kin. An example of this frequent contact came from one young mother who complained that her sister-in-law arrived with her baby, husband, and his mother every evening and had dinner with her family. Sometimes they brought their own dinner and sometimes not. She suspected the main reason they came was to watch her television set, since they had none. Another likely reason was that the sister-in-law was a cheery, lively girl who loved to laugh, and she was lonely as the only young woman in her house. Although the hostess had five children of her own and barely enough to feed them, the rules of hospitality and respect for relatives made it impossible for her to even hint to her husband's relatives that they not come over every night. While there, they were party to the disputes of the host family with their adolescent son and would add their own comments. They were not felt to have the same right as his parents to discipline him, but their interest and concern was expected and accepted; by being part of the same family it was in some sense their business.

Often the support provided by relatives is freely given and beneficial to both donor and recipient. One couple had three grown children, one of whom was a married daughter with her own children. When this woman's parents needed help at home she sent first her eldest daughter, later her next one. The girls lived with their grandparents a block from their own home and saw their mother and father daily. They still attended the same school, and the younger girl even said she preferred living with her grandparents because they encouraged her more in her schoolwork. This benefited the parents as well, since one child was fed and clothed by someone else. The same grandparents also had a boy of twelve, a country cousin on the wife's side, living with them so he could attend what his family felt was a better school. The boy's family clearly gained from the arrangement, and the wheat and vegetables they sent from their fields were helpful to their town relatives.

One must keep in mind, however, that such support between relatives is not universal; there are numerous exceptions. In another family, the grandmother of one household lived in two cramped rooms with her married son and his wife and six children, while her half-brother lived nearby in a three-story house. Even though he had a large family he was considered well-off, but his half-sister said he never gave her a penny. Adolescents grow up hearing complaints about family members who are felt to be failing in their obligations, so they come to expect both assistance and disappointment. Their attitude toward relatives is thus often ambivalent.

If one looks closely at the local families, one finds this sort of stress is not uncommon. However, two general statements should be made before closing our discussion of kin. One is that while strain among family members is frequent, in a real crisis relatives usually stick together. Second, while problems between families are often blamed on female in-laws being unable to get along, this may be a convenient excuse in a society in which (1) women are seen as more emotional and likely to get into fights, and (2) it is shameful to admit there is conflict between blood relatives, especially males.[12]

Another important function of the wider group of relatives is that it is seen, and used, as a resource for various kinds of needs. Much in Morocco is accomplished by means of "connections" (Rosen 1984), and relatives are the best means of connection. The petroleum company in Kabar formalized this resource in their policy of hiring employees' sons as their fathers retired, and the best-off family in our neighborhood managed to have both a father and son working there. Some sons worked in their fathers' businesses: two helped their fathers at outdoor markets, and one drove a taxi. A more explicit case of such kin networks is that all over Morocco, grocery shops are run by Berbers from the south; there are three such men in Zawiya. This system began when a few men started shops and accumulated capital, and then brought brothers or cousins north to help them; the network has even extended to France (Waterbury 1972).

Family networks are used not only to find jobs, but in any case of need. When a local extended family group claimed title to land that had been lost during the colonial regime, they hired lawyers to check into the records. However, they also contacted the daughter of a half-sister of one of the group: she was the cook for an important cabinet minister and it was felt that she could use her influence to help.

While family networks are readily activated, they do not always come through. We have noted that traditionally a divorced or widowed woman should be supported by her father or brother. Yet of the six women in this situation in our neighborhood, two lived mainly on money from grown children, two supported their children by agricultural day labor, and two were said to earn their living as prostitutes. We know that at least some of these women had brothers, but none was supported by them.

In general, adolescents grow up surrounded by family: in the household, in the town, in the nearby town, and on their summer visits to relatives in other parts of Morocco. Kin, both close and distant, are important sources of affection and support. In fact, when one becomes friends with an older person who is not a relative, one calls them *'ammi, khalli,* or *khalti*[13] (my father's brother, mother's brother or sister) to denote the closeness, and when adolescents described close friends they said they were "just like a sister or brother." One's closest relatives are the people one feels closest to and expects the most of, and as they get more distant in genealogical space, the relationship usually gets cooler. In spite of these high and often-met expectations, there are at times ambivalent feelings toward family members. Overall, most Moroccans are in contact with more relatives than are most Americans, and these relatives provide a source of support. They are the basic and most influential unit in Moroccan society. However, another essential source of support for adolescents is found in their friendships, to which we now turn.

■ 5
Friendship

For those Zawiya youth who continue in school, friendship and education are usually crucially interrelated. Youth who meet at school often become close friends, and some of the main opportunities to interact with friends occur when walking to and from school together, sharing a table in class, visiting at recess, or studying together. Friendship is much more egalitarian and exploratory than are family relations, with young people discussing their secrets and desires, sharing confidences and belongings, and trying to work out a way to deal with a world beyond the experience of their parents. However, this does not mean that young people turn to friends and exclude their parents, as some feel American teens do; parents remain an important influence. Friends fill roles that parents or other relatives cannot. [1]

Adolescents learn important cultural values through friendships, including the importance of reciprocity and of maintaining a good reputation. One aspect of a good reputation, especially for girls, is that one interacts only with peers of the same sex; this means that friendships rarely cross gender lines, reinforcing the cultural norm of separation of the sexes. The theme of ambivalence that we discussed with regard to the family appears again in relation to friendship: while one expects a great deal from friends, there are inevitable disappointments which lead to decreased dependence on or trust in friends. Further, it seems that this ambivalence about trust and intimacy with friends is more pronounced for males than for females, although it is experienced by both. [2]

Changing patterns of interpersonal relationships are a key feature of the picture of adolescence developed for Western culture by social scientists. The psychological literature on adolescence suggests that during this stage of life, relationships with friends undergo a number of significant and frequently stressful changes. The neopsychoanalytic theories of Erikson and Sullivan are particularly concerned with the importance of adolescent friendships for personality development. Erikson (1950) characterizes both same- and opposite-sex friendships as helping the individual to try out and master various aspects of the self enroute to the establishment of adult identity. Sullivan (1953) makes a persuasive case that the transition into full adolescence cannot be successfully made unless one attains an emotionally intimate relationship with a like-sexed "chum" in the preadolescent phase. Recent sociological investigations in the United States have underscored the importance of friends for the social development of adolescents. Seltzer (1982, 247) argues that the peer group is the "organizing dynamic core of the adolescent period," and Youniss and Smollar (1985, 3) emphasize that reciprocity among peers is a basis for learning the principle of fair treatment.[3]

One crucial and potentially stressful aspect of adolescent friendships was repeatedly mentioned by our informants in Zawiya: the difficult process of finding in one's friend(s) an object of trust and reciprocal sharing of feelings and possessions. A recurrent theme of Moroccan social relationships is the establishment of trustworthiness.[4] Distrust of most persons, especially those outside one's immediate family, is common in Moroccans' descriptions of their dealings with others. Yet some basis of mutual trust must be achieved with peers if one is to function successfully in society. Morocco is a country in which personal "presence" is absolutely pervasive and vital. One cannot achieve such presence without a very good sense of how one comes across to people. Interactions with friends help to develop and hone this sense—thus the great import of relationships with an age-mate and soul mate. Indeed, one could argue that the core goal of Zawiya socialization is to produce a person worthy of trust and able to command respect, one who respects propriety *(Hasham)*, displays mature judgment *('aql),* and stands by one's word *(kilma).*

Concern with trustworthiness and reciprocity was central in the responses of both male and female adolescents to our questions about friendship, but friendship is perhaps more deeply problematic for males. To the general concerns emphasized by both sexes—that a friend share, refrain from gossip, and not prove a bad influence—males add worry about competition and aggression of a more troubling sort than that generally described by females. Adolescent and adult males often state that everyone is basically out for himself and that friendships will be forgotten when the stakes are high. Males also expressed concern about physical aggression in the context of friendship: that one's friend would not back one up in a fight, or (worse) that the friend would himself let slip a remark disparaging to one's honor. The fear is that the friendship might then dissolve in anger, whether or not an actual fight ensued.

All these concerns occupy the attention of Zawiya youth during the teen years. The young men walking along the highway to Kabar hand in hand are trying to tell something about themselves, and see how it sounds echoed back to them. From these friends they expect (or at least hope for) loyalty and generosity. To them they give their own loyal and generous feelings, thereby expanding those emotions from an exclusive attachment to family. Boys talk about girls and jobs, anger and hope; they may construct and describe a fantasy future life for themselves.

NUMBER OF FRIENDS

The most commonly reported number of close friends was one.[5] While studies done in the United States have described adolescents as reporting fewer friends as they got older (Youniss and Smollar 1985), and while it appeared in Zawiya that children of nine and ten were often in groups of four and five while older teens were in twos and threes, our data offer minimal support of those observations. The number of reported close friends is generally small, and there is not a progressive decrease by age. However, if the sample is split at average age of puberty, we see a decrease in the number of reported friends for both sexes—from about two before puberty to one thereafter.[6] Thus most Zawiya adolescents report one or two close friends, always of the same sex, and there appears to be a tendency for older girls to report fewer close friends than do either boys in general or younger girls.

Only two male adolescents stated that they had no close friends. Both are the sons of a single woman who people say goes out with men and accepts money from them, and both are tough fighters, perhaps because of insults concerning their parentage. Two young women, both in their older teens, also reported no close friends.

Intensive interviews revealed more about the reasons for having only a few carefully selected friends. A young woman of nineteen gave one common reason for older girls: "There are some girls who are friends in groups of three or four, but in my opinion, it's better to be just two. A third raises a ruckus; she's a devil and gets one off course. She gets people fighting." A schoolgirl of twelve, asked about sources of conflict with her friends, emphasized the keeping of secrets. Another reason that older girls have fewer friends is that some leave the area or marry. Three of four informants reported having no close friends. Youniss and Smollar noted a decrease in the number of friends for older U.S. adolescents, but phrased the reasons in terms of a desire for greater intimacy and exclusivity, including the desire for self-disclosure and the sharing of problems and advice with one person (1985, 4). This is also true for Zawiya females, although they often phrase the desire for one close friend in terms of avoiding conflict.

SEX AND FRIENDSHIP

In none of the above cases was the friend of the opposite sex. This was due to both cultural constraints and the way in which we asked the question. Segregation of the sexes (except in the immediate family and in classrooms) is a strongly valued norm in Morocco, so a cross-sex friendship would be frowned on and suspected of having sexual overtones. Further, the Arabic language marks gender, so there is no way to say "friend" without indicating a male or a female friend (*SaHeb* and *SaHeba* respectively). To ask a girl if she has a girl friend is easy, but to use the masculine form in questioning a girl makes the question about a boyfriend, not a boy friend. Since there are strong norms against this, we doubted that anyone would respond in the positive even if she had a friend who was a boy.

As a general rule cross-sex friendships are rare and of low intensity in Zawiya. Although several young people said they believed cross-sex friendship might be possible, the texture of same- and opposite-sex friendships is very different, especially for girls.[7] Some older males, reluctant to share their uncertainties or fears with peers, may talk about such things more easily with girls. We heard of one case like this, but as the relationship went on, it also became sexual. The strong societal expectation that all male-female relationships are sexual causes tension in most of these friendships.

The following excerpt from an interview with Hurriya, a sixteen-year-old girl in secondary school, illustrates clearly the differences in the two types of male friends.

■ H: *One day a boy told me, "come here; I want to talk to you." He's a neighbor. . . . Well, I did not suspect anything because I used to go and have him help me with schoolwork. I didn't expect him to tell me anything. So I went to his house. He helped me with my homework and then said to me: "I want to talk to you." I said, "What do you want to tell me?" He replied "I want to talk to you and I want us to become friends."*

She told him she had to think about it, and after talking it over with her best friend she decided not to accept his offer and wrote him a letter saying so. Her explanation of that decision shows the difference between the two types of friend; it also shows that for girls to "talk" and to "laugh" with boys have different meanings.

■ H: *I don't want to be anybody's [girl]friend. I decided, and it is the right thing. I must really not talk to anybody. . . . It wouldn't be nice for me because everybody will know about it. It looks bad. That's why I want him to be like all our other neighbors' kids. We will laugh and all that. I don't want him to tell me that kind of talk. . . .*
S: *This is what I don't understand—the difference between talking and laughing.*
H: *The other guy [the SaHeb or boyfriend] will carry on, telling you "I like you, I love you, etc.," but with the other guys [Sadiqs] we only talk about school, and we tell jokes. . . . What I like are talks about studies, jokes. I don't like anybody telling me "I like you" and then taking advantage of me, as they usually do of others.*

Thus one "laughs" or kids around with a *Sadiq* and "talks" more seriously about romantic topics with a boyfriend or *SaHeb*. Hurriya's account also shows that norms are against the latter relationship when she says she turned her neighbor down partly because "it looks bad"; she wants to maintain a certain image.

THE IMPORTANCE OF RECIPROCITY

The sort of reciprocity valued by Zawiya teenagers in their friendships was illustrated in comments made by several of them, including Hakima and Abdelaziz, whose daily routines appeared in chapter 2. When Hakima at age sixteen was re-interviewed by Susan, she was still in school. She was asked to describe her "self" or "nature," and her response moved quickly to the topic of relations with friends and their reciprocal nature:

■ H: *I am not very tense. I have good relations with people. I help people who help me. I am nice to my girlfriends, to girl students and boy stu-*

dents. I treat [the boys] like brothers and deal with them correctly. They too are nice to me. But when they get upset with me, I get upset with them too. . . .

s: *OK. What do you do when you are nice to them?*

h: *I have fun with them. And when we have an exam and they need assistance I help them [i.e., show them the right answers], and they too show me the answers. I behave decently with them. If one of them refuses to help me when I ask her, the next time she asks me for help I refuse.*

As a nineteen-year-old high school student, Abdelaziz also mentioned reciprocity in terms of the sharing of answers in school and not admitting it to the teachers.

■ d: *Was there a time during the past year when you had to decide between two actions, and you didn't know which was the right thing to do?*

a: *Yes, a friend copied my work in class. The professor came over and asked who copied whom. I didn't want to embarrass my friend in front of the prof.*

d: *What did you do?*

a: *I kept quiet so my friend wouldn't be embarrassed, but the prof knows I work well and that my friend must have copied.*

The teacher then split the grade each had received between them. Both of these examples suggest that reciprocal reliance between friends readily takes precedence over the moral or legalistic requirements of the school system.

ACTIVITIES WITH FRIENDS

The activities typically engaged in with friends differed somewhat by sex: boys often mentioned engaging in sports activities together, while girls described embroidering together or helping each other with housework. Play groups begin to be composed of mainly one sex by the age of six or seven. Both boys and girls of those ages can be seen hunched in clusters near houses shooting marbles, or standing and encouraging their peers in hopscotch. It is more common for the boys' groups to play a version of soccer or to hit a ball or stone with a stick. While some younger female adolescents mentioned playing these games, by about twelve they turn to other activities.

Males, however, usually continue their intense interest in soccer. As one walks through Zawiya, the visible male teens are playing or watching soccer in the large field on the western edge of town, while the girls are gathered in smaller groups or are running errands. In the spring months of February and March, adolescent girls anxious to enjoy the sun sit on the edges of the greening fields and visit as they embroider. In other seasons, however, they are more apt than the boys to work and visit indoors, except for their daily trips to fetch water. Adolescents of both sexes who were still in school often mentioned studying together with same-sex peers. Older males were more likely than both younger males and females to indicate walking and/or talking together with their friends as a typical activity. Although females often mentioned talking, it was in the context of other work; they do not have the degree of leisure or mobility that allows boys to stroll and talk.

One of the major activities of young women and their friends is conversation, and often these conversations involve the exchange of intimacies. They may help each other with housework or do embroidery, but their main reason for getting together is to talk, especially about topics and feelings they would not discuss with others, except perhaps their mothers. A young woman of sixteen said, describing her relationship with her one best friend, "We don't hide anything from each other. . . . The things I talk about only with Suad are things like if I fought with someone at the well, or we laugh about the boys who talk to us there, discussing whether it's 'bad' or 'good' talk [improperly flirtatious, or innocuous]." Another sixteen-year-old said she and her friend discussed problems: one of them felt very sad about never seeing her father, who had left the household when she was an infant, and the other was concerned that she would not be allowed to see the woman who had raised her from infancy because of family problems. These were both deeply personal issues; that they were shared indicates intimacy.

The strongest friendships of the older male adolescents have a quality the participants sometimes compare favorably with their family relationships. Eighteen-year-old Rashid was asked about his best friends, and he said he and a lycée classmate had been close for four years. He shares with this friend secrets about his activities and feelings that he would tell no one else, including his older brother.

ORGANIZED GROUPS

One is struck by the relative absence in Zawiya of male or female peer groups with any clear structure or temporal stability. For boys, there are no hobby clubs, no class trip planners, no motorcycle gangs. One exception is the several soccer teams, although they include only a minority of older males. These are roughly neighborhood based and named. They raise money for uniforms and a ball, and they use the open stretch of ground bordering the neighborhood for competitions with other clubs. These are seldom regularly scheduled, usually occur in the late summer, and are intensely competitive.

Teenagers are increasingly known by the company they keep, and the collections of older teenage males beside neighborhood shops or the café in the Suiqa are sometimes discussed by older people as if they were "ganglets." These groups have little in common with urban gangs in the United States, but groups of teenage males do seem at times to goad each other on to acts of aggression or petty thievery. Females also have few visible peer groups, nor do they compete in athletics. There are informal groups of friends who get together to embroider or study, and these appear to be more explicitly recognized arrangements than male attempts to study together. The groups also are more likely to involve more than two teenagers at a time. Both girls and boys are likely to walk to school in small groups, starting in the elementary years, and perhaps these constitute a nucleus of "peer groups"; they are, however, variable in composition and unnamed, unlike the U.S. high school class's division into "jocks," "punks," and "nerds."

Because family ties are so strong and people have many relations in Zawiya, we thought friends might be selected from among an adolescent's relatives, but the majority of reported friends for both sexes were identified as neighbors. In general, it appears that closeness of residence is an important factor in determining one's friends.

BEGINNING AND ENDING FRIENDSHIPS

The most frequently mentioned reasons for close friendship in the larger group were agreement (or the absence of conflict), and the sharing or exchange of belongings and food. While both sexes often mentioned that their friends were close because they did not fight, girls sometimes also said specifically that their friends were those who did not gossip or tell tales about them. The desire to avoid gossip reflects for females the importance of maintaining a good reputation, a cultural value that is learned in youth and persists into adulthood. Other distinguishing qualities of friends mentioned by several adolescents included good character or general niceness, reliability, and readiness for mutual self-disclosure.[8] The reciprocity in sharing food and belongings in Zawiya is taken by adolescents as an indication of the closeness of friendship, and at the same time teaches the important social value of generosity.

Extended interviews provided more detailed information about the bases for friendship, causes of conflict, and reasons why friendships began and ended. Nearly all girls met their friends in school or through living in the same neighborhood. The majority wanted their friends to be similar to themselves, although the sorts of similarities differed. Hakima, quoted above, said she would like her friend to be like her in that they should both do well in school and not be envious of each other. A girl of fifteen said she wanted a friend to be similar in that she would live and dress well, and be clean. Older girls showed more concern both with their reputations and with psychological characteristics. A seventeen-year-old who had left school said she wanted a friend with "the same spirit" and similar behavior. An eighteen-year-old student wanted her friend to be "nice, not a loose girl who isn't a good student, running in and out of class and talking to boys all the time." Of her best friend she said, "My ideas are like her ideas. She agrees to study during class breaks; we have the same ideas. We study at the cultural center library; we don't walk the streets." Most said they wanted their friends to be about the same age, but only two wanted friends of the same economic level. Most said it was not important, and this view prevails in practice; we saw many cases of well-off girls with friends from poorer families.

Certain words were used to describe especially close friends. At fourteen, Hakima said she would tell a secret to "my friend from the soul [ruH]." A young woman in her twenties described her best friend as a "soul mate." Another young woman in her twenties said that friendships last if a friend "is good, acts on her real intentions [niya], and doesn't hide things. She should like me better than she likes other girls."

The fact that close friends are described as "soul mates" suggests an intimacy that many girls feel with their friends. However, we have noted that there is also an element of ambivalence and distrust in relations with friends; one almost expects to be disappointed. This came through in Susan's taped interviews, when she asked, "What does the phrase 'to depend on someone' mean to you? Who do you depend on?" Most young people of both sexes said they depended on their parents; many fewer depended on friends. Those who said they depended on friends gave examples such as trusting a friend to bring them barrettes from a trip to the city or to save them some sweets from a party; these were not major emotional investments. The following edited excerpt of an interview with a young woman in her twenties, one who earlier expressed great affection for her best friend and called her a soul mate, illustrates ambivalence about trusting friends.

■ s: *What does the phrase "to depend on someone" mean to you?*
a: *"Dependence is on God" not on "someone." You don't depend on people.*
s: *Really?*
a: *Of course. Let's say you tell someone "count on me to do such a thing for you" and you are not going to do it. In this case dependence is on God, not on a person. Suppose you had visitors after you promised some girl to get a dress ready for her [to sew it] that day—she needs it for the party—you didn't know about the guests before you promised her to do the work for her. So would you forget about them and fulfill your promise? I don't think so. The visitors will leave in an hour or two, and you reneg on your contract. Thus she is not depending on you anymore. Her dependence is dead. She won't trust you anymore even if you present your apologies to her and tell her about the visitors. Rather, she will think that you didn't do the work on time because you were jealous; you didn't want her to have a nice new dress for a party. You were not even invited to attend. She will also think you don't want her to look nicer than you do. So dependence doesn't exist.*
s: *It doesn't?*
a: *There is no girl who may rely or depend on another one.*
s: *Do you depend on your mother?*
a: *On one's mother, of course. . . .*
s: *At the moment does your mother depend on you? Does she trust you?*
a: *Of course she trusts me and depends on me.*

The way this young woman sees her mother as dependable, in contrast to the unreliability of friends, is typical of Zawiya adolescents and underscores the strength of family ties in general.

For young women, the main reasons that friendships end are conflict, a move to a different neighborhood or town, or concern that continued association with a certain friend may harm one's reputation. Given that many people mentioned conflict as a potential and frequent problem with friendship, it is interesting that there is a small but formalized ritual that marks the end of friendship, especially for younger children. It is literally called "cutting off" [qti'a]. If two girlfriends are really angry with one another, they "cut off" relations by linking their right little fingers and pulling them apart forcefully. After this, they do not speak to each other until they formally make up, which is often encouraged by other girls. Older girls do not use the finger motions, but also usually cut off relations by not speaking after a fight, and do not resume them without a somewhat formal reconciliation. A few examples demonstrate the process and illustrate some of the issues that cause conflict. A thirteen-year-old said that it was best for just two girls to be friends, because a third will cause trouble. "I fought with a friend who said bad things about me to another girl. That girl told me, and I accused my friend, who denied it. But I believed the other girl because she's a better person, and also because she's the one who raised the issue. Now I'm cut off, not speaking to my friend any more."

Fourteen-year-old Fateha said she never "cut off" relations with her best friend, but described the process with another friend. "Hayat and I were at the well, and she shoved my pregnant mother. I told her not to, but she didn't stop. So I told her mother, but Hayat said my mother and I wouldn't let her have a turn at the tap. Then Hayat wouldn't talk to me; I tried, and then didn't talk to her either. [They didn't use the finger motions because they're older; they just "cut off" using the word.] It only lasted about two days, because we always talk about schoolwork." She felt unhappy when she was cut off, and would ask about schoolwork and joke in order to make peace. They got back together, without any overt apology.

When Douglas asked thirteen-year-old Samir whether he ever fought with his best friend next door, Samir described an incident when they were in the third grade: "[We fought] about marbles. He said he was first and I said I was. We 'cut off,' and another boy made peace between us."

Najet, a girl of eleven, described how a classmate had insulted her by saying Najet had done a math problem wrong at school, even though it had been correct. Although they had been friends for about six months, Najet cut her off last year and has not spoken to her since. The girl even sent an intermediary to ask her to make up, but Najet refused and has not felt bad about it. Thus conflicts can sometimes end a friendship permanently, although more often they are resolved.

A young woman in her twenties gave an example of less-formalized cutting off. Once Kebira was waiting to go to the public bath, and her friend went without telling her. The baths are a chance to relax and visit, and are looked forward to and often shared with good friends. "It wasn't a big deal. We didn't insult each other, we just didn't speak. Or I'd insult her in a joking way, and she'd get mad. People usually make up on a holiday or some special occasion. You'd say, 'Here I've come to see you and you're still mad?' and you'd make peace."

The themes of reliability and reciprocal generosity mentioned by many adolescents were elaborated by several young people in discussing why some friendships last and others end unhappily. For example, when sixteen-year-old Sa'id was interviewed during the fall, he was asked about his best friends and indicated that these were now two boys from neighboring Douar

Doum. He volunteered that he had fought with one of his closest Zawiya friends from the summer period when Doug had first talked with him about friendship. The break occurred because, after borrowing many of his books and postcards, the friend had been reluctant to lend Sa'id a math book. He and his new friends, Sa'id said, both lend and borrow from each other constantly. He often lent them his prized newly acquired bicycle for long trips. When Sa'id was asked about the general qualities important for friends, he emphasized that when a friend asks to borrow something (he gave the example of a book) it must be given. He added that friends must not curse or insult ['iyyr] one another. Douglas talked later in the year with two of the former friends Sa'id had fought with, and they gave a similar account of the incident but felt that he had been childish to refuse to make up over so small an issue.

Another reason that friendships end is unique to older girls. Their friends marry and usually move out of the neighborhood. The remaining friend is often out of school and less mobile than younger girls, so it is difficult for her to make new friends. In this case she may spend time with a neighbor about the same age, even though she is not a best friend. These girls bear a double burden: they have lost close friends to confide in, and they are not yet married, often a source of much concern. This is one of the major sources of stress for older girls. Kebira, now in her twenties, described her problems with friendship:

Sabah is my only friend; we shop for vegetables together, and sometimes go to the public bath. But it's not a relationship of real affection; there are only we two girls this age on our street. There used to be [another girl, her best friend], but she moved [with her family, two blocks away] about a year ago. I still see her, we still visit at each others' houses, but only every month or so.

Even so short a distance has deprived Kebira of her close friend, and those who marry are usually even less accessible.

A final reason for ending a friendship, especially for young women, is fear that association with a certain person will harm one's reputation, and perhaps also lead one into unacceptable behaviors. These themes, as well as the topic of reciprocity, appear vividly in an interview with Aisha, a girl of eighteen in secondary school.

■ A: *How is my nature? Well, it is good. I like people who are nice to me. When people are not good to me I don't continue to like them. As for*

girls, I make friends with them but if I find they are not good, for example if they are sluts [qHb], bad, I leave them alone. . . .

s: And you . . . said some of the other girls are sluts, are not good; what
do they do?

A: They can have a bad influence on me.

s: How can they influence you?

A: For example: They have a bad reputation, and if I go with them
people will see us and say that person is not good. And if I go with one
of them they will say I am not good either. When girls are friends [ac-
quaintances], if one has a bad reputation the other will be seen as the
same. As they say, "One rotten fish makes the whole saddlebag stink."
. . . That is why I go only with nice people.

s: If you go with one who is not good, will you become like her? Or only
in the eyes of other people, even if you are nice?

A: Even if you are nice, people will judge you as bad because you go
with her and she has a bad reputation. She can have a bad influence on
you. She can tell you for example, "Go out, go out with that guy, he is
good looking." She will pressure you to do what she does. If a girl is not
mature or not intelligent, she can become like her friend.

s: And if she tells you to go out [prostitute yourself]? You know, that
word for a girl who goes with a man for money—but you may not
want to use it in that sense. I want to understand how you use it.

A: For example, if a boy starts following her, she becomes his friend. She
remains his girlfriend for some time. But then, later, he leaves her; they
split after a quarrel. Then she goes out with another boy. She goes out
with a lot of boys. She becomes friends with them.

s: Does she do it for money?

A: No. Not for money. He tells her, "I like you, I'll die for you." He tells
her, "I'll marry you." They remain together until the day he is fed up
with her. He just lets her go and looks for another one, without any
money.

Aisha's comments raise a point that both girls and their parents worry
about: association with bad companions can lead one into bad ways. While
this issue was particularly emphasized by adolescent girls, it also surfaced
in some of our conversations with males, as in the following exchange
with eighteen-year-old Mohammed, who works as an apprentice in Kabar
and was describing the good influence on him of a friend who is a college
student.

■ M: I was telling you about that friend of mine. We meet every afternoon. Then we part around 10:00 or 10:30 P.M.

s: *Does he work with you?*

m: *No, he is a student. I have a job; he is a person in school and he is a friend of mine. He goes to school in Fez . . . in his first year of the university.*

s: *What do you talk about?*

m: *Sometimes he brings up subjects from school. We also talk about good subjects.*

s: *Like what?*

m: *For example, he tells me, "Go with who is better than you. Don't go with a person who is stupid."*

s: *What does that mean?*

m: *It means someone who does not have sense [ʻaql], someone who drinks wine and who smokes. I should not become friends with someone like that. I should frequent someone who does not smoke and does not drink, someone who tells you not to do those bad things.*

Thus young people try to avoid peers with bad reputations, both to protect their reputations and to avoid damage to their character in a more behavioral sense. Zawiya adolescents and parents are aware of the important developmental influence of peers.

We see important similarities between Moroccan and American adolescents in the importance of adolescent friendships and in some sources of conflict between friends. Youniss and Smollar found that the four major sources of conflict for Americans, in order of frequency, were friends engaging in untrustworthy acts (like telling secrets), not paying sufficient attention to one, engaging in disrespectful acts (like putting one down), and participating in unacceptable behaviors (like moodiness or drinking) (1985, 111). We have seen examples of Moroccans worrying about friends spreading gossip or telling secrets, of a girl who wants to be liked better than others by her friend, and of a girl avoiding unacceptable behavior such as dating boys. Moroccan males especially worry about being treated disrespectfully by their friends; such behavior would include refusal to share goods, insults or physical acts, or failure to respect a friend's honor. Honor and reciprocity figure prominently in adolescent sexual relationships, our next topic.

■ 6
Sexuality, Courtship, and Marriage

Sexuality is recognized by Islam as a crucial and valuable, if sometimes problematic, aspect of human life (Bouhdiba 1985; Mernissi 1975; Musallam 1983). While the ideal Muslim adult should express and take pleasure in marital sexuality, for the male Moroccan in particular, sexual activity is regarded as an essential aspect of healthy adult life. We noted in chapter 3 that sexual maturity and specifically sexual potency are important signs of male adulthood in several schools of Islamic jurisprudence. At a personal emotional level, great pride is taken in potency, and great shame is felt at any sexual failure.[1] For the female, sexual pleasure in marriage is sanctioned. However, the strong negative view of sex outside marriage for women also often influences the experience of marital sex.

Adolescent sexuality has been a topic of great interest to twentieth-century psychology. Indeed, theories of sexuality have assumed a central place in the attempts of social science to explain the progress of culture and the rise of the modern industrial state and of bourgeois institutions (Foucault 1976). Foucault (1976) argues that it was with the rise of the industrial bourgeoisie in the eighteenth and nineteenth centuries that concern with controlling sexual outlets gave rise to the "repression" on which Freud based his theories. As a result, the private masturbation of the adolescent schoolboy became a subject for concerned parents and educators (Freud [1905] 1953; Foucault 1976). In a review of the Western psychological literature on the development of sexuality in adolescence, Miller and Simon (1980) note that the problem of adolescent sexuality has taken on special importance in industrial societies, where "young people are defined as sexually mature while simultaneously being defined as socially and psychologically immature" (1980, 383).[2]

Whiting, Burbank, and Ratner (1986) survey cross-cultural data and have noted that the management of sexuality becomes a problem in industrial societies where training for specialized occupations requires education and prolongs the period between puberty and marriage for both boys and girls. The youth of Zawiya now attend coeducational school, aspiring to secondary education and postponing marriage; for both boys and girls there is more opportunity and desire for heterosexual interaction.

It is assumed by most young people in Zawiya that one must conceal sexual experimentation from one's parents. In Zawiya over the past two decades there has been a substantial increase in opportunity for interaction with the opposite sex before marriage, partially because girls marry later; the mean age is 20.8 in rural areas and 23.8 in cities (Royaume du Maroc 1987, 27). These interactions have led to greater ambivalence with regard to interpersonal relations. Young women are placed in more situations involving sexual approaches by males, and young men attempt both to become sexually involved with neighborhood girls and to protect the reputation of their own sisters.

While at first glance it appears there may be a "sexual revolution" going on in Zawiya (see S. Davis 1984), data comparing past and current behaviors suggest this description of change is too extreme. It is important to note that in Zawiya "sexual" behavior encompasses a wider range than the Western reader may expect. In a society in which contacts between unrelated persons of the opposite sex are disapproved, any interaction has a sexual implication. Attempts to speak privately to the opposite sex are seen as the first step in a liaison that will ultimately become sexual.

In the parental generation, most marriages were arranged by families; now the increased contact of boys and girls has led many youths to form their own opinions of whom to marry, rather than simply accepting the match arranged for them. There is a fairly recent, and partly imported, aspiration on the part of both sexes to romantic love. There is evidence, however, of considerable ambivalence in both the young people's general attitudes toward the opposite sex and in the results of their own experience in this area. Coexisting with the male's desire to have a romantic liaison with a virgin is his readiness to exploit a girl who would be so "loose" as to let a boy date her. The ambivalence resulting from these attitudes is based on a conflict between ideals and reality. The ideal is that the untouched "good" girl should marry, while her dishonored sister is left single, in shame. In fact, it appears that girls who experiment rather freely with the new mores are more apt to marry than their peers who follow traditional rules and avoid contacts with males. Some mothers in Zawiya have noticed these trends and are discussing how to react; some of their conclusions suggest a change in norms.

We begin with an account of traditional practices, as experienced by typical parents of our adolescents, and then describe the situation for young people today.[3] This highlights the changes between the generations and indicates the issues to which today's adolescents are struggling to accommodate. To help our U.S. readers place the descriptions of sexual behavior in Zawiya in context, we refer to the findings of American researchers (Kinsey, Pomeroy, and Martin 1948; Kinsey et al. 1953; Frayser 1985). We also draw comparisons to recent surveys of adolescent sexual behavior in the United States (Coles and Stokes 1985).

TRADITIONAL APPROACHES TO SEXUALITY, MATE SELECTION, AND MARRIAGE

Sexuality and Islam

The reasons given by Moroccans for the separation of the sexes refer directly or indirectly to Islam.[4] The reasons for separation are discussed in detail in several recent works by North African social scientists (Bouhdiba 1985; Mernissi 1975; Sabbah 1984). As these writers explain, Islam does not have a negative view of sexuality per se; it is more positive than Christianity in general, and the Qur'an and Hadith state that sex in the context of marriage is both a duty and a pleasure. Marriage, and thus a sexual relationship, is the ideal state of the Muslim adult, and unmarried people are viewed as both incomplete and suspect. A similar argument is advanced by Bullough, who describes Islam as a "sex-positive" religion and notes that "whereas Christianity considered celibacy as the highest good, Islam accepted marriage as the highest good, ordained by God" (1976, 211). In a lengthy discussion of the advantages and disadvantages of marriage, the eleventh-century Muslim writer al-Ghazali notes that sexual pleasure provides a foretaste of the joys of paradise and may thus be an inducement to worship (Farah 1984, 60). However, sex outside the context of marriage is seen as threatening to the fabric of society.[5] It is felt that uncontrolled sexuality leads to chaos (*fitna*) because the believers are distracted from prayer and concern for the community and immerse themselves in sensuality.

Marriage is seen by al-Ghazali and other Muslim writers as important in preventing unbridled sexual passion, which, unconstrained by piety, will lead to "abomination" such as fornication, sodomy, or masturbation (Farah 1984, 61). Further, it is women's sexuality that must be controlled by seclusion, since it is believed that females are naturally lustful and cannot control themselves (see Burton 1886a; Sabbah 1984). This is the basis for the traditional segregation of the sexes in Muslim cultures. As Mernissi points out for her urban Moroccan sample, this segregation is now breaking down, with important consequences for individuals of each sex and for the society in general (Mernissi 1975, 81–87). Several recent Moroccan books contain vivid descriptions of rapidly changing female-male relationships (Alahayane et al. 1987; Naamane-Guessous 1987; Sbaï 1987).

Seclusion of Women and Arranged Marriages

Ideally in traditional Morocco females had no contact at all with males outside the family. Even within the household, the sexes were segregated in many ways. A woman was not supposed to speak even to other women; she could not buy goods from the peddler or go to market because she should not be seen by men. Although separation of the sexes was considered generally desirable, in fact it varied through the life cycle (S. Davis 1983a). Cross-sex contacts were more permissible for girls before menarche and women past menopause, while women just before and after marriage were the most strictly segregated. Marriages were arranged by both sets of parents, and unless a couple were related the young people might never have seen each other until their wedding night. On this night, part of the ceremony included a ritual display of hymeneal blood to demonstrate the bride's virginity.[6]

When most marriages were arranged by the parents of the bride and groom, the groom's parents took the initiative in finding a bride. All a girl could do was wait to be chosen. For the more traditional girls this is still the situation. When Susan asked two single sisters if their brothers in the army would bring home eligible bachelors to meet "the family," they were scandalized: it would be shameful for a girl's kin to even hint in such a manner. It is the male's mother who would do most of the prospecting; she asks relatives and friends if they know of a respectable young woman of the right economic level, and also keeps her eyes open at parties and in the public bath for eligible girls. Many Muslim cultures prescribe marriage to patrilateral parallel cousins, but this was rare in our own community.[7] The main concern is the girl's reputation. If she is a relative, her behavior and personal qualities are well known. When spouses are related the larger family provides an interested support group in times of marital stress.

The marriage of one of our sets of parents is a good example of the traditional style. The mother had finished primary school, which was unusual for a girl at that time, but her marriage was still arranged when she was about sixteen. She herself was interested in a young man who worked for her father, to whom she had found occasional chances to speak as he came by on errands. Before he could ask for her, however, neighbors requested her for their son who was a soldier; because he had been away in the French army, the potential bride had not seen him since she was a small child. His mother came to her home with a sister, and as their hostess prepared tea they examined the house to ascertain the general level of neatness and cleanliness. The prospective bride carefully served tea and cookies; while the purpose of such visits is not announced, when a woman with a marriageable daughter receives an unexpected visit, she always suspects such a motive and the household members are on their best behavior. The visitors observe the girl's attractiveness and, more importantly, demeanor. Since they expect a long and intense relationship with her, they want a bride who seems malleable and acquiescent, not a headstrong or independent one. In some cases the son has seen the girl passing and become interested, and sends his mother for an inspection. One wonders in how many cases a mother has reported the girl has bad breath or a filthy house, when in reality she was just a little spunky. In any case, if the groom's female relatives are pleased, they sound out the girl's mother to see if the family is interested. If they are, another meeting is arranged with the two fathers present to discuss the terms of the marriage: the date, the couple's future residence, and the bride-price. In this marriage, the two families knew and respected each other, so negotiations were quite easy. The bride's family asked for a settlement of about $300, half to be paid before the wedding and the other half to be paid only if there were a divorce. Her family used the money to buy her trousseau and some gold bracelets, and knew they would spend a roughly equal amount of their own funds on the wedding feast.

Once agreed, the parents and the couple went to make up the marriage contract at the office of the 'adl, a man trained in drawing up contracts. This is the legal part of a Moroccan marriage: if a couple should change their minds afterward, they need to get a divorce, even though they have never lived together. After the contract was written, the bride-to-be and her female relatives prepared for the marriage for another six months, buying furniture and clothing. Although this is usually a happy time for the girl, since she is certain of marriage but still living with her own family, in this case it was not. The girl wanted to marry her father's employee, and he belatedly asked for her hand, but the father had been unaware of this interest. He had given his word to the other family and refused to back down, saying, "I'm a *man*." The girl and her mother pleaded with him, to no avail. He had been a bit rushed to arrange the marriage for fear that his daughter would get into some kind of trouble—even though she was quite docile, it had happened to others. The groom was not well known to them because he had been away so much, but his family was honorable, and he would have a salary from France for his military service, so economically he appeared secure. Although he was a neighbor, he was older, and the bride never spoke to him until the wedding night. She recalled trying to get a glimpse of him from her roof as he passed during their engagement.

The couple's married life together began after the celebration that announced their union to the community. Reportedly in the past there were seven days of feasting; now there may be one to three days. Relatives and friends were invited, and the main event was a large dinner with musicians and dancing, held separately for males and females. Around three in the morning, the couple went into their bedroom with the party outside continuing. The groom was to deflower the bride, so that a bloodstained sheet could be displayed as evidence of her virginity (and of the groom's potency). In this case all went as planned, but if the bride had not been a virgin, the groom could return her to her family and ask that the bride-price be refunded. This would be both a great shame and a financial hardship for her family, and partly explains the great concern of family members with girls' honor.

The goal of these traditional marriages was to set up another household in which to raise children; the major aspect was reproductive and economic, certainly not romantic. Of course it was preferable if the couple liked each other, and there were marriages in the older generation in which the couple chose each other, and others in which arranged marriages were incompatible and broke up.

Sexual Segregation in Zawiya

The segregation of the sexes meant that few girls went to high school until recently, although many girls attended primary school. Daughters' sexuality is not threatening to their families until they near puberty. For example, in the mid-1960s Susan visited a number of Zawiya families whose daughters had left primary school and tried to convince them to return the girls to school. While she expected parents to resist because they did not want their daughters to attend classes with boys, not one parent gave that as a reason. Rather, in most cases the mother had a new baby and needed her daughter's help at home. Many girls did return to school, demonstrating that mixed sexes at this age did not disturb parents. However, by high school age there is danger of pregnancy, and the school is in the larger town, providing more opportunities for girls and boys to mix as they walk to and fro twice a day.

Since traditional norms stressed separation of the sexes, there was purportedly no opportunity for boys and girls even to meet and talk with each other, let alone engage in sexual activity. However, norms and behavior are two different matters, and to judge the amount of change in heterosexual interaction between past and present, we worked with well-known informants, asking them about each of fifty-three families in the neighborhood whether the parents or older siblings had been involved in sexual liaisons. Over the last fifteen years, eighteen of the older siblings and ten of the parents were reported to have had such relationships. For data from the more distant past, a woman in her fifties was asked if there were any illicit relationships in the nearby town of about fifty households where she grew up. She reported the details of eight cases that occurred about forty years ago: three involving single women, four married women, and one a divorcée. These informants were of course able to recount only instances of sexual misbehavior that had become the subject of local gossip, so these estimates may be low. On the other hand, such small traditional communities do not miss much. In the words of a common Moroccan saying, "What you breakfast on, the town lunches on." Expectations requiring segregation of the sexes were clear in the past, but these norms were sometimes broken.

In Morocco, the sexual behavior of males has always been less restricted than has that of females, and even in traditional communities men sought and found sexual outlets outside marriage. While the extramarital activity of a man could bring scandal on his family, or provoke violence from a cuckolded neighbor, it has been assumed by most Moroccans that males will on occasion consort with prostitutes or attempt to seduce married women and virginal girls.

SEXUAL SOCIALIZATION AND ACTIVITIES TODAY

Childhood

Heterosexual play in childhood is generally uncommon, although sometimes boys and girls between five and ten will play marbles or set up an imaginary store or house. Prepubertal play with a sexual theme is rare but does occur, usually in the context of playing "groom and bride" in small groups of children. These groups are often composed of five- to eight-year-olds, sometimes including siblings. This play takes place in the house (usually outside the scrutiny of the parents) or in an empty lot. Children attempt to re-create the ceremony, music, and dance they have witnessed at weddings, and the designated "groom" and "bride" may make contact with each others' genitals while playing at the defloration of the bride.

The river, used for washing of clothes as well as swimming, was mentioned by several male informants as a frequent setting for the awakening of sexual interest: young children of both sexes swim naked, while those who are showing secondary sexual characteristics wear underthings. Older adolescent girls and women occasionally swim clothed, and there are always adolescent males perched on the hill and bridge watching.

The sexual interest of a girl is more likely to blossom in the context of overhearing the married women in her family discussing sexual matters. While women do not discuss their own sexual activity in groups, they talk about the behavior of others and about such problems as impotence, infertility, and gynecological illnesses. In these groups of neighbors, children are nearly always present. After age eight or nine, boys will be chased out when these topics arise. Girls are allowed to remain, and especially those in their early teens listen with rapt interest, often being very quiet so as not to call attention to themselves. Sometimes a woman will say, "This isn't proper talk for children," and the girl will blush, but she will not be asked to leave. Thus while discussion of their own sexuality leads to great embarrassment and is avoided between a single girl and her mother, the topic in general is not taboo and such talk provides girls with important information.

Public Ceremonies and Sexuality

Other important settings for the development of sexual attitudes and interests include the celebrations surrounding the naming ceremony held a week after the birth of a child (as-sbu'), circumcision, and weddings. At these occasions music and dancing of an obviously sexual kind occur, and even where separate gatherings of adult males and females are held, prepubescent and adolescent children of both sexes are likely to be admitted. An example may help make the nature of such gatherings clear.

The occasion was a naming ceremony for a baby girl born to a family on our street. The celebration took place in late summer. A very popular musical group with female dancers (shikhat) from a nearby town was hired to provide the entertainment. The host, a local man employed in Europe, was clearly eager to provide a memorable gathering for his neighbors, and the group hired performed a number of popular songs in colloquial Arabic. We were struck by the obvious sexual "double meaning" of many of the lyrics, and the older adolescent males with whom Douglas was seated were clearly stimulated by these, and by the unmistakably sexual movements of the dancers. The women and girls sat on the other side of the roof, and most did not appear embarrassed by the sexual innuendos, even though they usually heard them only at all-female parties. An excerpt from Douglas's notes on the evening illustrates the mood:

> We arrived at about nine in the evening and were seated separately in the men's and women's areas and served tea. At about 9:50 the musicians began to tune their instruments. There were two women who danced and sang, and four men. One of the men played violin and did most of the humorous, sexual, and scatological recitation-type singing. Two of the others played small clay drums and sang, and the remaining man beat time on a large, deep-toned drum and sang loudly. Fat and grinning, he was a parody of male lustfulness: mimicking the older female dancer's movements, advancing on her and shaking his drum in her face, then retreating. They began to perform about ten, and the roof gradually filled over a period of an hour, until there were perhaps 150 people solidly lining the cushions along the walls and filling two-thirds of the floor space, which was occupied mostly by prepubescent boys and, behind them, adolescent girls. The older women were seated along the wall near the top of the stairs, farthest from the performers. The host himself stayed near the door at the head of the stairs, greeting guests as they arrived, keeping uninvited kids outs, assigning people to seats, calling on his son (whose newborn was being honored) to bring tea, and, later in the evening, heading off people trying to leave after an unseemly short stay of only four hours.
>
> The musicians took a few minutes to find their pace, but then settled into a routine of alternating standard songs and recitational pieces. One of the first songs featured the older, less attractive, but clearly more accomplished dancer singing an apparently well-known piece in which the prostitute/dancer is clearly alluding to her own fallen status. The refrain began with the singer asking, "Excuse me mother," for my various transgressions. The recurrent theme across the half-dozen verses was that the young woman's shameful behavior (sexual looseness, drunkenness, and a generally wayward life-style) was not really her fault, since it was related to her mother's rearing of her or finding her a bad husband, assigned to her by fate, and/or the result of generally difficult social circumstances. The refrain was always, "Mother, excuse me, but the fault's in you and not in me."
>
> The audience was in various stages of consciousness and atten-

tiveness. Many of the younger men were apparently already rather drunk and were surreptitiously passing a bottle of wine from which they filled tea glasses and quickly drank; other young men and adolescent males were smoking *kif* (marijuana mixed with tobacco) in a small pipe or emptying cigarettes and refilling them with a mixture of tobacco and hashish. The adolescent girls seemed fascinated but a little giggly with embarrassment, particularly when the dancers approached. Many of the younger boys watched literally openmouthed. The older women were mostly impassive as far as I could see. The most obviously enthusiastic spectators throughout the evening were late adolescent males, who often clapped in time to the drum and chanted familiar refrains. The group had played perhaps four sets by the time we left at two in the morning, with pauses to rest and smoke [the male musicians smoking kif and the older female dancer cigarettes]. Three times the dancers worked the crowd for money, with the older dancer approaching one person after another and dancing directly in front of him. This places her midriff directly in front of the seated male's face, and given the nature of her movements has the unmistakable implication that she's taunting him with her sex. At one point a boy in his late teens was coaxed by the dancer and his friends into standing and dancing, and he had an obvious erection.

We were the first to leave, after a hasty taste of the *tajines* [stews] prepared for the party. We learned the next morning that most of our neighbors had stayed until dawn and that the party warmed up in the wee hours, with one of the male musicians donning a female dancer's robe.

The dancers featured on such occasions are also prostitutes, and the knowledge of their sexual availability adds to the excitement. At celebrations where dancers are present, it is common for arrangements to be made for all interested males to pay for brief access to them in a nearby room at the conclusion of the party. The adolescent male's first heterosexual experience is likely to be with a prostitute, often at the conclusion of such a wedding, circumcision, or naming ceremony.

Sexual Outlets

Most Zawiya residents regard marital heterosexual relations as the most natural and acceptable form of sexual expression, and consider other sexual activities as temporary substitutes for heterosexual relations.

Male Homoeroticism

The alleged sexual practices of the Orient have been a source of fascination to European observers for centuries (Burton 1886b; Said 1978).

Particular interest has been directed to male homosexuality. Earlier ethnographic accounts of Morocco have described male homosexual activity as both tolerated and common (Westermarck 1926). However, as Moroccan sociologist Taher Benjelloun notes, while homosexuality is a "current practice" in Morocco, it is typically concealed and is associated with shame (1977, 73). For Zawiya at least, male homoeroticism (sexual arousal or release in company of other males) must be clearly distinguished from homosexuality in the sense of an ongoing preference for males as sexual partners. Homoeroticism is tolerated and fairly common in late childhood and early adolescence, while homosexuality is typically strongly censured and quite rare in Zawiya. The homoerotic contact that seems to occur fairly commonly among teenage males is usually casual, sporadic, and of short duration. Local adults tend to regard such activity as childish play, and the boys involved do not consider themselves homosexual. Both juveniles and adults expect that such homoerotic activity will give way as opportunity permits to heterosexual intercourse, and if it does not do so individual shame and community censure are likely.

Before puberty boys sometimes play at mutual masturbation, particularly after swimming naked in the river. Such masturbatory play is likely to be the first "sexual" activity of the boy who participates. The boys involved will typically be prepubescent or near the beginning of physical puberty (roughly nine to fourteen in age). Younger boys may also watch older ones masturbating. Estimates about the percentage of boys who experience some form of homoerotic activity before or during early adolescence varied widely, but it seems reasonable to assume that more than half of local boys have had at least some experience of group masturbation or exhibition. This contact is earlier in time, more common, and less negatively viewed than homoerotic contact involving interfemoral, or occasionally anal, intercourse. Colloquial Arabic distinguishes homosexual activity on the basis of activity/passivity: *zamel* (lit. "companion") describes the passive, and *Hawwa'i* the active partner.[8] The passive role is clearly associated with more shame than the active, and Benjelloun asserts that the active homosexual role may be seen both as a demonstration of virility in a male who is also heterosexually active and as an acceptable substitute when heterosexual activity is impossible (1977, 74). Indeed, Benjelloun suggests, in a manner reminiscent of the personality theorist Sullivan (1953, 256–258), that sexual contact with other boys in early adolescence may be a normal consequence of the separation of the sexes (Benjelloun 1977, 74–75). In any case, the shame associated with reputed homosexuality in Zawiya is focused particularly on the alleged passive participant. Boys will poke fun at others by writing on walls that so-and-so is a zamel and so-and-so his Hawwa'i, and the supposed date of their activity; and word zamel is the most frequent graffito in Moroccan public toilets. Such contact is usually confined to genital activity, without kissing or other expressions of affection.[9] We suggest, though this topic clearly needs further investigation, that whereas early homoerotic experiences have often been emotionally problematic for U.S. adolescents (Group for the Advancement of Psychiatry 1966), they are less likely to be so for their Moroccan agemates. In Zawiya, passing homoerotic encounters are viewed as a stage, not a pathology.

Female Homoeroticism

All male informants agreed that female homosexuality, as an ongoing sexual preference for females, was viewed much more negatively than male homosexuality, and that it was in fact rare. Several informants argued that female homosexuality did not occur at all in Morocco, although they had heard it was common in Europe.

Females also said that female homosexuality was rare, although one local case was cited in which a young woman was said to love another girl and could not be discouraged by the protests of the latter's parents. However, the first young woman was ultimately married, reportedly against her wishes. No cases of adult women living as homosexuals were cited, and no homoerotic contacts between adolescent girls in Zawiya were mentioned.

We can only speculate on the differences in male and female behavior in this area. Perhaps the greater reluctance of females to discuss sex led to their reporting less activity—yet they did describe other sexual activity. Perhaps female sexual desires were less strong than those of males and thus not acted on. Or perhaps females' contact with siblings, friends, and the children they care for (carrying, sitting close, holding hands) largely satisfied their needs for physical intimacy.

Autoeroticism

Like American teenagers (see Coles and Stokes 1985), Zawiya youth are generally reluctant to discuss masturbation. This is partly the result of Muslim child rearing. While the Qur'an does not discuss masturbation explicitly, there is a general sense among Muslims that sexual experience without a partner is shameful. There is little training of bodily modesty for boys during early childhood: male toddlers often run about wearing only a short shift, small boys may urinate in public, and pubescent males sometimes swim nude in the local river. With the onset of seminal emissions, however, a new ambivalence is felt because of the association of emission with impurity and because of the prevalent view that masturbation is an accession to dangerous temptation. We emphasize that masturbation is discussed only very covertly and with great shame. This was also true of the North African Muslim workers in France described by Benjelloun, for whom the idea of masturbation seemed frequently to be connected to impotence. Benjelloun also suggests that the shame older Moroccan males feel about masturbation may be because they understand it as a "regression to the stage of adolescence, as a return to an earlier stage of sexual misery" (Benjelloun 1977, 86).

Only one young woman would comment explicitly on female masturbation (although the fact that this girl was not shy in general and did describe male masturbation lends credibility to her view). When asked if females masturbate, she responded simply, "How could they do that?" There are some locally known jokes alluding to female masturbation, however, and we infer that it does occur.

Other Outlets

As in other farming cultures that employ animal husbandry, Morocco probably has a moderate prevalence of sexual contact between animals and adolescent males.[10] Male informants found it easier to discuss animal contact than to discuss masturbation (although this may have been because subjects believe masturbation practices described are more likely to be attributed to them). It is clear that animal contact was regarded as a shameful activity, that it was considered rare among older adolescents and adults, and that it was emotionally equated with masturbation. Sometimes small groups of boys participate. Among older adolescents and adults the activity is carefully kept private. The female donkey (*Hmara*) was mentioned as the most common animal.[11]

Not only is sex with animals viewed with distate by most adults, but several local cases of physical deformity or apparent insanity are attributed to the male sufferer's supposed prior sexual activity with animals. Neither males nor females described female sexual contact with animals. Sabbah (1984) discusses male fantasies of female-animal copulation as a feature of medieval Arabic sexual books which are still available in Morocco, but no informant of either sex mentioned such fantasies to us.

Heterosexual Relationships

Gender Differences in Data Collection

Overall, we were struck by the difference in tone of the conversations we had with male and with female teenagers in Zawiya about sexuality. The males, if they were willing talk explicitly about their own experience, talked about sexual behavior, while females, even when they were obviously trying to be completely open with Susan, avoided describing behavior and concentrated on trying to portray the feelings involved in relationships.[12] Although this means that the information on girls' sexual activity is necessarily secondhand, the fact that several girls gave similar accounts, and that these fit with what we were able to observe, makes us feel that we are presenting an accurate picture of the situation.

Love and Courtship

The themes of change over time and ambivalence are both present and interrelated to how girls feel about contact with boys. One area in which this is clear is the topic of romantic "love." In the last fifteen years, more girls have become literate and more have had access to television, both of which are channels for the presentation of a kind of romantic love to which most traditional females have had little exposure. Although the concepts of platonic love and the chivalrous male come from early Arab poetry, it was mainly educated males who were exposed to that tradition; little filtered into local popular culture. Popular reading material for girls with a basic level of literacy is the *photoroman*, a magazine with a layout like a comic book, except that photographs are used instead of cartoons. The plot is almost inevitably boy meets girl, mutual longing develops, their relationship encounters an obstacle, the obstacle is overcome, and the couple live happily ever after. Many of these publications originate in Italy, with the captions changed to either French or Arabic. Girls see the two sexes involved in earnest conversation about their problems, dancing, embracing, and kissing—all things they do not see in Zawiya, but about which they fantasize. The romantic interactions of married couples in Zawiya are seldom observed, and the unmarried may have more opportunity and some increased pressure to interact, but no overt models. These magazines are one source of information for girls. Movies present similar themes, but most of the girls we knew had never attended: the theaters are full of rowdy males and it is not appropriate for respectable girls to be seen in them.

Another source of information on romantic love is television, especially the serial films made in Egypt. In the last five years or so there has been an increased amount of Egyptian programming on Moroccan television, which the majority of girls we knew watched daily. In the past most television films were French, but now half or more are from Egypt. Egyptian Arabic is much better understood than French by most girls. While French films were divided between romance and cops-and-robbers, the majority of those from Egypt are romantic. These present less direct sexual interaction than the *photoromans*, but more sentimental musing on relationships that are usually thwarted. There is no "explicit sex" in Western terms, but the characters dress in Western clothing which is sometimes sexually suggestive by Zawiya standards, and the "traditional" Egyptian belly dances which are often included are seen as sexual.

Males are also exposed to the ideal of romantic love. Many adolescent males over fifteen attend one of the three cinemas in Kabar once a week, and there they see a variety of films including Western action and romantic types, Indian, and Far Eastern kung-fu. Although not justifying an "X" rating, some of the European films were soft-core pornography, providing visual information not available elsewhere in the culture. The implication of these films is that unabashed consumerism and unrestrained lust are the desirable hallmarks of Western culture. Young men also listen intently to a variety of music, including light classical and popular Middle Eastern, European and American popular, and reggae. They are fascinated by the varied romantic images presented. Several young men asked Douglas to explain the English lyrics of a Bob Marley or a Dolly Parton song.

Thus both sexes are exposed to materials (from the West and the East) that present them with a picture of male-female relationships quite different from the traditional one in which the spouse is chosen by the parents and couple's goal is to raise a family, not primarily to have a sexually satisfying or emotionally fulfilling relationship. Of course such traditional couples hope to get along well, and many develop a close and caring relationship over the years, but this was not their primary goal in marriage and there was no attempt to choose a partner with this in mind. Now, however, girls think a great deal about how they will relate to their future husband, how much of a role they will have in choosing him—and if, when, and how they (rather than their parents) should begin looking for a likely male.

The following edited excerpt from an interview with Farida, a girl of fourteen who had a primary school education, illustrates a young woman's interest in and feelings about beginning to interact with the opposite sex. While this is a matter of concern for all girls, only Farida discussed it overtly.

■ s: *What's important to you these days? . . . I want to know what you have on your mind, what preoccupies you most.*
F: *What interests us*[13] *is to see how girls meet boys, so that we learn too. We do want to start getting together with boys. However, if we do now, we won't know what to do. . . . We're still learning step by step.*
s: *So what do you want to learn?*
F: *I want to learn to hold a discussion, how to become shrewd [mTuwwra].*

s: *Who is going to teach you? How do you expect to learn? Do you want to date and learn gradually, or does your friend show you, or other girls who are knowledgeable, or what?*

F: *No. She [my friend] watches girls from her own family and from my family and we teach each other. I learn from relatives in cities. . . . I learned from my sister when she was still a girl [i.e., before she married.] She was shrewd. . . . She on the other hand learned from her [older] sister and her sister's friends. To learn well we teach each other.*

s: *Did you discuss things with your sister before she got married, or did you ask questions?*

F: *No. I was just watching. . . . If I had asked her, it wouldn't have been appropriate. I would have looked bad. . . . She wouldn't like me. She would say, "You are starting to learn at this age?" I have to be older so that becoming shrewd will help me accept what a boy would tell me. At the same time, one's parents won't fear for her. For example, we're too young and our parents worry about us. . . .*

s: *Your girlfriend teaches you. Are you going to talk to boys to learn also?*

F: *Little by little. You start first with young ones. . . . If you are young you select [boys] your age so that you get trained. Once you learn from young boys, then you move to older ones.*

Although most young women did not begin to meet with boys until at least the age of fifteen or sixteen, this fourteen-year-old indicates that she gave considerable attention to forming relationships before then. Her statement that she could not openly ask her sister about dealing with boys indicates that the norms against interaction are still strong, even if belied by behavior. It also shows her "managing" how she presents herself to a family member, her sister, while she is more direct and self-disclosing with her friend; the conflict of old and new values about heterosexual interaction leads to different self-presentations in different contexts.

Both sexes are ambivalent about heterosexual interaction. Girls want to make contact with boys but know most people will disapprove. Girls fear that boys are apt to entice them into sexual activity and then leave them. They phrase this as a fear that boys will "lead you on" (*itfella 'alik*).[14] Most girls over sixteen can give specific examples of this occurring locally. Girls also fear physical punishment or possibly rape as a consequence of their heterosexual activity, if discovered. Several older adolescents said that a couple found in an isolated setting by a group of young men might be physically or sexually abused. One instance reputedly occurred at the time of the fall festival (*moussem*) of the local saint in 1982, when we heard the girl was raped and the boy beaten. Neither dared to press charges because their sexual activity placed them in violation of the law. Whatever their frequency, such widely (if covertly) discussed instances serve to discourage girls who contemplate clandestine meetings with boys.

Boys are also ambivalent about heterosexual relations. While there is little social stigma for them (indeed, they may have increased status with male friends) in appearing in public with a young woman, they fear that a girl who would go out with them would do so, or has already done so, with others, and thus is not "pure" enough for marriage.

For girls then, interacting with boys means they must defy tradition and hide their activities, and while they have romantic aspirations they simultaneously expect males to lie to seduce them. Boys find they feel romantic about and suspicious of a young woman at the same time. These are not the bases for a trusting, mutually nurturing relationship, and indeed what we could discern about most adolescent couples led us to feel that the major component of these relationships was sex.[15]

Heterosexual Behavior

In Zawiya there is no such thing as socially acceptable dating, so adolescents must arrange other ways to get together.[16] The first contact of a girl with a boy is usually outdoors, while she is running an errand, walking to school in Kabar, or getting water at the well. Groups of older adolescent boys often form to talk and watch the "action" in front of stores, on corners, or near one of the water taps. They make comments on, or to, passing girls who are old enough to be interesting. They may kid younger girls (around fourteen) who are pretty and show some sexual development, but they expend their more serious efforts on girls sixteen and over, who are more apt to keep a rendezvous with them. At first a girl will ignore all comments, lest she appear to be "loose." If she responded right away, a boy would think she talked to everyone, which might make him drop her. She will continue to ignore boys in whom she has no interest, but she will smile briefly at one she likes when he calls out that she is pretty. Next she will begin to respond to his comments, often in a joking way; some girls are said to "laugh" or "kid around with" boys in these public settings, which is not seen as serious as long as things go no further. Another setting for casual flirtation is the walk to Kabar to visit the shops or the Thursday open-air market; those attending junior or senior high school typically walk along the train tracks. There are often one or more teenage girls walking along silently, with a male or males following twenty feet behind. The male will be trying to persuade a girl who has struck his fancy to deign to talk with him.[17] The walk to school along the tracks is an especially active setting for flirtation, as it is the near-exclusive domain of teenagers during the hours when sessions are beginning or ending. The high embankments along both sides of the track also afford some privacy from the eyes of passing motorists or a talkative younger sibling.

If the boy and girl are interested in getting together, the next stage is to arrange to meet away from the usual bystanders; this first tryst is usually right in Zawiya, but on a residential street after dark. Many of the local streetlights are out, and the need of couples for a place to meet unobserved is probably one of the causes. They arrange this meeting with a quick word at the edge of the group, or sometimes with a note carried by a younger sibling—one young enough to be easily intimidated by threats, so there is little risk of tales to parents. At this meeting they can talk more about their interest in each other, and as such meetings continue, they may progress to embraces and kissing if the setting is private enough. Contacts may also be arranged and pursued by letters delivered by friends.

Greater physical intimacy cannot occur on a streetcorner, so a couple desiring intimate relations may arrange to meet in another town (for those who are more mobile) where they can obtain the use of a friend's house or go to a hotel. They may also plan to meet in the fields to the west of town after dark. Girls will use an errand or a visit to a relative as an excuse, and often a girlfriend will cover for them by going along until they meet the boy. There may be an intermediate step for those who go to town; girls like to "promenade" and look at merchandise in shops, and boys often offer to buy them things like a dress, a scarf, or a watch. While this carries a hint of obligation, some girls feel one can accept gifts without having to "pay" for them later. If the couple meets in a town, the girl is likely to try to delay the sexual aspect of the relationship and continue the "courting" for awhile, so that both the boy will not think she is "easy" and and she can remain a virgin. It is more difficult to pursue other activities in the fields, where less sophisticated girls are apt to go, so for them there will be a shorter resistance to sexual activity.

In general, the physically mature and attractive girls of Zawiya are approached regularly in a sexually suggestive manner by males of adolescent age and beyond. To be known to have walked in the fields beyond view of the houses, or to have been seen in conversation with a boy in Kabar, or to have visited his house when his parents were not there is taken as evidence of loss of sexual purity. The resulting tensions are in some respects reminiscent of the situation in the United States before the last several decades, in which the girl suspected of sexual activity was stigmatized while the boy was excused or envied. Many attractive girls were said to have had to leave the community after becoming known as sexually active, and in most cases the community assumes these young women will become prostitutes in other towns or cities. Informants mentioned disappointments in love or premarital pregnancy as reasons for suicide by both sexes. The only known recent case of suicide involved a young man driven to despair over a fatal illness that would take him from the girl he loved.

From the male point of view this situation, while not directly punishing of sexual activity as in the case of the female, is hardly comfortable. The lack of opportunity for a prolonged, romantic relationship with a girl is a direct contradiction of the goals fostered by the music, magazines, and films most popular with adolescent males. Some of the older males we knew mourned the loss of relationships with girls they claimed to have loved but could not consider marrying because of the dishonor brought on the girl—by the male's own seduction of her. The male simply assumes that since the girl gave in to him she will (and perhaps has) to others. Such views are certainly not unknown in our own society, but in Morocco they stem in part from both Islamic tradition and popular belief in the sexual desire and deviousness of women.

As noted above, there is no real Zawiya equivalent to the U.S. notion of a dating couple. Rather the term *friend* takes on on sexual connotations when applied to an unmarried person of the other sex. Precisely what the sexual activity involves varies. Among "dating" couples some sexual intimacy is apparently frequent, but a variety of attempts are made to forestall pregnancy by avoiding full vaginal intromission of the penis. There are girls who have full intercourse; although none admitted it, we know the reports were not idle gossip because of several instances of abortion among unmarried Zawiya girls. A boy who has full intercourse with a girl is said to "break her" (*ikhesserha*), since her hymen is no longer intact. Girls try to prevent this, and pregnancy, by other methods. One is mutual caressing until the boy ejaculates, and another is interfemoral intercourse without intromission. The latter may occur with the couple partially clothed and is called in local slang *iy'ishu* or "they live [like man and wife]," but the girl retains her virginity. Sometimes the girl will leave her underpants in place; sometimes the boy will caress himself in the girl's labia without insertion (a practice referred to by males as "painting"), or will be careful to penetrate only a little and try to withdraw before ejaculation. Another possibility is anal intercourse, which is apparently less negatively viewed than in the United States.[18] On this topic we encountered some disagreement between the sexes. Some males indicated anal intercourse was fairly common in unmarried couples, and others said it was rare; some females said it occurred rarely, while others felt it was unnatural and never occurred. Some male informants argued that girls enjoyed this type of contact more than vaginal intercourse, but the practice was also usually mentioned as a way of avoiding pregnancy. Frequent anal intercourse is thought to enlarge the buttocks, and boys speculate about the activities of girls so endowed. If a man attempts anal intercourse with his wife it is one of the few situations in which she can initiate a divorce, suggesting a strong cultural aversion; this may mean that it seldom occurs, or that if it does, it is another source of ambivalence (see Westermarck 1926). Condoms and birth control pills are also available, but seem to be used by only a minority of sexually active unmarried couples, perhaps because their purchase is likely to lead to gossip.

The atmosphere surrounding premarital sexual experience in Zawiya today can be seen in the related vocabulary. Several girls mentioned that a girl who wants to meet and talk with boys can do so and still preserve her honor, but must "watch herself" (*Hdi rasha*). She must be very careful of each move she makes, both to keep the relationship covert and to keep it under control. A word used by both sexes to describe how boys make contact with girls is *Siyyed*, which can be used to mean fish or hunt game in another context. When we questioned informants, they said that *Siyyed*, applied to girls, was much like fishing because one entices the girl as one does a fish. Another word we heard used repeatedly this trip, but did not recall from a decade previously, is *wa'iya* to refer to a girl. It is derived from "awareness," but the way it is used implies "sophisticated" or "knows her way around." A girl who is "sophisticated" is contrasted to one who is ignorant or clumsy in dealing with males. The latter girl may be taken advantage of by a smooth talker, and perhaps be convinced to go out into the fields and have sex; a sophisticated girl would string him along awhile, get some benefits for herself, and have enough sense to arrange a liaison in another town or someone's house, where she would likely not get caught. This sounds like *wa'iya* carries the connotation that a girl is "fast," but not so. The word can refer to a girl with a good reputation who "knows her way around" in the sense that she travels to cities, is well educated, or is skilled in dealing with people; there is no automatic sexual connotation. On the other hand, a girl who does something to compromise her reputation, such as having relations with many men or getting pregnant, is said to have "gone out against her future" (*kherjet 'ala mustaqbel dyalha*), to have sacrificed her future for present pleasure. It may also be said that she "knocked down her reputation" (*taHet sum'a dyalha*).

An overview of the terms related to sexual behavior suggests an attitude toward premarital sex similar to that in the United States in the 1950s, hey-day of the "double standard." Girls are enticed, "fished for," by males; but they must guard their reputations and behavior, and be "smart," or they will be broken or ruined. Many girls seem very interested in heterosexual rela-tionships, but their activity is constrained by both lack of role models (a girl cannot ask her big sister what to do on a first date and whether to let the boy kiss her; the big sister would call the girl a slut and tell their parents!) and fear of social censure which may lead to permanent spinsterhood.

Consequences of Heterosexual Relationships

Premarital flirtation is thus an area of conflict for many young people and leads to a general ambivalence. Males were, as noted, less likely to talk to us in detail about the contradiction between lust and love. For the more articulate, however, there is some awareness that they too are caught in a bind where each new conquest may be doomed because sexual success sours romance. Shy and more traditional girls still avoid conflict by staying close to home and following community norms. For girls, the main opportu-nity to discuss the opposite sex is with their girlfriends, and some feel even that is unacceptable. Several teenage girls said they discussed other girls or their plans with friends, but not "that bad stuff," suggesting they would drop a girl as a friend if she wanted to talk about sexual matters. It was usually girls under fifteen who said this, perhaps reflecting their mothers' instruc-tion; for older girls, romantic involvement is often an important topic of con-versation. Older, more adventuresome girls are torn between remaining "good girls," maintaining good reputations in the hope a suitable marriage with an attractive male will be arranged, and experimenting by going out with some of the boys who flirt with them. This is the more risky course: one may meet a desirable young man, fall in love, and be married even after hav-ing a sexual relationship with him; or one may be dropped as "loose" after the male tires of the relationship. Further, if word of these activities gets around the community, it may well compromise the girl's future chances of marriage. The situation is made even more difficult by the fact that several neighborhood girls between twenty and thirty were still unmarried (for rea-sons we will discuss below). The temptation was even stronger for them, since they saw themselves approaching spinsterhood even though they were "good," and probably feared they might never have any fun if they did not have it now, while they were still young and attractive. The conflict, and resultant ambivalence, is poignantly clear in the following edited excerpt from an interview with a young woman in her twenties who has a primary school education. Amina was asked to describe something that had happened to her that was not right or was unfair.

> It concerns this matter of marriage. A boy will tell you "I trust you, I care for you. . . . If I don't see you for just half a day I go crazy; it seems to me I haven't seen you for a year." And at that time, the boy does have feelings. He cares for you. Truly. Powerfully. But he doesn't have any money [to marry], and you just keep sacrificing yourself for him, talking to him, laughing with him. And you lose your value—and your family's. Okay, people see you together, but you say, "They don't matter to me. Because even if I'm standing with him, he'll marry me, God willing."
>
> And finally, he doesn't marry you—how do you feel? It feels like a calamity, like a "psychological complex." You feel angry at home, and you're always upset, because you don't trust anyone, even your parents. You sacrificed yourself for that boy, talking to him even in public, . . . and in the end he marries someone else, when he has a good job and he's well off. How do you think you would feel? . . . You will remember your times together and what you went through in the past. You see how things happen. . . . That a boy gives you his word of honor and later doesn't keep it is not right. That is what makes a mature and intelligent girl distrust a boy. She doesn't trust boys—never.

The male view of the ambivalence felt toward sexual and emotional intimacy by Zawiya-reared youth is suggested by the following interview excerpt. This young man was in his midtwenties at the time of the interview, had completed some college education, and was responding to a question about what "love" meant to him. He did so in a way that combined romantic ideals with the expectation of some problems—over which he expected to triumph. He emphasizes his own dominant role in the relationship, the interference of gossips, and the preoccupation of the community with the girl's reputation.

> To love a girl is to give her, or to advise her, to help her, to take care of her, to show her the wrong things and the right ones. Not let her do the worst things but only the best and to be perfect. To tell her to ignore what people say to her because it's all lies and meant only to destroy her. . . . If that girl for instance is a good person, and she is working when people learn that I am going to marry her, they'll start gossiping about her. They will start telling me how bad she is, that she is not serious, that she talks to many boys [goes out with them], and that I should reconsider and try to find another girl. . . . But the people don't really know what kind of relationship I have with her. I take what they say as

lies because they may be just taking revenge for whatever misunderstanding they may have had with her, or something of that nature. But I do what I like.

In another conversation, he presented a less idealistic view of relations between the sexes, reflecting the view that females are often deceitful in satisfying their lust.[19] When asked how a poor man could get expensive medicine for his dying wife (the "Heinz" dilemma used by Kohlberg 1984), he said it would be very hard for the man to get money, but much easier for a woman, who could use "sex, for instance": "I know so many women who do that, and not even to buy medicine for their husbands, but only to buy a fancy dress to wear for a party or to buy a *jellaba* [long outer robe] or to buy new shoes or what have you."

Another consequence of sexual behavior is the "mistakes"—illegitimate pregnancies. The way these are handled influences sexual behavior. If correcting mistakes is fairly easy, there is less constraint on sexual activity. In Zawiya, there were several alternatives for girls who got pregnant before they were married. Although illegal, abortions are available from some medical doctors, and also from midwives or other women who know folk medicine. Medical abortions are expensive by local standards (around $200), but if the male has an income, he may help out; if he will not, the girl may claim paternity and try to force him to marry her. Abortions can also be self-induced. Another alternative is for the girl to have the child elsewhere, leaving town on the pretext of visiting a relative (which is usually plausible) before the pregnancy is obvious. She may have the baby and give it to a childless couple, who are often contacted through obstetrical nurses. A girl may arrange with someone in her hometown to "adopt" the baby, asking them to tell people it was gotten "at the hospital"; in this way she can still see the child. Or she may keep the child and return home with it after a year or two, saying she was married and divorced in the meantime; divorce is common enough to make this plausible. Thus while cultural norms find pregnancy outside marriage a very serious offense, in current practice there are several ways to deal with it. Girls do not want to get pregnant, but it is not so threatening as to forestall any sexual activity.

These findings for our Moroccan community contrast with those for other settings in the Harvard Adolescence Project. Among Eskimo teenagers, Condon (1987, 150–151) found remarkably little sanction attached to the birth of children out of wedlock, and such children may be raised by the unwed mother, her parents, or other members of the community. In the rural Romanian town studied by Ratner (forthcoming), on the other hand, teenage dating is accepted and encouraged by school dances and other mixed social gatherings, yet an illegitimate child is a great source of shame and community censure for the girl and her family.

MATE SELECTION AND MARRIAGE TODAY

While many aspects of traditional mate selection and marriage have continued into the present, we see changes in some areas. Being together in high school, as well as exposure to ideas of romantic love, make some couples more interested in and able to pursue heterosexual relationships, which in turn leads to choosing their own spouses. The availability of jobs makes it possible to live apart from the groom's parents and to be less controlled by them (especially his mother) after marriage: parents may thus have less motivation to select the bride themselves. The possibility of contact between the sexes has changed the defloration ceremony somewhat. A large change is the number of females between twenty and thirty who are not yet married; in the past only 1 or 2 percent of girls over twenty-five were unmarried. We examine these changes below.

Adolescent Hopes and Expectations

There were only two married adolescents in our neighborhood,[20] so we describe young people's stated desires, their attitudes, rather than their actual behavior with regard to marriage. Nearly all said they wanted to marry, although some girls were hesitant to say so. There is an exaggerated shyness around such topics early in adolescence, for some girls. Susan also learned not to ask this question in front of fathers: the sexual shyness between generations makes even such an apparently innocuous question risqué. Girls were a little shy on this topic with their mothers, but much less so.

Young peoples' descriptions of the ideal spouse emphasized characteristics that could be perceived by one's parents in arranging a marriage: a woman should be beautiful "in body and mind," or a man should have a good job. Other responses noted the need for a good relationship, a quality parents could not judge unless the young people knew each other prior to marriage. Sixteen percent of males and 33 percent of females defined the ideal spouse in terms that involved the relationship, such as, "I have to like her—to agree with her," and "He should be good; he should have a good personality, and we should respect each other and be honest with each other, not insulting each other." Responses about the ideal spouse suggest that at least some young people hope to have a voice in selecting their own spouse, that they worry about marital harmony, and that they are concerned about the character or personality of a prospective marriage partner. About twice as many females as males stressed the importance of a good relationship.

In response to our direct question, "Who should choose the spouse?" most Zawiya youth (64 percent of females and 55 percent of males) said their parents should choose.[21] A sizable minority of adolescents, however, want an active part in the decision.[22]

Older youth were more eager to choose their own spouse, as were youth with a higher school status. Both these findings may be due to the fact that for older youth, marriage becomes more of a real issue and less an abstract question, and by this time they may have met people of the opposite sex they would like to marry. The results are also consistent with our view that schooling is an important factor in changing attitudes.

In response by age, sex, or educational level, there were no significant differences in preference of residence after marriage. About half the young people said they wanted to live with the groom's parents; somewhat over a third said they wanted to live as a couple. More girls than boys preferred not to live with the groom's parents. Girls as young as eleven said they preferred their own household because otherwise they would probably fight with relatives, especially their mother-in-law.

Marriage Arrangements

Nearly all Zawiya young people plan to marry and have children. The majority of those we asked said they hoped to have two children, a boy and a girl; the highest number of children desired was four. This was noteworthy because these young people came from families with an average of 5.8 surviving children. This stated preference is probably due partly to the media: many television dramas as well as the literature and posters of the family planning movement suggest that the ideal couple is over twenty and has only two children. However, the average Moroccan woman bears 6.9 children (Royaume du Maroc 1984).

In actual practice, most marriages are still arranged by parents, with the girl's family waiting for the boy's to approach them. Even if a couple should meet independently, they still ask the parents to arrange things; a woman must still legally be "given away" by a male relative. Nearly half of their older siblings chose their own spouse while only a quarter of adolescents surveyed said they wished to do so.[23]

Some examples of recent marriage arrangements provide a clearer picture of the situation in Zawiya today. During our residence a girl of about fourteen was married off by her parents. It was quite a topic of conversation, with most people feeling she was too young, even though she would not live with the groom for another year. A young woman of sixteen had finished her primary education and was felt by some to be ready for marriage, but her mother turned down two offers from relatives with health problems without telling the girl. In another case, a girl of seventeen was to be married to a young man of twenty-nine. Both lived in our neighborhood: they were not related but both families were quite well-off, and the mothers were friends. The young man had a job and thus met the prime requirement for being ready to marry. The girl had never been to school, so there was no concern about finishing her education, and she had had time to learn all the necessary housekeeping skills. With the parents' and the couple's agreement, the contract was signed and the girl began to work on her trousseau. However, a problem soon arose. The groom's two older married sisters came to town, and people said they "gave her the once-over." Apparently there was some problem, because the couple were divorced before the marriage was consummated. This was doubly serious because the bride's brother (who worked abroad) was to marry the groom's sister (who was in high school); that marriage was also canceled. The cause of the breakup was never clear.

These examples show the importance of the family in mate selection, but as young people have more contact with each other, the couple is increasingly involved in this process. The following excerpts from an interview with a mother of Zawiya adolescents, one of the more educated young matrons, illustrates other ways young women can influence the choice of a future spouse.

■ s: *I would like to ask you why Latifa [a neighbor] is not married.*
n: *You know why: it is because she does not talk. She is too shy—she must be talkative, participate in this and that. She must have fun, talk to boys. . . .*
s: *I find it strange that a girl who is conscientious, religious [is not married]—*
n: *Everything good. She is a very decent girl—*
s: *And there are other girls who people criticize, "That girl dated, she went out with this and that, she was a whore," and they do get married. . . . What should a girl do if she wants to get married? . . .*
n: *What does she need to do to marry him by hook or by crook?*
s: *Yes.*

N: *She starts talking to him, dating him until a problem arises, either she gets pregnant or whatever, and she does marry him, by force. She warns him either to marry her or to face justice [the government can force marriages in some cases]. And he marries her; that is a forced marriage.*

S: *You mean she chooses of her own free will to become pregnant in order to get married?* . . .

N: *It happens a lot—*

S: *And do [girls] succeed with this scheme?*

N: *For some it works; for others it doesn't.*

S: *You gave me the example of [your friend]. For her it didn't work.*

N: *It didn't work for her. Although they got married and had a child, they ended up with a divorce.*

S: *Are there some for whom the scheme works? Do you know any of those for whom it worked?*

N: *A lot of them, there are lots of them.*

S: *What would you estimate? Do many succeed, do many fail, or is it fifty-fifty, or what?*

N: *I would say it does not work for the majority. Afterward their marriage becomes sour. They split.*

The ceremonial part of the marriage, with separate parties for males and females, still follows tradition. Women often play for each other, and men may hire nonlocal musicians and dancing girls. One change is the addition of a band of local young men who may play for the dancers at either male or female parties.

Recently, some couples have had a party at the time the marriage contract is signed; it is smaller than the traditional delayed party, and usually just relatives and a few close friends are invited. We attended such a party in Kabar, and although the couple was educated and both had jobs, the sexes still sat in separate rooms. After the party the couple moves in together and often forgoes the larger celebration. They explain that this saves them thousands of dollars, which they prefer to spend on furniture. This kind of party also eliminates the defloration of the bride while wedding guests wait for the results, which may be desired by a couple who are already acquainted sexually.

Virginity

Zawiya today, like most of Morocco, continues to prescribe premarital sexual abstinence for women. In Moroccan Arabic the term "girl" (*bint*) implies virginity, while to refer to a female as a "woman" (*mra*) implies that she has lost her virginity. The public display of sheets stained with the hymeneal blood at the conclusion of wedding celebrations continues, despite the not infrequent premarital sexual activity of girls.[24]

One sophisticated young adult male informant told of a variety of attitudes and behaviors concerning the handling of the display of the bridal sheets. Sometimes the male himself has taken his fiancée's virginity, loves her, and wants to marry without embarrassment, so he either cuts himself on the wedding night to produce blood or collaborates with the girl in some way. Alternatively the couple may forgo a formal wedding and simply complete the legal-papers phase of the marriage before beginning to cohabit. In other cases the bride's brothers know ahead of time that their sister is not a virgin, and, suspecting the groom may not know, they stay close to the bridal chamber to calm or threaten the groom so no scandal occurs. Finally, in some cases neither the brother(s) nor groom knows the bride is not a virgin and all hell breaks loose, with groom and/or brother(s) berating, beating, or conceivably killing the bride. Neither we nor this informant could cite any cases of such violence locally. The informant mentioned several local examples where the bride's nonvirginity was well known before the ceremony and either "bloody" linens were produced or there was in any case no outcry.[25] He reported that doctors can now re-create apparent virginity, and claimed many girls experiment freely and then avail themselves of this procedure.[26] He said some couples claim to restrict themselves to kissing between the legal and the public ceremony, but he found this hard to believe.

Females also said that couples who expect trouble producing the hymeneal blood can still have a traditional wedding—with proper preparation. A relative or midwife can make a small cut inside the bride's vagina that will tear and bleed during intercourse. We also learned of a doctor who agreed to draw a blood sample to be used later on the bridal sheets. Several people reported that a surrogate for hymeneal blood is available through drugstores. One local bride who used this method was the object of covert ridicule: she was around thirty and known to have had at least two abortions. When the groom brought out a pair of bloodstained underwear, the women guests laughed behind their hands at the bride's "drugstore panties."

The various subterfuges available to the former virgin demonstrate that in spite of changing behavior, the ideal of virginity is still important. Some girls have examinations by medical doctors when they become engaged, either to assure the fiancé that they are virgins or to provide evidence that any future lack of virginity is due to the groom, not another man.

The display of blood-stained sheets as proof of the male's potency is also important. There have been local cases of failure to break the hymen due to the groom's loss of erection, and frequent recourse to magical protection of the groom before and during the ceremony testifies to this concern. During the summer wedding season in Zawiya, a local magician was promoting his services based on such fears; he announced that he would place a *tqaf* (spell to limit sexual productivity—here, to cause impotence) on any bridegroom who did not pay him a large "fee" (roughly $30) for a protective amulet.

The experience of the wedding night may be quite tense for both bride and groom. He has to be able to penetrate and break the hymen, and she must cooperate to produce the hymeneal blood, being sexually initiated when she is perhaps frightened. Both bride and groom are likely to be exhausted from days of preparation and entertaining, and both can hear the crowd just outside the door, waiting for results.

We had a local young woman ask two Zawiya brides about their experiences. The first bride, in her late teens, was marrying a young man in his twenties who worked in construction. When Susan and her assistant spoke to her at her wedding party (about three hours before the defloration), she was enjoying being the center of attention of the women and girls. She appeared a bit shy, but not fearful, when asked if she were afraid of the events to come. The next morning she said her first experience of intercourse had been fine and seemed quite relaxed. Later, our assistant said she had heard that the girl and her fiancé had been seen walking in the fields outside Zawiya, so perhaps her wedding night was not her first sexual experience. The second bride was a bit older, in her twenties, and more educated than the first. She had an office job, while the first did not work outside the home. Her family was economically better off than the first, and the wedding was more elaborate. Our assistant said the bride seemed fairly apprehensive on her wedding night. The next day, when she tried to interview the bride, the latter was so upset that she could not speak with her. She learned later that penetration had been difficult for the groom, that he had been quite forceful, and that the bride had been very fearful and upset.

Life after Marriage

The behavior of recently married couples has changed over time, and these changes suggest limited movement toward more egalitariian roles for the sexes. Instead of the wife walking deferentially behind the husband, many young couples now walk side by side; sometimes the husband will carry a baby in his arms instead of leaving it in the traditional sling on the wife's back. Young wives may work outside the household, even after they have children. Their contribution to the family budget is important, and childcare is readily available through relatives or hired help. A few husbands help with childcare and housework, but that is still uncommon; in general a working wife bears a double burden, especially when she lacks hired help. Overall, most marriages are quite traditional. New brides are expected to be secluded and to observe the husband's wishes.

A Marriage Problem

While in the past nearly all Zawiya girls were married by age twenty or twenty-two, in 1982 we found many young women between twenty and thirty still single.[27] This may be the result of a shortage of men, both because the war in the Sahara requires many soldiers and because many men work abroad, especially in France and Belgium. However, working men and soldiers commonly marry and leave their wives with parents or in their own home (when children are older), so these factors would not necessarily prevent marriage. Some young women suggested the reason was that young men wanted to avoid the responsibility of a wife and children, and thus delayed marriage; the accuracy of this is harder to assess. A final possibility lies in the economy. Inflation has hit Morocco as it has the rest of the world, causing commodity prices and bride-prices to rise, but jobs are difficult to find for young men, and the wages are often low. Thus young men may find their first job later and have to work longer to amass the bride-price. The fact that many couples prefer to forgo the large wedding celebration and to have a smaller engagement party instead, saving the money to furnish their home, suggests that money concerns are important. Such economizing would allow a lower bride-price to be set, and since the bride's parents are expected to spend a like amount for the bride's trousseau and the wedding party, both sides of the family would benefit. We believe economic difficulties are at the root of this problem.

While delayed marriage seems a reasonable solution to economic difficulties, it may cause a long-term problem. If the men of Zawiya married girls in their twenties once they had saved up enough money, things would be fine. However, in the past a girl of twenty was already a little "old"; even with higher education delaying marriage, twenty-five is usually the upper limit of female marriageability in Zawiya. By her midtwenties, a young woman will also have become an individual in her own right, no longer used to unquestioning obedience to others. Strong individual preferences are not a desirable characteristic for a traditional wife, so these young women are likely to be passed over as brides. This is also a problem for more educated people, as we saw when talking to a young man from Zawiya who had grown up in France and was studying for an advanced degree. He was with his "girlfriend" who was in high school, and he said he definitely favored marrying an educated girl. She could discuss ideas with him—the only problem was, sometimes she did not agree! For the more traditional girls who are unmarried in their twenties, it is possible that a whole cohort will be passed over for marriage if and when the economic situation adjusts itself. Since they were raised when girls were educated only at the primary level, they cannot turn to careers as an alternative to families. Instead, they are likely to spend their lives caring for their aging parents, a sad prospect for young women who want and need a family of their own to reach full adult status.

Sex, Love, and the Future

Today's sexual experimentation is not a revolutionary departure from the past, but there does appear to be a steady increase in both the opportunity for and the amount of heterosexual interaction.[28] With more girls attending secondary school and making the twice-a-day walk this entails, it appears that opportunities for sexual liaisons are readily available, while they were very difficult to arrange in the past. However, when we suggested this to a local girl, she said no, her mother had told her about meeting goatherds out in the forest when she went to get water or wood for the family.[29] Living in Zawiya today, however, it is both easier for girls to leave the house and less likely that a relative will see them talking to a boy, partly because of the town's size.

The standards for interaction with the opposite sex are definitely in flux, especially for females. Thus it is difficult for them to decide how to act—whether to "talk" to boys and how far to go after beginning a flirtation. Decisions about sexual activity are made more difficult because, while cultural norms were traditionally against interacting, there are many recent local examples of girls who have done so and later married happily. While these women were gossiped about at first, their current situations are comfortable, and certainly preferable to the life of a spinster. On the other hand, girls are aware that word of their "talking" with boys may get around and hamper their chances for a good (or any) marriage, and many wonder which path to take. This is seen in their ambivalence about males. Men are desired and romanticized, and they are necessary to the childbearing women value so highly, but they are also untrustworthy and will deceive a girl if she is not careful. For their part, men lust after the young beauties who are each year more visible on the streets of Zawiya and Kabar, and they try all the persuasive means at their disposal to seduce these girls. Yet most of them expect to marry virgins and to insist on fidelity from their wives. The implicit contradiction in these expectations is seldom discussed.

The topics of sexuality and mate selection are as complex, and potentially productive of conflict, in Zawiya as in an American community. The sharp double standard concerning heterosexual relationships for males and females and the prevalence of shame and potential dishonor as consequences of female sexual activity are reminiscent of much of our own literature on the adolescent period. Recent questionnaire, clinical, and time-sampling studies of U.S. teenagers have emphasized a similar tension between the demands of a newly developed body and the romantic hopes engendered by the adolescent culture (Coles and Stokes 1985; Csikszentmihalyi and Larson 1984). Nor are Moroccan and American societies alone in displaying a greater negative sanction of female than of male premarital sexual activity: a review of the anthropological literature on sexuality (Suggs and Marshall 1971) shows that a double standard is a very common societal response to the sexual maturation of males and females.

The most poignant dimension of adolescent sexuality in Zawiya is the tension between the emotional intimacy teenagers have increasingly learned to crave and the physical desire they can satisfy only at the cost of shame or potential dishonor, desire that coexists so tenuously with romance and that may indeed doom the relationship in which it has found expression. As Thompson has noted (for U.S. teenage girls), the issues of "sex, intimacy, and permanence are fused" (1984, 369). This fusion has been emphasized in Gilligan's reexamination of personality theory, which treats the maintenance of attachment rather than the establishment of autonomy as central (1982); it is a fusion increasingly at issue for Zawiya youth as they accommodate to a broader international culture of adolescence.

Popular music illustrates the widespread hope of Zawiya youth for future "love," in spite of their doubts and ambivalence, and suggests changing gender roles. The airwaves of Morocco are filled with songs of romantic passion—in Arabic, French, and English. Somewhere in this melange of images the young people of Zawiya, like those to the East and West, hope to find someone with whom they can live as adults, sharing passion and family life. A colloquial Arabic song that was newly popular in the fall of 1982, heard on tapes and sung by girls when they got together (Susan heard it from a fourteen-year-old) went as follows:

> Oh, him with the eyebrows that meet
> Oh, the one with the lovely mole
> He leads the girls on—the days gave him good fortune.
> Pour for me, so I can drink from that pool
> Next year the virgin will ask for the hand of the bachelor.[30]

■ 7
Stress and Deviance

Most theoretical writing about adolescence as a life stage treats it as coincident with increased conflict between youthful emotions and adult social norms (Freud [1905] 1953; Erikson 1968), and such conflict may lead to stress or deviance. Our treatment of adolescence in Zawiya has focused on the balance between autonomy and hierarchy implicit in the concept of 'aql. Much of the conflict Americans associate with the adolescent years has been attributed to children's attempts to demonstrate autonomy by refusing or contradicting parental advice. In Zawiya, autonomy was not such a source of conflict. People do not expect the degree of autonomy many Americans seem to feel is their due, if by autonomy we refer to independence of others' needs and expectations.[1] Moroccans are aware that they are part of a larger kin network; the individual's desires are seldom the first, and almost never the only, consideration. Rather, the mature adult is one who balances responsible social behavior with the maintenance of individual honor and the satisfaction of basic needs.

Limited expectation of autonomy is paired with great respect for age. One does not openly question one's elders, and there is less open conflict between parents and adolescents than one hears about in the United States. However, as young people have greater knowledge, and more choices of life courses than their parents, conflict between the generations may increase.[2] Zawiya is an interesting setting since so few parents and so many adolescents attended school. In addition, while the older generation works in agriculture, unskilled labor, or sales, with a few men in skilled jobs such as welder, driver, or mason, the young have many more options—at least theoretically. Most aspire to white-collar jobs such as teacher, lawyer, and doctor, although none of their parents works in those professions. Yet overt conflict between the generations was uncommon in Zawiya, and the traditionalism of their parents was not a major complaint of young people.

CONFLICT

We both asked teenagers about conflict with parents and looked for examples; sometimes we heard of conflicts from parents, and sometimes we witnessed them. Nearly half of the Zawiya youth questioned said they never disagreed with their mothers. In more detailed interviews, however, only one denied disagreeing with her mother.[3] The others all gave examples of conflict with either or both parents. Younger girls, ages eleven to sixteen, got in trouble if they refused to run an errand, fought with their siblings, did not study, or got bad grades. Their parents might strike them with a hand or a belt, or "insult" them. There is a term for "scold" (*khaSm*), but the word *'iyyer* (to insult, reproach) is stronger, suggesting an attack on a person's character. This term is also used in fights with non–household members. Girls seventeen and older had problems because of not doing chores correctly or coming home late. They were not struck, but rather reproached.

These types of conflict or disagreement are mild. We did not expect people to readily tell us serious offenses they had committed, but in fact serious offenses seem relatively rare. A few examples of those of which we learned give some idea of the range of more serious problems in this semirural part of Morocco.

One girl of eighteen had left home for a week and gone to a city with a neighbor girl; they told no one they were leaving and their families feared they had been kidnapped or enticed into prostitution. The families were desperate and asked all close family (they did not want outsiders to know for fear of compromising the girls' future marriage chances) if there were any clues to their whereabouts. They even went to the outdoor weekly market, where they would see country relatives who might have some news. They were about to go to the police and have the girls announced over the radio as missing, despite the consequences for the family reputation, when the two girls turned up. The one we knew best offered no explanation, and when her mother began to complain the girl told her to shut up or she would choke her. This case was unusual in that the mother was a single parent and in ill health; otherwise, the girl would not have escaped unpunished, as she did. The whole story was hushed up and people who asked where the girl had been were told she had been visiting country relatives.

In another example, a girl who was in her late teens had gone to the fields to meet a boyfriend. Their relationship was reportedly not sexual, but nonetheless, someone saw them and reported to her maternal aunt, with whom she lived. The aunt came rushing to the scene and, as our informant said, did not "protect" the girl. Instead of taking her home quietly and covering up, the aunt shouted the whole story in front of all the onlookers, and the girl was thoroughly shamed. Since that time she has avoided trouble and become respectable once again.

The conflicts boys have with their parents are both more varied and less subject to control than those of their sisters. Instances like staying out without notifying parents are the source of scoldings for younger boys, but such behavior is fairly common among older male adolescents and would usually be passed over with a plausible explanation from the youth on his return. Minor conflicts concern completion of homework, running errands, and arbitration of disputes with siblings. In all of these the Zawiya father is expected to insist on obedience and good behavior from his children. More serious offenses we heard about included drug and alcohol use, theft, and school disciplinary problems. While all of the girls' serious offenses were related to their propriety, this was not an important area of concern for boys.

One boy of sixteen was reported to be terrorizing his secondary school. He talked back to teachers, disrupted the classroom, and threatened to strike anyone who inhibited him. He had failed primary school, and his parents had paid for a year at a private school in Kabar so he could continue his education. However, he told the school administration he was an orphan, so they had no one to whom to send disciplinary notes. While he was not punished by his parents, most of his peers looked down on him and on his parents for failure to correct his behavior. Hence males too can influence the whole family's reputation.

In another family, the sons had reputations as thieves. One had even been to prison. A brother of fifteen was the current thief, mainly robbing nearby gardens and selling the produce. We heard that he gave his family the money to buy him clothing, for which they somewhat reluctantly admired him—it was better than gambling or buying wine. We also heard that his younger brother was learning the "trade." These boys were not disciplined, perhaps because their father worked abroad and their mother could not manage them. Neighbors disparaged their behavior, and in this, as in several other cases of delinquent sons, lack of paternal supervision was blamed.

Alcohol or drug abuse were not a large source of conflict with parents, not because the parents approved but because such behavior was both partially expected and difficult to control. Some mothers deplored the fact that their sons came home drunk and sick, but there was little they could do about it.

In general these young people were not in conflict with their parents, and most of them stayed out of trouble with legal and school authorities. There were minor skirmishes over daily routine, but neither group took them seriously. Most girls interviewed said their parents generally understood them. On the other hand the expectation of explicit verbal empathy for one's deep inner feelings did not exist. An indication of minor disagreement with parents appeared when the majority of girls said they wanted to be different as parents. The differences, however, were seldom related to the way the girls themselves were treated; some wanted fewer children, others to apply more discipline or teach better manners. Boys asked about similarity to their parents most often spoke of their parents' illiteracy and the lack of understanding of modern educational and economic pressures as sources of conflict. Some educated males said they were embarrassed by their parents' attitudes and could not hope to explain their aspirations to them. Generally, however, these Zawiya adolescents respected and got along well with their parents.

SOURCES OF STRESS FOR ADOLESCENTS

We found relatively little overt stress among the young people of Zawiya, despite rapid change in several aspects of local society, but there was evidence of stress for some youths. Secondary schooling, different expectations for males and females, and relationships with the opposite sex were all often stressful.

Heterosexual Relations

For girls both in and out of school, relations with the opposite sex are stressful (see chap. 6). As girls reach about fourteen and approach menarche, many become interested in boys, but have to find a way to meet them that will not be found out and ruin their reputation. A further stress was girls' belief that most boys, although they said they intended to marry a girl when they got involved, would "love 'em and leave 'em." The main stress for males is that they are interested in heterosexual relationships for several years, during which they have inadequate access to respectable females and must therefore seek satisfaction elsewhere.

Gender Ambivalence

Many adolescents appear to have mixed feelings about both their own gender and the opposite sex. While this was not a consuming passion and rarely came up spontaneously in conversations, it is an area of some stress for many adolescents, and probably more for girls than for boys. We saw indications of this ambivalence in the results of the draw-a-person test—with many young people drawing the opposite sex first, as well as in response to direct questions.

We asked Zawiya adolescents to "draw a person" (we used a term that was gender neutral) and then to turn over the paper and "draw the opposite," and we noted which sex was drawn first. This task, which has been employed for many purposes (S. Davis 1983b), was used as a type of self-portrait. If a person draws the opposite sex first, this may indicate that they feel ambivalent about their own sex and may prefer the gender role of the opposite sex.[4] Among the samples included in the Harvard Adolescence Project, Zawiya was rated as having much constraint on females' premarital freedom, and Zawiya girls made the largest proportaion of cross-sex first drawings (60 percent). Zawiya boys also made the largest proportion of cross-sex first drawings (28 percent) among the studied groups. This suggests a relatively high degree of ambivalence by both sexes about their gender roles in Morocco. In contrast, the Inuit females studied by Condon were rated as the least constrained of all the groups with regard to premarital sexuality, and they also had the lowest percentage of females drawing males first, 9 percent (Condon 1987, 134). Some adolescents were asked whether in general they felt it was better to be a boy or a girl in Morocco, and specifically whether they themselves had ever wished they were of the opposite sex.[5] All males and about half the females said it was better to be a male. In each of the groups (boys, girls who chose females, girls who chose males) there were adolescents both in and out of school, so age or school status is not clearly associated with one type of choice. There seems to be a general preference for the male role, supporting the suggestion of such a preference in the draw-a-person results.

Young people's responses to questions on gender role preference clarify the reasons for their predominantly male choices and sometimes also give an indication of ambivalent or negative feelings about the opposite sex. The following excerpts from an edited interview with Aisha, a young woman in secondary school, raise issues mentioned by many adolescents.

■ s: *In your opinion, what's better here in Morocco, to be a girl or to be a boy? . . .*

a: *I [would] prefer to be a boy.*

s: *Really?*

a: *Well, the girl is only at home. When it gets a bit dark, she cannot go out. They don't let her out. She shouldn't go to the movies. . . . She cannot do much. As for the boy, he is under no constraints. He can go out, he can go to the movies. Nobody in his house will criticize him. If he wants to get involved with a girl, they won't ask him why.*

s: *They don't hear about it? Or even if they do, they don't say anything?*

a: *They hear about it, but they don't say anything. He makes girlfriends, goes for a walk, goes to the movies, goes out at night, stays out until midnight or 1:00 A.M., then comes back home. He fears no one.*

s: *Did it ever happen to you that you said to yourself: "If only God had made me a boy, not a girl"?*

a: *Yes I do, I say it. But only when I am alone and all that. For example, when I am alone at night, I say, "Look, now I am alone. If I were a boy I would be outdoors. I wouldn't be alone. I would be outside with boys having fun. At the movies, taking a walk and doing anything and come back and all that." Not like a girl; as soon as it gets dark, she has to get back home and that's it. . . . It is also that the girl does a lot of housework. The boy gets up, has breakfast and leaves. He comes back at lunchtime, has lunch and leaves. He does not care about anything. That is not the case for the girl. She has to do the laundry, sweep the floor, and cook. She gets exhausted by work.*

The themes of boys' greater freedom of movement and fewer household responsibilities were often mentioned by girls as advantages of the male role. However, girls who said they had never wished they were boys presented what they saw as negative aspects of the male role. Hakima was sixteen and in school when she said she preferred to be a girl.

■ h: *It is better to be a girl. Girls are better; they are different than boys. Boys go to jail; they fight with knives. . . . They aggress against each other, but girls don't do these things. Boys use cigarettes and damage their lungs or catch other diseases. They also stay outdoors late at*

night and end up being picked up by the police. Girls do not go out;
they stay at home, and this is why it is better to be a girl.

Hakima emphasizes negative characteristics of boys (smoking, fighting), and the increased freedom that Aisha sees as desirable, Hakima sees bad.

Mohammed, a young man of eighteen who has left school, believes it is preferable to be a male but indicates that some of his friends feel differently.

■ s: *In your opinion, in Morocco is it better to be female or male?*
M: *Male.*
s: *Why?*
M: *Because here in Morocco, girls don't have so much value.*
s: *How? Give me an example.*
M: *For example, if a girl is always out around the town. . . . She spends her time touring the town; she's like "extra"* [zayda]. *A man would be working and he would have his family. A girl just idles around and makes a bad reputation for herself. She stays wherever she goes, and she spends her time hanging around in Kabar, and that's all. . . .*
s: *Why do you think that, in Morocco, it's better to be a boy than a girl?*
M: *A girl, if she's outside her house, without her parents, or if her parents stay at home and don't work, she does the same because she doesn't find a job. If it were a guy and his parents can't work, he would go out and work. He could do construction work. A girl can't go and work outside. The boy can find a job anywhere, whereas the girl can't.*
s: *So girls are only accepted in certain jobs. Have you ever said to yourself, "I wish God had created me a girl"?*
M: *No never. There are girls I hear in the market say, "We wish we were born guys," and there are a lot of guys who say, "We wish were girls." A lot of my friends say so.*
s: *Why do they think it's better to be female?*
M: *Each one has his own character. There are those who envy good things. For example, a girl who is very lucky, and who gets married to some rich man who can take her abroad. Then they say, "We wish we were girls." Or again, when one sees a girl here in Morocco with her own riches and who has a lot of money, he says, "I wish I were a girl." . . . It's as though they are jealous.*

While Mohammed admits elsewhere that there can be good girls like his sisters, what comes to his mind first are girls who compromise their own and their families' reputations. He also mentions an important basis of the cultural preference for males: they are expected to work and help support the family. Finally, his report that some of his friends envy rich or lucky females gives us a clue about why 28 percent of Moroccan males drew female figures first, suggesting that they preferred or were especially interested in the female gender role. The male household head in Morocco carries the heavy responsibility of supporting his family, something that is increasingly difficult for young men to do when jobs are hard to find. The fantasy of being supported by someone else, as in the traditional female role, must be appealing to some young men confronting this challenge.

Education

A major concern of adolescents in Zawiya is education; they are constantly thinking about doing well enough in school to pass to the next grade. Remaining in school has become more of a problem since we left town because of a new law that requires a student who has failed more than two years of school to drop out. In our sample of about a hundred young people, those in school had failed an average of almost one year for every two that they passed; for example, a child in fourth grade would typically have failed two years and been in school for a total of six. Although most adolescents do not appear overtly anxious about school, most work hard and prepare diligently for exams. Older boys spend the majority of their out-of-school time studying; their sisters would too but for the demands of housework.

Moroccan education is different from that familiar to most Americans in several ways. Classes are taught in literary Arabic, rather than the colloquial language spoken at home and with friends. The relation between literary Arabic and the Moroccan dialect is like that between Latin and Italian: the former is recognized as a prototype and ideal for the latter, but one that must be learned through formal instruction as a foreign language. Research on schooling and cognitive development in Morocco has underscored the early importance of language of instruction (Wagner and Spratt 1987b).[6]

Classroom relations in Zawiya are hierarchical, with the teacher exercising unquestioned authority, and the students rather tensely waiting to be called on. When the teacher puts a lesson on the board, students copy and memorize it. The emphasis is on learning the given answer, rather than on the process of discussing a problem to arrive at a solution.[7] With a large school population (roughly thirty-five students per classroom in the primary school) attending in split shifts nationwide, the traditional approach is efficient but sometimes stressful. As in the family, the threat of physical punishment is an effective inducement to orderly behavior, but the controls learned may not generalize to other settings.

We sat in on a math class in the junior high school in Kabar. As in most Moroccan schools, the class was coeducational. Boys wear normal street dress, but girls are required to wear either a smock or a traditional long robe, less to ensure that they are modestly covered than to assure that poorer girls do not feel they must have a large wardrobe. The class was orderly and attentive, and students raised their hands to give solutions to problems on the board, rising to speak. The class was conducted in French, as are many higher-level classes in the sciences.[8]

The school system is a microcosm of the state bureaucracy, and cynicism is sometimes expressed about the workings of this complex hierarchy. Students who failed often said it was because they had not bribed someone or that their good exam was exchanged with the poor exam of another student with better connections. Others said they failed because certain teachers did not do their jobs well, skipping classes or refusing to explain points or answer questions. These complaints, though common, came from students who needed to justify failure. Such stories reveal students' concern that even if they learn well, they may not succeed.

The probability of finishing high school in Zawiya is low. Our rough estimate is that when a Zawiya child enters elementary school, the likelihood of completing high school and receiving the coveted *baccalaureate* diploma is not more than 3 percent. In one recent year, fewer than a dozen youth from this community of eleven thousand persons passed the standarized national examination for the baccalaureate, despite the fact that the vast majority of their peers in Zawiya had already failed or dropped out in earlier years, so those who remained were probably the most talented and serious students. Such low success rates, combined with very poor job prospects even for the lucky few who continue on to college, have produced increasing frustration and cynicism among Zawiyans and Moroccans generally.[9] Returning to Zawiya after several years absence and inquiring about the children of our friends has often been a painful experience, as we learn that the bright and hardworking child of previous years has now left school after several failures.

Although the majority of the adolescents we talked to aspired to white-collar jobs, these aspirations are quite unrealistic. We attempted to judge the fit between aspirations and prospects by examining the jobs held by adolescents' older siblings as a sample of types of work done by people from this area.[10] A maximum of one-fifth have or can hope for white-collar jobs, while about one-third have unskilled jobs and many are under- or unemployed. On the one hand, adolescents are encouraged because they have neighbors or siblings who have gotten an education and won white-collar jobs; such success stories also inspire many of their parents to make the sacrifices necessary to send their children to school. On the other hand, a minority of older siblings hold these desirable jobs, and it is much more difficult to get them now than in the past. When the French left Morocco in 1956, they left a large number of jobs in government and business to be filled by Moroccans. By 1965, these jobs were mostly filled, and limited economic growth has meant there are not many new job slots available. When the junior high school principal was asked what he thought were problems for adolescents, his first response was that they are "uncertain of their destiny." This is not because they neglect to plan, but because the economic situation in Morocco is very difficult, and even able students often cannot find a job.

The commitment of the Moroccan government to mass education has thus become a source of contradictions, with an increasingly literate and ambitious populace frustrated in its hopes for improved prospects through education (see Spratt 1987). While these stresses now affect adolescents of both sexes in almost every family, on the whole males have probably felt the frustrations of failure in school more keenly and in greater numbers, since it has been the hope of families that a son would land a secure white-collar position adequate for him to support his aging parents and help his younger siblings. In spite of these difficulties, parents and students still strive for academic success. Education is a source of further stress for females, because in the context of coeducational schooling they are more likely to form a romantic attachment to a boy, potentially leading to some degree of sexual activity and resultant dishonor.

DEVIANCE

Deviance is represented as a reaction to stress in much of the psychological literature, and Americans often expect or fear some deviant behavior by adolescents. We approach the topic with some diffidence, however, because in the nature of ethnographic fieldwork one usually has primary contact with local persons who, although "deviant" in the sense that they are more open toward or interested in foreigners, are unlikely to be themselves deviant or to be able to accurately portray those whose behavior is seriously at odds with community values. Zawiya adolescents often see on television or in films deviant behavior involving sex and crime. While we cannot say how this affects their behavior, it appears to figure prominently in the fantasies of at least some local youth.

Our discussion of deviance applies almost exclusively to males; major deviance for the Zawiya female occurs almost exclusively in the realm of sexuality.

Drugs and Alcohol

The use of drugs or alcohol is disapproved by Islam. In the past, the deviant use of drugs and alcohol was quite limited, especially among adolescents. Alcohol was consumed by some teenagers as a form of rebellion against cultural rules, in the same way that a few might eat ham in violation of the Muslim prohibition against pork. Older men might drink wine or beer on occasion, and whiskey was drunk by the upper classes and thus seen by middle-class men as a status drink when they could afford it. Most adult men smoked cigarettes, and a few older men smoked a mixture of tobacco and marijuana, called kif. Today, some adolescent males smoke kif or the marijuana resin hashish, and a few experiment with other drugs.

Tobacco

Cigarette smoking is a common, but on the whole a negatively viewed, activity of adolescent males; it is almost unheard of among teenage females in rural settings like Zawiya. Boys in Zawiya between the ages of fifteen and twenty often experiment with smoking in order to appear grown-up, much like their counterparts in the United States. While many adult males are chain smokers, some youth consciously try to avoid starting to smoke for health reasons. Smoking by males is not seen as seriously deviant unless they are very young or (regardless of age) smoke disrespectfully in front of their fathers.

Alcohol

Our impression is that more and younger teenagers are experimenting with drinking in Zawiya. The government has limited the number of stores that sell alcohol, but it is not illegal. There are no bars or stores selling alcohol in Zawiya itself, but both exist in Kabar. The most frequent drink of young men is cheap rouge, red wine sold in plastic bottles for about 15 DH ($2.50); wine in glass bottles costs over 20 DH and is too expensive for most Zawiya youth. One occasionally sees or hears drunks in Zawiya, and they are one reason women fear to go out at night.

A few local men drink heavily and regularly and are probably alcoholic, but most drinking occurs at celebrations. Young men in particular will have paper bags containing bottled alcohol to pour into their tea glasses (as we noticed at the naming ceremony described in chap. 6) or will drink from the bottle. The goal of such drinking is explicitly to produce intoxication, to "heat one's head" so one can overcome feelings of self-consciousness and enjoy the party. A boy's drunkenness is seen as deviant behavior only if it is frequent or occurs without a ceremonial excuse. Only a few young men in our neighborhood were known to regularly drink too much, and they were viewed with disdain. These males were at the older end of adolescence. Younger boys may experiment with alcohol, buying a bottle and drinking it in a group, but do not use it enough to be considered deviant.

Kif *and* Hashish

Cannabis (marijuana) has long been grown and consumed in Morocco, and has been used for centuries for medicinal purposes and as a mild intoxicant. The most common traditional Moroccan use of cannabis was as kif, a powder of leaves from the plant mixed with tobacco and smoked a small amount at a time in a small pipe. Both kif and hashish were formerly used almost exclusively by males past middle age, who were sometimes seen lounging by the river or on public transport. This drug use was regarded by many pious older Moroccans as religiously "reprehensible" (*makruh*).[11] Habitual users were often seen as irresponsible by members of their families, and they were the occasional objects of ridicule by street children.

Now, however, hashish—although illegal—is sold to young men in Zawiya who mix it with cigarette tobacco and refill the cigarette. The dosage tended to be small in the traditional kif smoker, but many of these maintained a slightly intoxicated state almost indefinitely. Today's adolescent male "hash" user probably consumes a much higher dose per session, but has fewer and shorter sessions than the traditional adult user. A piece of hashish the size of a pencil eraser cost 10 DH (about $1.60) in 1982, placing it well within the budget of older adolescents. Hashish was available in Kabar and was also often brought back by teenagers from trips north to coastal resorts. Although we cannot give precise estimates, everyone in the community would agree that drug use has increased among teenagers, and perhaps half the young men have tried these substances. Knowledgeable informants identified about 20 percent of neighborhood teenage males as regular kif or hashish users.

It is difficult to be precise about the local rationale for drug use. One local man in his midtwenties from outside the immediate neighborhood was widely known in Zawiya as a regular kif smoker. Several young men mentioned his humorous behavior when under the influence, and he was quoted during Ramadan as saying, "I'm going to smoke kif and remain *faTar* [i.e., eating rather than fasting] the whole month, so I can go to Hell and be with Bob Marley!" There is tolerance in many families for some adolescent experimentation with marijuana, and some teenagers talk casually about smoking a *jwan* (joint). Musicians and members of curing brotherhoods may make uncensured public use of kif, as in the case of the dancer-musicians described in chapter 6, or like a local teen music group that sat outside the house where they were performing and smoked between sets. Some older young men said they used it to forget their problems. Boys who smoke every day, or who smoke at school between classes, are seen as deviant and are disparaged by their peers, who often suggest that they will ruin their health—or even lose their sanity—as a result.

Other Substances

Adolescents told us about several other intoxicants, some of which were used locally and others that were found in large cities. None is common, compared to kif. Other drugs included shoe polish and the glue used to repair bicycles; both were inhaled. We heard of a few adolescents in the high school taking pills to get high or "dizzy," but did not hear about specific types. Another kind of substance abuse involved extracting an intoxicant from the exhaust of city buses, which are not found in Zawiya. More locally available methods used to get high included brewing mint tea with fermented figs, one of the few drugs said to be used by girls (at parties), and eating the spice nutmeg. An older woman described eating hashish cookies at a party years ago.

A few local young men were clearly deviant in terms of drug use. One of the wealthier families in the neighborhood is headed by a middle-aged man who has for many years worked abroad. He returns each summer, and the money he brings with him has provided his family with a large house and a fairly high standard of living. Two of his teenage sons have been in frequent trouble because of fighting, however, and the older of these, aged eighteen at the time of the research, was regarded by many in the neighborhood as thoroughly bad. He was expelled from school, is frequently involved in serious fights with other young men, is believed to steal, and makes frequent and excessive use of alcohol and marijuana. When his name came up in conversation we were told several times that he was bad because of lack of paternal supervision at home.

Another recognized deviant was a twenty-year-old who occasionally ran a one-room café nearby. This establishment had a hand-operated soccer game and card tables, and during the irregular evening hours when it was open it was a gathering place for some of the tougher older adolescent males. The smell of marijuana could frequently be detected coming from this café, and the teenage proprietor was perceived as a hardened and cynical deviant. This was also blamed on the lack of strong paternal guidance, although the father resided in the household. While both of these cases may be in part explained by the family situation as neighbors perceived it, the majority of father-absent households in Zawiya do not seem to have produced deviant children.

Crime

Serious crime is rare in town in general, and especially among adolescents. The only female behavior that might be seen as criminal is prostitution, and none of the adolescents we knew was involved in it. There were older women who were considered prostitutes or who arranged liaisons in town, but not teenagers. The main crime we found that involved adolescents was petty theft by boys, usually of fruit or vegetables from the isolated gardens along the river, and sometimes from shops. We heard of a few cases of young men around twenty trying to break into shops to steal things to get money for their girlfriends. In general, stealing fruit is seen as something many boys do on occasion and is not considered serious, while stealing other property is seen as deviant and requiring punishment, either by parents or by the law.

Crises

Although they were rare in our neighborhood, one hears of young people suffering "crises" (called *une crise* in French by the more educated; *mrd nefsani*, psychological illness, by others; or simply *medrub*, struck [by spirits]). These are illnesses that incapacitate the individual, rendering him or her unable to function for months, with no apparent physical cause. Among the approximately 150 young people we worked with, none was currently suffering a crise, although several were mildly retarded or brain damaged.

However, one young woman was afflicted after we left in 1983, and a man in his twenties from outside the neighborhood described his earlier illness to Douglas. The young woman, in her early twenties, was being a great help to her mother in running the wedding celebration of an older brother. Suddenly she was unable to move, began to shout and cry, and was put to bed. She became quiet after a few days, but laid in bed lethargically, unable to function normally. Her mother tried many approaches, taking her to medical doctors and to magical and religious curers. After about a year, the girl began to function normally and was felt to be recovered. The women of the family decided that probably a jealous female relative had placed a spell in the girl's path and that she had recovered because of a counterspell. We wondered whether the girl's singleness and lack of current prospects were made especially stressful by assisting with her brother's wedding, and whether her illness was a way to temporarily escape this stress.

A local young man became ill at about thirteen, after he and two friends had made fun of a Sufi curing ceremony. He said he felt like someone picked him up and dashed him to the ground, and that he remembered nothing until the next day. He was incapacitated for months, during which time his parents tried various supernatural cures. Finally, a ceremony by one of the Sufi brotherhoods was effective; today, as a young adult, he earns a living working with another curing group.[12]

Suicide

Suicide in Zawiya is not the serious issue it is among American adolescents. Only one recent case was well known—that of a young man who had thrown himself off a roof on learning he had a fatal illness, after a prior disappointment in love. A less clear case involved a young woman some people said died of a mysterious illness, while others said she was unmarried and pregnant and had taken an overdose of medication. Someone said a young man in nearby Kabar had drunk poison on hearing he failed his baccalaureate exam; such actions are sometimes contemplated, but rarely carried out. Suicide, or the deep depression that can lead to suicide, is rare among adolescents in Zawiya.

A CASE OF ADOLESCENT CONFLICT

One sixteen-year-old boy, Sa'id, may serve as an example of stress and interpersonal conflict, at least among favored male children, although the intensity of some of his conflict with his family is rare.[13] When he was a toddler, Sa'id, whose biological father is a withdrawn, underemployed man, was taken to live in the home of his maternal grandparents in another part of the neighborhood. This couple had a son of their own, already a young man, who lived abroad during much of Sa'id's later childhood, and Sa'id was raised by his grandparents as if he were their son. He was taught to call his grandparents "father" and "mother," although he knew they were his mother's parents. His biological parents were frequent visitors to the household, and he seems to have treated his mother as if she were a much older sister, and indeed sometimes referred to her as "sister."

Sa'id was constantly indulged with playthings and the best morsels of food, and his misbehavior was almost always greeted with a smile by the grandparents. He was a very attractive child, and his sense of himself as the center of so much doting activity produced behavior of the kind labeled "spoiled" in the United States. Although Sa'id's success in school was important to the grandparents, they apparently found it impossible to discipline him, and in spite of being bright he has failed several times.

During the past several years his behavior toward both his grandparents and his mother has become increasingly aggressive and demanding, and early in the period of our residence he moved out of the grandparents' household (shortly after taking over as his private room what had been the family's kitchen) in a rage after being denied money for a purchase he wished to make. He subsequently moved back in with the grandparents after a money quarrel with his parents, only to move back to the parents' household weeks later in yet another money quarrel. Each of these conflicts had as an apparent cause the denial to Sa'id of what were sizable sums given the resources of both households. In responding to our structured interviews about closeness to family members, he described as the person most dear at home "my father," meaning his biological father. In discussing his dreams and fears, he several times referred to the maternal uncle whose place he seems to have filled in his grandparents' affections as "my brother," and the interview from which we quote contains many references to "father" or "mother" which are ambiguous (to the listener) as to whether the parent or grandparent is intended.

What is most striking about Sa'id is his combination of shyness, even cowardice, toward nonfamily members, combined with abusiveness toward family members when angry. On several occasions during our fieldwork Sa'id struck his mother, even during the later months of her pregnancy. This was seen as shocking and reprehensible behavior by neighbors, and it was intensely embarrassing to the other family members involved. In the company of nonfamily adults, however, Sa'id was often acquiescent and deferent to a fault and presented a picture of one so shy as to be incapable of any display of negative emotion. Several of his regular companions were younger than he, and with them he could be assertive, but with boys his own age and older he was often fearful. His fearfulness was the subject of comment and some ridicule in the neighborhood, since he would not walk a block unaccompanied after dark and was even afraid to enter his grandparents' unoccupied house during the daytime.

We quote at length from an edited interview tape-recorded in late 1984, when Sa'id was eighteen. This interview is atypical for the apparently confused thinking it shows at some points. On the other hand, Sa'id illustrates more general adolescent tensions. We join the interview after Susan has been pressing Sa'id for several minutes to tell her about his "nature" [*Tabi'a*]. In this instance, and throughout the interview, Sa'id often answers with apparent reference to people in general when asked about himself, and describes relations with his father when asked about his mother. His grandfather, the central male figure in his childhood, had died the year before this interview.

■ s: *Let's go back to your nature. Can you say something besides the way you live, which you said is fine, but which is not your nature.*

SA'ID: *The way I live, correct. Living is not just eating, but if you feel that your parents support you and provide you with what you need. That's what parents do. There are parents who have only one son and they are proud of him. They love him a lot and they provide him with all he needs. Even if they don't have much, they borrow and secure his living and his other needs.*

s: *And is your father that way?*

SA'ID: *Whatever I need he gets it for me. . . .*

s: *Can you tell me how you are doing with your mother?*

SA'ID: *Well, I won't say our relations are that great. I would say, however, that my relations with my father are 100 percent better than with my mother. . . . Because to tell you frankly, I like it when I am respected. I live with my [grandparents'] family and we live all right, especially since I lived here since my childhood and they provided for all my needs. They had the money, and that enabled them to spend it on me.*

s: *Who are you referring to?*

SA'ID: *Grandpa. He raised me since childhood and he brought me all I asked for. So I got used to such a life-style. As for my [grand]mother, even when I get upset she calms me down by giving me something. She gets me calmed down by satisfying me, and by giving me advice and hugging me. She keeps using this approach until I cool down. Let's say I want something immediately, a cassette recorder for example, they do buy it for me. Well—she keeps telling me they'll buy it for me, I should wait a bit, and she does this until I cool down.*

s: *You're talking about your [grand]mother Zohra?*

SA'ID: *My mother Zohra. She is good to me. She is nice. As for my other [biological] mother, she gets upset with me sometimes and I just don't like anybody getting angry at me—*

s: *What do you do when you are angry? If you don't like her getting angry at you, what do you do when she does?*

SA'ID: *It is the same with me. If somebody shouts at me I get upset, especially when I invite a friend of mine. I welcome him to my house because he is my best friend. My [biological] father understands the situation and says hello to my guest but my mother behaves in such a way as to show him that he is not welcome. Why does she do this? She says to me, "You bring boys here!" This makes me mad. Why does she have to treat me like this? If I were dealing with my [grand]mother she would understand my situation and wait for the guy to leave to ask me why I invited him and give me the reason why I shouldn't invite him to my home. But she makes her comments on the spot. It is a shame.*

. . .

s: *Can you give me an example about what happened as a result of such a disagreement?*

. . .

SA'ID: *This one does not satisfy my needs. For example if I want something—even when I say something she knows how I react when I am upset—my mother, my grandmother Zohra, she takes her responsibility. She knows that when I am upset I swear—I insult her, argue with her, and this is a habit that goes back to my childhood. Since then I was yelling at her. But when she comes to hug me, kiss me and calm me I forget the problems I have and laugh with her. But with regard to this one [biological mother] it is different. She too shouts and confronts me. If I say one word she answers me back and that upsets me a lot. I tend to break whatever I find in front of me.*

. . .

When we have a disagreement I like to go out to "change air" and try to forget all that happened between us. Then I go back home.

s: *You forget it. OK. So the worst thing that could happen between a son and his father and son and his mother is if he answers them back. This is the worst thing.*

SA'ID: *Yes.*

s: *Sometimes this happens to you.*

SA'ID: *It does happen to me sometimes, but with regard to my father. . . . For my father it is all right—I know his very nature, whatever I do, he can do nothing to me. And I don't shy away from him. I can talk to him about any topic and he won't say no. There are some—a man who doesn't give his son a chance to speak. I can talk to him, hassle him, and he wouldn't say anything. He doesn't want to upset my plans.*

s: *And what's the best thing that could happen between a son and his father?*

SAʿID: *As I told you, he can squabble with him. But of course if the son insults his father the latter wouldn't stomach the fact that his own son insults him, he may kick him out.*

s: *Who, the son?*

SAʿID: *The father can kick out his son, and the son leaves to wander in the streets.*

s: *And this is the nicest thing that could happen between a son and his father?*

SAʿID: *Yes.*[14]

s: *This is nice? I asked you about the nicest thing.*

SAʿID: *The nicest thing? If his father kicks him out that's it. He becomes a hooligan. The sheer number of problems can lead the boy to lose his mind. He can lose his memory and end up with some mental problems. . . . There is a guy for example who is upset. If he is a smoker and has no cigarettes and no money he loses his temper. When he goes home he may get into an argument with his father. His father starts beating him up. But the boy doesn't like being beaten up at that age so he feels he has to face the dilemma.*

s: *What is "to face the dilemma"?*

SAʿID: *To face his father. He says something to him to make him stop beating him up. He can raise his hands and tell him to stop hitting him, and that he should mind his own business and not that of the son. The father wouldn't permit this kind of behavior from his son. He'll get very upset and tell his son to leave his house.*

s: *How would he kick him out?*

SAʿID: *He will tell him, "Go away. I'm not your father and you are not my son." This occurs this way. A father just tells his son, "You are not my son and I'm not your father." The son then just leaves and heads toward the streets where he starts bumming around. He goes to—*

s: *And is this a nice or bad thing?*

SAʿID: *A bad thing.*

s: *OK.*

SAʿID: *The kid becomes a hoodlum, especially if he has no mother to protect him. If he has no mother and his father marries another woman, and the father loves this woman: he loves her very much, and the son is not from that mother. He is from the mother who died. A disagreement may occur, the woman then reports to her husband about it. She tells him, "Your son answers me back," and what have you. The father feels bad about this, he gets upset and kicks his son out. The son leaves the house and becomes a hoodlum. He is on his own, alone. He doesn't find anybody to assist him. No father or mother to help him. The only mother he got died. So he loses his temper. He starts talking to himself, sometimes he steals. He stays this way until he becomes a bum.*

The major themes of this interview appear to be almost narcissistic preoccupation with being cared for and indulged; ambiguity as to whether parental responsibilities for emotional and material support are to be met by his parents or grandparents; preoccupation with (and fear of) his own rage and aggression; inability either to characterize his mother in realistic terms or to admit to the level of his aggression against her; and fear of conflict with his father leading to rejection, delinquency, and insanity. Sa'id's claim that he can "hassle" and pressure his father without fear of contradiction may appear as closeness, but in Moroccan terms it shows a lack of proper respect and deference from a son to his father—the same lack of respect toward him he resents in his friends.

This interview illustrates several issues. It shows what types of disagreement lead to conflict with parents. Sa'id wants his mother to show she respects him, an important sign that one is no longer a child. Such respect is usually awarded for mature behavior, including facing problems courageously and showing self-control in situations of stress. Yet Sa'id praises his grandmother for coddling him like a child when he is upset and criticizes his mother for confronting him on issues in a more adult way. In fact, confronting someone indicates lack of respect in Zawiya; one should accept the behavior of a respected person. However, Sa'id's mother's confrontations threaten his shaky self-control; he is apt to fly into a rage, something a mature person should never do. Although Sa'id is unusual in that he still acts out these issues at the age of eighteen, such conflicts are concerns for other young men in Zawiya.

Sa'id's vivid images at the end of the interview seem to be driven without regard for Susan's questions, and we have wondered whether he may be reporting part of a plot from a film he has seen, and which he has incorporated into his own fantasies of what it would be like if he and his father really quarreled. Deeper than this fear of external circumstances (loss of financial support, conflict with parents) is Sa'id's fear that he, like others he knows of, will lose emotional control, will become crazy. Sa'id also shows concern that his temper is more than he can handle. He speaks of this possible loss of control impersonally, and his language is rather psychological. Most of his

Zawiya neighbors would probably express the danger as possession by spirits (*jnun*). Thus this midadolescent boy vacillates between childish fears and aspiration to adult prerogatives. He wants to be indulged as a child, mothered, even while commanding the respect of his father and mother and others in the community. Of such contradictory behavior, his relatives and neighbors would say, "He hasn't yet incorporated his ʿaql."

Several sources or potential sources of stress for the adolescents in Zawiya include the difficulty of completing one's education and the high and perhaps unrealistic aspirations both students and their parents have with regard to future jobs. Other sources are concern with managing heterosexual relationships in a culture in which they are negatively sanctioned, and ambivalence about one's gender role, especially for females. Conflict between the generations is not a general problem, despite broad differences in level of education and in typical life-style. The expectation of a limited degree of individual autonomy, combined with a strong respect for elders and the importance of the family, makes the generational conflict that occurs in many American households both less common and less serious in Morocco. Serious deviance is uncommon in this community. Generally the young people of Zawiya, like the adults, appear to be coping with a sometimes difficult and rapidly changing social and economic situation with dignity and self-respect.

■ 8
The Zawiya Individual

We conclude our presentation of coming of age in Zawiya with the more personal and subjective side of Zawiya adolescence—the nature and development of adolescent self-awareness.[1] We emphasize here the individual's perspective on late childhood and early adulthood in Zawiya: self-perception, the changing quality of problem-solving and moral thought, aspirations for the future, and the expression of personal concerns in dreams and fantasy. Of course no experience is purely personal, and each aspect of individual experience must be understood in light of the social expectations and constraints afforded by Moroccan society and the neighborhood setting.

Reflective thought emerges as an issue during this time of change in the lives of Zawiya adolescents. New reasoning skills allow the older youth to reflect on the relationship between personal experience and community values. The theme of rapid change is again important here, at both a sociocultural and an individual level. First, shifting social reality includes increased exposure to public education, the administrative personnel and political institutions of the larger society, contact with relatives and friends familiar with very different settings than Zawiya, and constant exposure to electronic media. Family relations, friendships, heterosexual relations, and the expression of deviance and conflict are all affected by these pervasive sociocultural changes. Second, the physical and behavioral changes that young persons experience individually, and the reaction of others to these changes, cause them to think about themselves with a new awareness. This new self-awareness is frequently described by them in terms of 'aql; we now return to the import of this term in Moroccan society and to its use by young people in Zawiya.

SELF-AWARENESS IN ZAWIYA

The concept of self is an increasingly interesting and controversial topic in anthropology, and we were especially concerned with the development and expression of self-concepts in Zawiya. A major task in moving from childhood to adulthood for these Moroccan youth involves developing 'aql: learning to interact with the wider society in an appropriate way, and learning the complex process of maneuvering skillfully among various relationships. Indeed, the complex and subtle interactions of some of our friends made us feel like social Neanderthals by contrast. Young people learn to control their individual desires at most times, to interact correctly with older and younger, richer and poorer, and male and female kin, neighbors, merchants, teachers, and others. The area of heterosexual relations is especially revealing, since new norms for behavior have not been articulated. Managing these relations in a society whose traditional norms posit that no such relations should occur for unmarried youth requires very skillful maneuvering indeed. As we have seen, sexual experimentation involves acting in some relationships as a person who does have such interactions, and one's own knowledge of those interactions informs the self-concept. However, most of the time, to most audiences, one presents and lives a self either unconcerned with sexual relationships (males) or virtuously abstaining from such relationships (females). Thus changing gender relations present a real focus of concern for the Moroccan youth discussed here, and conceptions of an internal agentive self informed by social values and a socially constructed self are relevant in explaining Zawiya adolescents' behavior. To see one of these aspects of individuals' behavior as real or central and the other as superficial or duplicitous is to overlook the complexity and subtlety of Moroccan social interaction.

Changing patterns of relationship characterize the teen years for Zawiya youth, and changing interpersonal settings for behavior prompt new reflectiveness about one's position in the family, the community, and the larger society. New relationships may prove stressful or may bring to light contradiction between the young person and his or her family. In any case, the older teenager is more likely to reflect on the problems of simultaneously satisfying the expectations of family, friends, and teachers; in this reflective thought we can discern new cognitive styles and new personal aspirations.

ʿAql

Adolescence in Zawiya involves new and increased self-awareness, and the self-awareness that adolescents develop at this time and the Moroccan concept of ʿaql are closely related. Theoretical accounts of adolescence as a time for reconciliation of more powerful needs for emotional and physical intimacy with increased sensitivity to social expectations seem relevant to the development of ʿaql by Zawiya youth (Freud [1905] 1953; Erikson 1968; Sullivan 1953). The idea of a fundamental tension between emotion and reason, lust and prudence, has become since Hall's work at the turn of the century (Hall 1904) the central conception of adolescence in Western social science literature, and it was in large part to test the universality of these claims that the pioneering ethnographic studies of Mead (1928, 1930) were undertaken. A similar conception of the maturational problem is suggested by the "*nafs-ʿaql* paradigm" articulated for Morocco by Rosen (1984), in which persons are seen as having varying amounts of passion and reason in precarious balance. People in Zawiya described individuals as having more or less ʿaql, and therefore as being more or less able to control themselves, although they seldom used the term *nafs*. Borrowing Abu-Lughod's reading of ʿaql as "social sense" we examine the way this sensitivity to society's expectations manifests itself in the thinking and behavior of the young people of Zawiya.

CHANGING SELF-AWARENESS

Western psychological depictions of adolescence emphasize change in the subjective and social experience of the self. Adolescents are described as needing to reconcile new desires and new roles with their inner sense of sameness (Erikson 1968). This aspect of Zawiya adolescence is illustrated by examples of the responses of young people to direct questions concerning how they had changed in their thinking about themselves.[2]

Female Self-Awareness

Most girls' responses to questions about themselves and how they had changed in the preceding year suggested a concern with how they related to and were perceived by others in the community. Such awareness of themselves and of the effects of their behavior is not expected of younger children.[3]

One kind of answer focused specifically on interpersonal relations, on getting along with others and not fighting; this was one of the stated goals of adolescent friendships.

An eleven-year-old schoolgirl said, "I get along well with girls; I don't fight with them, and I don't learn their bad habits." A schoolgirl of fourteen indicated: "I don't fight with people; I get along well with them, and them with me. If they give me something, I'll be willing to give them something too. But if they won't share and then ask me for something, I won't give it to them."

Another kind of answer is characteristic of older girls and reflects a cultural expectation that girls of about fifteen become concerned with their appearance. People assume this is related to their new interest in boys. A schoolgirl of sixteen remarked, "I've changed a lot since last year. Then, I just wore whatever was around; this year, I only wear nice things." But a sixteen-year-old who had not attended school said: "I didn't pay attention to myself. Last year I used to play out in the street, things like marbles, hopscotch, soccer, and jumprope, with boys and girls. This year, I just felt I'm older, and don't play like that any more. I could tell because I'm bigger, I have breasts."

For some girls this preoccupation with appearance seems to pass; a twenty-one-year-old said she was less concerned with her appearance than previously, and she and a seventeen-year-old said they went out less than they used to. Their behavior was culturally appropriate for older girls, who are expected to be reticent about displaying themselves in public.

Another dimension of one's relation to others is shown by older girls, who responded that one of their characteristics was that they paid little attention to what others thought or said about them. This seemingly contradictory view in fact shows awareness that gossip is widespread, and there are apt to be many untrue rumors; if one is easily upset by them, she is apt to lose her temper and get into fights, characteristics of one with no ʿaql. This apparent lack of concern about the opinions of others therefore shows an inner strength and maturity, a sense that one's own behavior and opinions are what are important, and an ability to weigh the importance of various social contexts. The person with developed ʿaql is sensitive to the expectations of the social environment, but not overwhelmmed by them. A girl of seventeen with some primary education said:

> Yes, I've changed. I used to go over to people's houses—I thought they were like me; we just joked around. Now I see that people are perfidious; they say I "laugh" too much. It's better to stay home and have only

a little fun. They said, "She became aware of her different aspects" [*faqet m'a jnabha*], meaning that I began to dress well, and also to think about boys. Whatever you do, you're insulted. If you don't dress well and comb your hair nicely, they say you look sloppy. If you do, they say, "She woke up [to the presence of boys]." If I hear someone talking about me, I don't pay any attention. I didn't used to like to dress well because of that talk. I know they're jealous.

A twenty-two-year-old, also with some primary education, described how she had changed in a similar way: "I've cooled off [in terms of temper]. I don't care; let people talk, I've become a responsible adult [I developed my 'aql]."

A young woman of twenty-eight described in more detail the importance of developing sense, although she did not use the word *'aql*, but another word, *nefkha*, that literally means swollen or expanded, and can also refer to pride.[1] In describing the development of 'aql for some local young people, she said that in some cases it was due to the way the family had raised the young person, sometimes it came after a troublesome young man had a stint in the army, and sometimes a person just developed it by him or herself. She said of all these young people, "Pride [*nefkha*] has grown in them: Whatever the economic situation of their family is, they don't mind it. Such a person minds his own business. *Nefkha* is good, better than anything else. A person who is *menfukha* thinks about herself, and doesn't pay attention to others and get involved in their problems."

While the number of cases does not allow broad generalization, these data suggest a trend in which younger adolescents attempt to exhibit 'aql by immersion in and conformity to social context, while older adolescents develop a balance between the ever-shifting context and their own values.

Male Self-Awareness

For older teenage males in Zawiya late adolescence is a period when one is supposed to demonstrate control over one's emotions, deference to manifest authority (i.e., to give respect), and a well-modulated ability to elicit support from other males (i.e., to command respect). These demands can be stressful and contradictory.

As males seek support from friends, they also entangle themselves in a web of obligations. One of our friends often set out for what he hoped would be a one-hour errand to Kabar, only to return late that night. He would then recount how one friend after another had met him on the street and demanded an extended conversation, a visit to a café, and his attendance on some errand the friend needed to run. Moroccans sometimes describe the hospitality extended to them by friends or relatives as having been "imprisoned" (*Hbsu-ni*), and this jovial "capture" is very demanding of both time and patience. Yet such is the stuff of Moroccan social relations, and most young adults have learned to handle these demanding interactions with skill.

The central theme of the accounts of older males, when asked about how they had changed in the past year, was typically that they had become in some way more self-reflective, more aware of the consequences of their actions and the influences upon them, and more able to steer their own course. Thus eighteen-year-old Rashid said to Douglas, "My thinking has changed. When you are doing bad, associating with bad people, and you see the problem, you change." Sa'id, two years younger, said he had changed a lot: "Last year I didn't understand anything, like about dressing well or [being serious about] my studies."

COGNITIVE DEVELOPMENT IN ZAWIYA

Full self-awareness is not possible at early stages of cognitive development. Much of the Western literature on adolescent thinking is based on the results of various tests of mental functioning administered to high school and college student subjects. Each of the field teams in the Harvard Adolescence Project collected several sorts of test data concerning problem solving, self-perception, and moral reasoning. Our interview and structured test materials provide evidence for fairly pronounced differences in the styles of thinking displayed by older as compared with younger teenagers. The results for our Zawiya sample illustrate both the difficulties of cross-cultural comparison and the powerful role of formal schooling in structuring the types of thinking evoked by Western psychological tests. These results are more fully reported elsewhere (D. Davis 1989), but we summarize and discuss them here.

Formal Operational Thought in Adolescence

The major cognitive change alleged to occur during the adolescent years involves the emergence of what Piaget (Piaget 1972; Inhelder and Piaget 1958) has called "formal operations." Formal operations are reflected in increased ability to reason hypothetically, independent of concrete situations, and to describe one's own reasoning processes. Among the Swiss children studied by Piaget (1972), formal operations became established between the ages of twelve and fifteen. Piaget noted, however, that the rate of progression through developmental stages appears to vary from culture to culture. He also acknowledged that while formal operational reasoning is in principle independent of the content to which it is applied, empirical studies have indicated individual and subcultural differences in the contexts in which such reasoning is displayed. Much of the cross-cultural research on the development of formal operations has shown large cultural differences, with schooled Western samples consistently showing superior performance (see Snarey 1984). Males have also tended to score higher on a variety of measures of formal operational reasoning. Both the cultural and the sex differences have recently been seen as evidence of cultural assumptions or biases inherent in these concepts. We employed two standardized measures of such reasoning with a subset of Zawiya young people: a problem-solving task developed by Neimark (Neimark and Lewis 1967), and the Kohs block test of spatial reasoning from the Wechesler Intelligence Scale for Children.

The Problem-Solving Test

The task used in Neimark's test involves matching a pattern concealed under a set of eight shutters arranged in a circle to one of a set of eight patterns of white and black dots (Neimark and Wagner 1964; Neimark and Lewis 1967).[5] In Zawiya older, more schooled, and male subjects tended to do better on the test when the other effects were statistically controlled.[6] Formal schooling and maturation also appear to be important contributors to test performance. The poorer performance of girls tested may be due to the fact that so few of them had reached the secondary school level at which formal reasoning is taught, although it is also possible they were more anxious at being questioned by males. Even among male subjects, however, the average level of performance was not much above chance. Douglas kept detailed notes on the way each of those tested approached the task, and he was in several cases startled to note that a boy who was a skilled card or checkers player (both skills tapping similar problem-solving abilities) was utterly confused by the Neimark test. On the whole these results convinced us that such a standardized measure of problem solving was inadequate to detect the kind of reasoning of which we know Zawiya youth to be cabable as they solve the real personal dilemmas of their lives.

It is hardly surprising that these Zawiya youth did not perform as Western subjects have, both because of the cultural limitations of the tests developed and because of lower levels of schooling in Zawiya. We do not believe the lower average scrores can be used to infer differences in native ability. The pervasive failure of research to discover formal operational thought in non-Western settings is revealing primarily of the limitations of our theories and methods. Adults in Zawiya reason as subtly about their social world as do Americans or Europeans about theirs, but they do not typically express this social intelligence in easily recognizable expressions of the formal didactic or syllogistic thinking Piagetians have described. This "failure" seems to us primarily due to cultural differences and to the recent introduction of and low persistence in Western-style formal schooling in Zawiya.

The Block Design Test

The Kohs test involves reproducing a set of designs printed on cards, using a set of nine two-colored blocks. The results showed even more clearly the critical role of formal schooling. The average score for twenty-four females tested was not significantly different from that of the twenty-two males.[7] Only the number of years of formal schooling made a significant difference in the score when other effects were statistically controlled, with more schooled youth doing better at the test.

The results from both tests confirm the strong role of formal schooling in establishing even modest levels of performance on standard measures of cognitive performance. What is of special interest for our purposes, however, is how these formalized test results relate to the responses of Zawiya youth to more realistic questions concerning social and moral reasoning.

Social Cognition in Zawiya

Following the example of our colleague Mitchell Ratner,[8] who studied a Romanian town as part of the Harvard Adolescence Project, we asked the group of adolescents we interviewed at length a set of questions requiring formal reasoning in everyday situations.[9] Although the sample tested (nine males and thirteen females) is too small to permit statistical generalization, there is a substantial difference in the sophistication of the answers among the older teenagers questioned.[10] Correct responses are correlated with years of successfully completed schooling: more educated youth did better on the average. This effect was produced by the males, however, since both age and school effects are greater for males than for females. As with the more structured tests, the effects of schooling on females and on males are difficult to compare: many fewer females reach secondary school, and those who do are probably unusual in other ways having to do with motivation and family characteristics. It is likely that the traditional expectation that girls would spend the later teen years at home helping out and preparing for marriage has, until recently, kept many capable young women from receiving the training that would have enabled them to cope in a familiar way with these questions.

Younger children tended to answer each "social counterfactual" question in the negative: a teacher could not teach falsehood, a policeman cannot steal. Older adolescents not only realized that such generalizations could easily be false in a particular instance, but they also frequently couched their answers in terms of a realistic (if rather cynical) awareness of the subtle requirements of correct behavior. Abdelaziz pointed out, when asked whether a teacher could teach something that was not true, that the teacher might well teach something he himself believed (giving fortune-telling as an example) but that was not really so. Older adolescents often responded to questions about whether authority figures could violate their trust with variations on, "Are you kidding?" When Kabiri was asked whether a judge could jail an innocent man he said, "Yes. Think how many innocent men are in jail." Several younger children, however, gave a simple no to all seven social counterfactual questions. The role of formal schooling was strikingly obvious in the responses of several of the males Douglas tested, as they thought briefly about a complex problem, asked for paper, and then worked out the answers as Cartesian products!

Moral Reasoning in Zawiya

We were more concerned with the relationship of formal reasoning to social issues in the lives of adolescents, and we were especially interested in moral judgment as a form of social thinking. The most influential cross-cultural work on moral reasoning has been that of Kohlberg and his associates (Kohlberg 1964, 1971; Kohlberg and Gilligan 1971; Snarey 1984). Kohlberg's treatment of moral reasoning draws heavily on Piaget's stage theory of the development of formal thought (Piaget 1932). Kohlberg's theory emphasizes the transition from conventional rule-following to increased reliance on internalized moral principles as adolescence progresses. We did not strictly apply Kohlberg's testing procedures to the Zawiya sample, since it would have required a more extensive study than time permitted. We did present to our "clinical" informants a modified version of a social dilemma used by Kohlberg and Gilligan, however, and we asked several other questions related to social and moral cognition.

We posed a problem Kohlbergians have often used, the "Heinz" dilemma of a man whose wife is dying of a disease for which the only medicine is controlled by a druggist who demands more money than the man can raise. We did not, as has been usual in Kohlberg's research, ask directly whether the man would be justified in stealing the medicine; rather we asked our adolescent informants to suggest what he might do. Zawiya adolescents typically did not mention the possibility of the man's stealing the drug until all other options had been exhausted. Most often it was suggested that the man could surely reason with the druggist and get him to take payment over time or that relatives would lend the necessary money. Several of these answers showed the elaborate and subtle ways Moroccans enlist the support of others.

Each adolescent was also asked to suggest a personal moral dilemma,[11] and the responses gave us some insight into personal styles and preoccupations. Several secondary school male students responded, like Abdelaziz, by recalling instances in which a friend wanted to copy their work in school. These examples were not discussed in terms of universalizing conceptions of the general good ("What would happen if everyone cheated?"), but rather in terms of a realistic assessment of the relative cost of disappointing a friend or being punished by a teacher. Abdelaziz, asked to make up a dilemma, said "You might know somebody who's fleeing the police and comes to your house. If you tell the police, they'll send him to prison for twelve years, and people will say you did a bad thing; but if you don't tell, the police might punish you, perhaps with three years in prison."

In this "prisoner's dilemma," as in his real examples concerning school, Abdelaziz asks whether to follow a legal rule and both hurt a friend and suffer censure from the community, or to break the law and be severely punished. Such responses leave Abdelaziz sounding "conventional" in Kohlberg's terms, but they also reflect vividly the actual content of Zawiya ethics, in which reciprocal obligations to friends and family are central.

Females were asked to recount a moral dilemma from their own lives, and they and a few males were also given a hypothetical dilemma concerning choice of a spouse. While the content was varied, the personal dilemmas often focused on maintaining relationships. A girl in her early twenties had been told by her father to stop being friends with a neighbor girl who he felt had a bad reputation, and was torn by her conflicting loyalty to her family and to her friend. Her solution tried to satisfy both, still seeing the girl, but less than before and out of view of her family. A girl of sixteen had fought with a good friend and they were not speaking; her dilemma concerned who should make the first move in settling things. Finally she did, since the relationship was very important to her.

The marriage dilemma was phrased as follows: "A couple is in love and wants to marry but their parents oppose it; what should they do?" It elicited a variety of creative responses and an interesting variation by age, as well as echoing the emphasis on maintaining relationships, especially with family. The girls questioned ranged from fourteen to the late twenties, and both the younger and older ones said the girl should follow her parents' advice and not marry the young man, while four sixteen-year-olds said the couple should marry in any case. Three young men (fourteen, eighteen, and eighteen) were also asked this dilemma, and all said the couple should make their own choice. However, no one suggested an open break with the parents, and it was in preventing this break that much creativity came into play. Thus a sixteen-year-old suggested that the young man could sneak into the girl's room and stage a mock argument, including the girl's saying "But what about the baby?" At this point the parents would probably rush in and insist on the marriage they had opposed. Another sixteen-year-old said the couple should enlist the help of a doctor, who would explain to the parents that the daughter's health would fail progressively unless she could marry the man she loved. More realistically, four girls and one boy said the couple could run away and return and beg for reconciliation after they married and had children. A young man of eighteen gave several alternatives that would allow the couple to marry without alienating the parents. First, he said they could wait until the parents "were not there," that is, had died. When it was suggested that that might be a long wait, he said the young man could beg his parents to change their minds—daily. He finally said that the young woman could lose her virginity and force the marriage, but this was the least desirable alternative. Thus maintaining relationships and paying attention to the effects on all involved, rather than adherence to an abstract principle like "it is the couple's right to choose," was the main goal in solving these moral dilemmas (see Gilligan 1982).

ADOLESCENT ASPIRATIONS

Zawiya is primarily a traditional rural community with but a handful of persons occupying white-collar jobs. When they are asked what they hope for their own futures, however, the youth of Zawiya readily imagine a very different set of circumstances and project themselves into skilled trades and the professions.

Career

We asked 102 adolescents, "What do you hope for in your future?", purposely making the question general to see what range of answers we would get. Still, most young people answered in terms of a job they hoped to have. Table 8.1 shows the way boys and girls responded.

Perhaps the most striking feature of these responses is that over 40 percent of these young people hope to be teachers. This is understandable for several reasons. For most young people the teacher is probably the most salient nonfamily adult, and the source of powerful new hopes and frustrations. Several families in the neighborhood had young men who were currently teachers, so role models were readily available. Furthermore, for young people of this social level, it is more likely they can complete the level of education necessary to be a teacher (two years of post–high school training for a primary teacher, in 1982) than pursue a higher degree in medicine, law, or an academic field. Being a teacher is especially an ideal of the young, who have not yet reached the secondary school level they must complete in order to teach. In fact, since only a small minority of students finishes high school, it is unlikely that many of these young people will become teachers or be able to pursue other professional occupations.

Similar proportions of males and females wanted to be teachers or to pursue other professional careers. Among the professions, both boys and girls mentioned doctor, lawyer, and school principal; one girl mentioned pharmacist. In this culture where many (both Moroccans and outsiders) assume that the sexes are not equal, at least the schooled young women have the same high aspirations for their futures as their male counterparts.

More boys than girls mentioned nonprofessional jobs, especially crafts like carpentry and welding; for girls, such craft jobs would consist of sewing or embroidery—and such jobs can seldom provide more than a partial income. Many of the boys and girls who wanted these jobs were sixteen or

TABLE 8.1
Adolescents' Future Aspirations

Response	Males (N = 45)	Females (N = 57)
1 Teacher (primary, secondary, or college)	47%	37%
2 Other professional jobs (including engineer, doctor)	20	16
3 Nonprofessional jobs (sales, police, crafts)	27	9
4 Good family life	2	9
5 Well off materially	0	12
6 Other responses	4	18

older and already practicing a craft. Thus in general, interest in these jobs is more realistic than the more widespread desire to be a teacher.

A total of twelve girls, but only one young boy, explicitly aspired to a good family or material life. Boys too are interested in a good material life, but they express this in terms of job aspirations; some girls still expect to be supported and do not focus on job roles. Several young people (including one boy) said their hope for the future was "nothing," since they were not educated or had failed out of school. As one girl of sixteen said when we asked "What do you hope for in your future?" "How [could I have a future]? I'm not educated."

Future Residence

We wondered whether young people planned to stay in the same semi-rural area all their lives and thus asked where they hoped to live after they married. In general, more girls than boys wanted to live in a city (57 percent versus 36 percent), while more boys than girls wanted to stay in Zawiya or Kabar (55 percent versus 35 percent). This sex difference is probably related to two things: boys expect to live with their families in town after marriage while girls may move with their husbands, and girls are more eager to escape Zawiya since it is they who have to wait in line for water and mop up the dust that blows in from the unpaved streets. When we looked at the average educational levels of the persons making each choice, they were quite similar except that the girls choosing Zawiya or Kabar were relatively less educated than the others.

Whether the new couple will live with the groom's family or in a separate household is another aspect of residence after marriage. We expected that more educated young people would prefer to live by themselves, but we found no clear difference in the preference to live with parents or by themselves based on age, sex, years of school passed, or school level (primary, secondary, or out of school). There was a tendency for girls to say they preferred to live separately as a couple more frequently than did boys.

BEING ALONE

An observation often made of American adolescents is that they want to spend a great deal of their time alone, whether to withdraw from the pressures of social or family life or to think about the future. The time-sampling research of Csikszentmihalyi and Larson with suburban Chicago high school students, for example, found that they both emphasized the importance of having time to spend alone and did in fact spend 25 percent of their waking hours each week in their rooms or in other solitary settings (1984, 59).

A dramatic difference between American and Moroccan society is that in the latter, few people of any age spend time alone. A person who wanted to be alone very much would be considered suspicious or a deviant. Indeed, when Susan worked in the Peace Corps in Zawiya and tried to substitute standing in the corner for the supposedly more severe corporal punishment for preschoolers, it had to be stopped at once. Small children were terribly upset by being separated from the group, even in the same room, and cried as if heartbroken. To be set apart from the group—to not comform—is a problem for many American adolescents; in Morocco, being apart physically seems relatively more upsetting.

Although we were aware of this general trend, we wondered whether adolescence might involve increased desire to be alone. In our intensive interviews we asked, "Do you ever want to be alone?" For girls, the answer in general was no, although a few older girls expressed some interest. An eleven-year-old said, "No, never," while a twelve-year-old said, "Where? Sometimes I go back and forth to school alone, if I'm mad or don't find anyone to walk with. Sometimes I sit alone at recess, if I don't want to play because I'm sick. I don't think at all then, and I've never wanted to be alone at home."

The latter answer both expresses surprise at the idea and reminds us of one important constraint on being alone: very few homes have any extra space.

A few older girls indicated some interest in being alone. A nineteen-year-old said, "I never wanted to be alone, . . . although yes, sometimes recently, I'm alone and embroider. I don't think about anything then." Her demeanor was revealing; she laughed a little as she answered. We knew from other conversations that she was very concerned about getting married, and her giggles suggested she may have been thinking about that.

An older (age twenty), more educated girl seemed to have the closest pattern to American adolescents: "Yes, I've liked to be alone for quite a while now, in the house but not outside. I read, listen to music or just sit. Sometimes I think about my future; I want to be a pharmacist." This response was uncommon, even among older girls. However, this was the most educated girl we worked with, her family was one of the most well-to-do, and she and a sister had their own room, unlike most girls, who share with several siblings. More typical was the response of a twenty-one-year-old: "No, I get bored alone at home. I never want to be alone; I want company."

Generally, Moroccans of all ages and both sexes expect to spend most of their time in company with others. Teenage boys, like girls, are usually found in pairs or larger groups when they are outside the home. Older males have much greater control over their own time, however, and while they choose to spend much of it in the company of one or a few friends, they may also decide to spend some of it alone. Increased reflectiveness, and an occasional desire to perform this reflection in private, appears to be somewhat characteristic of at least male Zawiya adolescents. Continued schooling is associated with this desire, whether as cause or effect, and as a result the more educated cohort of Zawiya males is more likely to mention wanting to be alone.

DREAMS

We asked young people about their dreams, both because dreams have figured so prominently in Western (Freudian) thinking about personality and because Moroccans themselves are interested in dreams and their interpretation. Many Moroccan interpreters say a dream usually means the opposite of its contents, so dreaming of getting money may mean one will lose it. Others interpret such a dream more literally to mean one will get rich. Other conventional dream meanings mentioned by Zawiya friends include various associations, such as a lost tooth with the death of someone known to the dreamer, black and "white" (green) olives with bad and good omens respectively, and the snake with the Ramadan fast. Dream interpreters who will translate the symbolic content of one's dreams into prescriptions and predictions for one's life are still common in Morocco, and literate young people are likely to have seen one of several traditional dream books in Arabic.[12]

Susan collected sixteen dreams in some detail from girls. This is a small sample, and although we knew these girls quite well, we do not claim to be able to do a clinical analysis of the dream material. However, the themes give us some idea of these young women's concerns. Some of the girls who reported their dreams had asked female relatives known to be good at "unraveling" dreams to interpret them, while others paid their dreams little attention. Among the dreams reported by girls, the majority included frightening contents.[13]

A nineteen-year-old girl, much concerned about getting herself married, had the following dream.[14]

It was like I was at BL's wedding [a girlfriend about her age who had recently married], going to her husband's house. The bride was wearing long blue trousers, a long white net dress under which the pants showed, and a white cape. The bride and groom were in Kabar, in the street in a car, with others following on foot [the dreamer included]. I heard people, the bride's neighbors, coming along and saying, "All our water bottles [plastic, to carry water from the public well to the house] are torn." They didn't have the bottles with them. I heard them and told B, and her husband overheard and said, "Don't say anything. Shh—people will hear. Here's some money, if they're sad about the water bottles [i.e., to get new ones]." He gave me several ten dirham notes [about $1.60 each] and I passed them out to A, X, and K, who were helping with the wedding. [The first two are close relatives of the dreamer, and all 3 did help with the actual wedding.] B's husband said "You helped a lot, here's twenty dirhams"—and then I woke up. I asked my aunt about it, but she didn't know how to explain it.

Young women love to go to weddings, where they have an opportunity to dress up and enjoy themselves dancing and singing, and perhaps to be glimpsed by a young man seeking a wife (or by his mother). Indeed, the dreamer had attended the wedding in her dream a few months earlier and had embarrassed her relatives by wearing much makeup; there had been a recent death in the family so she should have been more subdued. In her own mind, and perhaps in the minds of others, there was also some question of the dreamer's virtue, as she decided on the best strategy to find a husband. One wonders if her concern about torn water bottles in the dream, namely, damaged containers of an essential fluid substance, could be related to concerns about her own reproductive system.

A concern with protecting virtue or with physical safety was apparent in several of the girls' frightening dreams, as were the negative aspects of relating to males. These dreams also reflect some ways for girls to deal with unrelated males.

A fourteen-year-old girl related the following dream, which she said she had had repeatedly. "I dreamt a young man was following me; I didn't know him. My feet were heavy, like they were stuck and I couldn't move them. I don't know where I was, but I found a sea. I walked into it; it was better to die in the water than to be killed by that guy, or . . ." She was too shy to say sexually molested, but the pause conveyed that concern. [15] A fifteen-year-old's dream has a similar theme, but in it she has the presence of mind to extricate herself from the threatening situation. She also portrays the role of male relatives in protecting young women.

It was night, and I was walking along the road to Kabar, approaching the small train station, with my little sisters [ages five and seven], carrying a bag of oranges. A car stopped; it was light blue and there were three men in it with cloth over their faces, so only their eyes showed. They wanted to "steal" the three of us. I saw a shop open and ran to it with the girls, and softly told the man in it to say he was my father, so the others would go away. I said "Father," and he said "Yes, daughter?" and the thieves went away. I gave the shopkeeper an orange and went home.

A twenty-two-year-old with a good reputation, but unmarried and quite concerned about it, had the following dream. Again we see the importance of male relatives, this time in an idiom that will delight Freudians.

Last night, I dreamt my oldest brother was sleeping in the kitchen on the second floor. I was going up the stairs, and saw a snake stuck on the ceiling, with just his head sticking out. He was big and old, with a wide head like a fish and something stiff like knitting needles sticking out, two from the top and two from the bottom lip; he was about a half a meter long. I called out to wake my [older] brother and he got up and came over, but it didn't bother him. I ran past, up the stairs to the roof. My brother tried to pick up the snake with a stick, but he couldn't—it just followed me. My younger brother [age eighteen] followed me up; I was crying and screaming. Before I saw him, I was on the roof and it had no wall around it, and I saw our next door neighbor and her husband on their roof. She said, "Come over here—what's the matter?" I said, "You're not a good woman, and your daughter isn't good. I won't go there; it's better to let the snake bite me." She asked me to come again, and then my younger brother appeared, and I didn't even answer her. My brother picked up a big stick with a nail in it, slammed it into the snake's head, and lifted it up and threw it into the vacant house across the street. He said, "It's OK; I've thrown him away." I was quiet, but I watched the snake: it lifted its head and looked at me. Maybe it was dying, maybe it was still alive, but it was far away, so I wasn't frightened of it anymore.

There are several interesting aspects of this dream. In reality, brothers are supposed to protect their sisters from attacks on their honor, represented in the dream by the "phallic" snake.[16] This girl in fact gets on well with her eldest brother and fights with the one who saved her in the dream, so that aspect is puzzling. Around the time of the dream, the female members of her family were feuding with the neighbor she refused to speak to on the roof. Her concern in the dream that the woman and her daughter were not "good," and her refusal to join them, reflects the cultural concern that girls may be negatively affected by peers with loose morals. Finally, one wonders if there is a wishful aspect to this dream, frightening as it seems. This girl was at the upper end of the age range for marriage and had no current prospects. She was unlikely to meet such a threat in reality, due in part to the combination of her own proper behavior and her family's stress on their honor. She would likely have welcomed a male's expression of interest in her.

When considering the frightening dreams and how many concern male aggression against females, it is noteworthy that several of Susan's clinical informants described local instances of rape to her; one of the most detailed accounts was from an eleven-year-old girl, who told of both male and female victims. We do not take this to mean that rape is necessarily common, but that the possibility is made known to girls who might be vulnerable, both for their protection and to frighten them from taking any chances. Yet, as we have noted, some girls do take chances when they decide to meet boys secretly. On a conscious level, they are less concerned with male aggression than with being "led on" and having their reputations ruined, as was poignantly described by Amina, in chapter 6. However, a fear of male aggression appears in their dreams.

The dreams told Douglas by male informants reflect several of the same concerns as those of females. While many of the males' dreams concerned mundane occurrences such as school events or conversations with friends, most that were recalled at length or after the passage of time involved frightening or uncanny themes. Particularly striking were dreams of being immobilized in the face of a terrifying assailant or mysterious force. These dreams are typically considered to be the result of a spirit-creature, the *bughatat* (rather like the older European sense of an animal nightmare or incubus), who seizes the sleeper and may cause physical harm if he or she does not awaken. Males often named and described the bughatat, while females did not. The recounting of such nightmares illustrates the ambivalent reactions of educated older adolescents toward the "folk" beliefs of their parents. On the one hand the high school student who feels himself a part of the modern scientific world is disdainful of the seemingly superstitious and magical practices of his parents; on the other, he has just had firsthand experience of the power of the bughatat and therefore of the world of the unseen. Under such circumstances several young men we knew remained skeptical about much of their parents' beliefs while accepting the copper rings, iron knives, or salt for the pocket offered to control the bughatat. These traditional remedies were described as effective by each of the persons who told us of using them, and almost every male Douglas asked knew at least secondhand of experiences with nightmare visitations. We suspect, though no systematic study has been done, that these problems begin or drastically increase with puberty. One informant said specifically that little children were not bothered, since one needed 'aql, reasoning power, to conceive of the bughatat.

Rashid, one of the older male adolescents we knew best, reported dreams at various times during the year. Earlier we discussed his seeking his mother's help against troublesome nightmares. He also dreamed he had died. When he told his mother this dream, she said it meant the opposite—that he would have a long life. In a manner typical of our conversations about possession, Rashid alluded to spirit-creatures (*jnun*) but did not say the word, which was characteristic of the circumspection with which Moroccans discuss those they call "the owners of the earth."

Another of Rashid's dreams, from late in the summer vacation, involved the school setting (as did many fragmentary dreams from other male informants).

> He found that it was the first day of school. He was at home and had breakfast, took his cousin's taxi to Kabar and went to the junior high school, where he had to wait an hour and a half or more for the gates to be opened. There were friends of his there, and they talked about who had passed last spring's exams, and probably about other things. Then the students entered and the officials were reading class assignments off a list. He entered his class, but did not recall any content from there. He woke to find he had only dreamed this and was angry it was not true that school was beginning, because he was bored with having nothing to do.

Later in the fall, Rashid dreamed that a jailed relative had been released. He mentioned the dream in the morning to his mother, and she said she had dreamed the same thing. Such experiences, retold to family and friends, probably serve to sustain the belief that dreams are real communications rather than the result of unconscious fantasies (see Freud 1900; Kilborne 1981).

The last dream report comes from Sa'id, who was sixteen when he recounted this dream. Although Sa'id is unusual, even unique in a variety of ways, his dream illustrates several issues we found expressed by other adolescents as well: fear of aggression and injury, impeded movement, and desire for support from relatives or friends.

On this occasion Sa'id said he seldom dreams, perhaps twice a month. Douglas emphasized that he thought dreams were very interesting in a study like ours, and Sa'id said he had had a dream when his "brother" (i.e., his maternal uncle) was away from home several years previously:

He was out alone at night and a thief [shfar] chased him. He ran into the neighborhood flour mill [taHuna], then ran out the other door. He ran to the Suiqa with the thief chasing him and, by Hamad's shop, he fell. The thief was catching up, but his legs "stuck" [i.e., he could not make them move, often a sign of the bughatat]. He saw his "brother" [uncle] coming and tried to warn him, but couldn't talk. He turned and saw a number of thieves (about five). He and his "brother" were caught by them, and they all got in a big black car and drove into a kind of tunnel under the earth. Here he saw many dead people who had been slaughtered and skinned. He was terrified and got out somehow with his "brother." Then his "father" [grandfather] came with police and caught the thieves, and he woke up.

This dream repeated some aspects of a family story Saʻid had heard when he was younger, concerning the sister of a distant cousin who was allegedly kidnapped and taken to Casablanca, where she was held captive in a basement. Saʻid's account of this dream followed his recounting of that kidnapping incident. The dream reflects the wishful role of the grandfather who was so important in raising him and casts his feared uncle as a brotherly collaborator. The dream also expresses clearly Saʻid's fearfulness and sense of uncanny influences.

SPIRITS AND POSSESSION

Males in Morocco typically explain nightmares by referring to a spiritual being that attacks the sleeper. The subject of jnun or spirits came up in a number of interviews with male adolescents, and the existence and powers of jnun and local saints was the most frequent topic mentioned by male adolescents when contrasting their own religious views with those of their parents. While female adolescents also typically believe in jnun, the power of local saints, and magical practices, these topics rarely arose in interviews, although we heard many stories about girls visiting a magician or a saint's tomb to increase chances of marriage. When Abdelaziz and Kabiri described their experiences, both knew about the characteristics of bughatat but said they personally had had no trouble. When asked about jnun, Abdelaziz began telling of an experience of his that happened roughly five years ago (when he was about fourteen):

He was walking alone just near the flour mill near his house. There was a party, probably a wedding, in progress, and he saw what seemed to be a cat in the street ahead of him. It meowed at him, then seemed to be trying to block his path, and grew much larger (he held his arms out indicating perhaps three feet in length). He turned to run, and suddenly found it blocking his path behind. He was terrified, but somehow got past and ran home.

Abdelaziz then elaborated about jnun generally: they can take human form, even looking like someone one knows well, but their feet are usually those of a camel (others said the feet are those of a cow); if one looks at them in a mirror one sees their true form. Abdelaziz and Kabiri had heard of an event nearby involving two truck drivers from Fez.

They stopped late one night for a beautiful young woman who flagged them down. She was dressed up, wearing white, and got into the truck. The driver's companion was sitting by her (probably trying to make a pass at her), and she "struck" his arm. He called out; the driver laughed at him, and she then struck him in the eyes so he could not see. He drove the truck off the road, and when the police came they could find no evidence of her having been there.

Most Moroccans would understand this story to refer to the powerful and ubiquitous female spirit (*jinniya*) Aisha Qandisha.[17] "Lady (*lalla*) Aisha," as she is also called, is frequently mentioned as the possessing spirit responsible for a person's strange behavior or (in males) loss of sexual potency. Treating the problems she causes her human targets is the business of the Hamadsha, a Moroccan "Sufi" brotherhood with numerous adherents in Zawiya. Their music and dance place stricken men or women in a trance which helps to control or satisfy the possessing *jinn* (Crapanzano 1973). Like many of their schoolmates, Abdelaziz and Kabiri are skeptical about the practices used to deal with spiritual influences or to summon the help of a (deceased) popular saint; they believe much of the invocation of the spiritual power (*baraka*) of local saints borders on the sacrilegious. On the other hand, they have seen friends and relatives "struck" with a variety of unexplainable physical and psychological troubles, and often these appear to be reduced or eliminated by the help of the Hamadsha, other Sufi groups, or by recourse to various traditional magical practices. Thus they are ambivalent, and they will probably maintain their skepticism until they or a family member needs help, at which time traditional remedies will be tried along with European-style medical treatment.

MAKING SENSE OF ZAWIYA

In conclusion, we place our description of adolescence in this small Moroc-can town in the context of the broader comparative questions with which we began: To what extent does adolescence exist as a life stage in Zawiya? How do the experiences of Zawiya youth correspond to those hypothesized by Western scholars?

While physical puberty is recognized for both sexes, adolescence has no clear or universally agreed-on counterpart in Zawiya. The concept of ado-lescence as a life stage and a more general readiness to associate subtle psychological changes with the physical period between childhood and adulthood are relatively recent importations to Zawiya and are directly asso-ciated with formal education. In several ways, education is a major variable in determining the extent and quality of the "adolescent experience." Young people who had attended secondary school were much more likely than oth-ers to name a stage of adolescence when we asked them to describe stages of the life cycle in Zawiya. They also cited psychological changes in adoles-cence, while others usually cited only physical changes, we assume because secondary students study adolescence at school. The availability of new types of jobs for educated people means that now virtually all families try to have their sons and daughters complete primary school. While in the past many would have married in their late teens, now many continue their edu-cation. Hence their lives contain one of the key features of adolescence—a lengthy liminal or borderline period of physical maturity before the individ-ual becomes an employed and mated householder. In a superficial sense, many of the youth of Zawiya have experiences with family, friends, lovers, and teachers that parallel those of Western young people the same age. Since fewer girls than boys attend high school, not as many of them experi-ence these conditions. The parents, older siblings, and teachers of teenagers expect some thoughtless or unreasoning behavior from youth, but they do not expect, nor do they usually encounter, serious problems.

One reason for the limited intergenerational conflict in Zawiya is the value placed on the family instead of the individual as the basic social unit. Young people are part of a nuclear or larger family, with many relatives liv-ing nearby, and they usually subordinate their wishes to those of the group. Relations among family members are usually very warm, and most youth said they felt closest to their mothers. While siblings may squabble, intense arguments with parents are rare and showing respect for elders is important.

Both sharing and reciprocity are major values in Moroccan culture, and they are learned especially in the realm of friendship. One finds these values within the family where they are obligatory, while in a friendship the application of these principles is more open to negotiation, as will be the case in much of adult life.[18]

Young people want friends who will show an interest in them and with whom they can share both material goods and their feelings and secrets. Friends are nearly always of the same sex, mainly because of the expected social separation of the sexes. Girls often talk to each other while doing housework or embroidering, while boys may just stroll and visit. Boys may spend time together participating in sports, especially soccer, while only young girls play games together. In friendship one can both experiment with social roles outside the family and seek self-validation from peers—who have more current social values than parents and who are not charged with guarding one's virtue as are siblings.

Both sexes in Morocco desire trust and reciprocity in a friend, but at the same time feel ambivalent because they fear their friends will disappoint them. However, the ambivalence and distrust seem stronger for males; it seems that females are less often or less seriously disappointed by their friends, and that in general it is easier for them to maintain intimate relationships with same-sex peers.[19]

While the norm in Zawiya is that single males and females should not interact with each other, they currently often do, in school or in other public settings. Dating is disapproved, but couples manage to spend time together, with very different consequences for males and females. Girls who agree to spend time with boys risk their reputations and perhaps future chances of marriage, while the boys involved are not censured. Girl enter a relationship hoping for marriage, but expecting much less. Boys are socialized to admire secluded females, but also to pursue relationships with them. Thus if they succeed in the latter, their desire for the former is dashed.

Although couples interact today much more than in the past, most marriages are still arranged. Traditional girls wait for their families to be asked, and even more adventuresome girls and boys must seek the approval of their parents. One cohort of females appears to have been skipped over by males looking for partners during a period when bride-prices rose rapidly and jobs were hard to find; they face a problematic future in a town where one is not really a grown woman without a husband and children.

Deviant behavior, often seen as resulting from stress, exists in Zawiya, but it involves a small minority of adolescents. Female deviance consists mainly of openly breaking rules of sexual propriety. Male deviance is more varied and includes the excessive use of alcohol, marijuana, or hashish; occasional use by older adolescent males is tolerated. Petty thefts by young adolescent males are also frowned on but tolerated, while more serious crimes are rare. Mental illness was a rare form of adolescent deviance in the neighborhood we studied, but we heard of a few cases. Youth sometimes react to the stress of delayed marriage, end-of-school exams, or other problems with what Westerners might call a hysterical illness—one for which there is no apparent physical cause. Symptoms often include being bedridden and asocial, unable to function normally. Both medical and supernatural cures are sought, and often these are effective. Suicide is rare.

The teen years in Zawiya are a time of changed self-awareness and of the formation of a newly sophisticated sense of oneself as a social actor. The successful older adolescent, the one with 'aql, will be aware how he or she comes across to others, will have a clear conception of how his or her behavior is judged by the context in which it occurs and by the company a person keeps, and will know how to enlist the support of neighbors and avoid conflict while reconciling often conflicting expectations of family, friends, and the larger society. These skills may not translate into superior performance on standardized tests, but they indicate a well-honed sensitivity that allows the Moroccan adult to see a wide range of possible motives and consequences of each person's actions and to take moral considerations into account in a practical way.

Sociologists have usually written about adolescence or related concepts from an American or European perspective, while anthropologists have tried to move beyond it. Although Margaret Mead stressed the cultural influence on adolescence, the factors she cited as important in her analysis of the period in Samoa and America would not predict the generally calm nature of the adolescent years in Zawiya. She felt that traditional Samoan youth lacked many of the problems of their American peers because Samoans' futures would be very similar to those of their parents. Zawiyans are more like Americans than Samoans in the sense that they live in a period of rapid change and cannot turn to their often uneducated parents for advice about schoolwork or about the details of the professional careers to which many aspire.

Zawiya youth do not exhibit the level of rebellion or conflict that many Americans seem to feel is natural in this age-group. One reason is the hierarchical nature of Moroccan society, fostering the great respect shown to the aged. Another is the importance of the family unit rather than the individual. Zawiya youth generally do what is best for the family rather than what is best for themselves as individuals; this eliminates many of the sources of the conflict Americans expect.

While Morocco produces many strong and dynamic individuals, an orientation of individualism is uncommon. For Americans, to whom individual autonomy is important, it may be difficult to grasp Moroccan ideas of self and self-awareness which are developed during and immediately after the teen years. We noted that the average Westerner may think of self as an independent, individually constituted unit. American social scientists, especially those of the symbolic interaction school, corrected this perspective by pointing out that our ideas of self are also necessarily influenced by our social environment.[20]

Goffman, in *Presentation of Self in Everyday Life* (1959), uses the idiom of the theater to illustrate the influence of social context. His description of an individual actor portraying a character evoked through social interaction with the audience was used in chapter 1 to illustrate two aspects of self. While we have found Goffman's analysis useful in some ways, it is not fully appropriate to characterize Moroccan social reality.[21] Goffman emphasizes "impression management," thus introducing a moral aspect of the social performer: "Instead of attempting to achieve certain ends by acceptable means, they can attempt to achieve the *impression* that they are achieving certain ends by acceptable means. . . . The observer's need to rely on the representation of things itself creates the possibility of misrepresentation" (1959, 250–251, emphasis added).

Goffman's use of "misrepresentation" suggests deceit, as does the phrase "impression management." This is often an inappropriate description of varied self-presentation in cultural settings where social context is very important.

Several recent writers on the Middle East have stressed the importance of the social construction of self as a corrective to too much emphasis on the individual aspect.[22]

Abu-Lughod refers to the self in her discussion of the discrepancy between the sentiments expressed in poetic and in mundane discourses by the Awlad 'Ali Bedouin in Egypt's Western Desert. For example, a woman may react to a divorce by saying she really did not care for her husband, showing a culturally approved stoicism that brings her honor in people's eyes. Yet on another occasion she may recite to her close friends a short poem that bemoans the loss. Abu-Lughod argues that "consideration of the messages conveyed in the two discourses and the relationship between them reveals much about the 'self' in Bedouin society and ultimately about the relationship between culture and individual experience" (1985, 246). She does not claim that the poetic discourse reveals a "true self" as opposed to a more socially influenced honorable self, but rather that "there are at least two ideologies in Bedouin culture, each providing models of and for different types of experience" (1986, 258). These discourses are not rigid templates, "but rather languages that people can use to express themselves" (1986, 258). Thus Abu-Lughod reveals two aspects of self for the Awlad ʿAli, both socially constructed. She also states that people are not automatons but use these two aspects to "express themselves"; she describes something that sounds more like the Western individual view of self, one that chooses among social constructions. The difference from most Western treatments of self is in the balance of individual and social constructions, with the social aspect more important among the Awlad ʿAli.

Criticizing the moral evaluation implicit in Goffman's discussion of impression management, Abu-Lughod notes that this view "misconstrues and devalues the meaning of social conformity in Bedouin society. . . . There exists no source of self-definition or evaluation other than the [moral] standard. . . . The fusion of self-regard and the respect of others makes meaningless Goffman's distinction between realizing moral standards and giving the impression of realizing them" (1986, 237–238).

The necessity for these Bedouin to fit into their local community is more intense than for the youth of Zawiya, who have somewhat broader social options, yet lack the range of alternate ideologies and life-styles available to American youth. Still, the respect of others is very important to self-esteem in Zawiya.

However, some recent accounts of Morocco emphasize so strongly the importance of context for the Moroccan self that it appears people are "determined" by context and lack individually constituted selves. Geertz's influential work treats Moroccans as "contextualized persons": "The selves that bump and jostle each other in the alleys of Sefrou gain their definition from associative relations they are imputed to have with the society that surrounds them. They are contextualized persons" (1983, 66). A similar perspective is found in Rosen's (1984) *Bargaining for Reality*, also based on work in the Moroccan town of Sefrou. Moroccans as characterized by Rosen live in a social context that they have "negotiated," that is, that they have implicitly or explicitly defined in their interactions with others, and this is closely related to their concept of self:

> The image of the self that emerges is not . . . one of a personally fashioned entity—an individual who has by whatever spiritual or psychological means created an inner self distinctive from all others. Nor is it a concept of the self as *persona*, a mask presented to others that conceals the deeper domain of one's true self. Rather, the Moroccan concept of person is one in which the individual is *always* a situated actor—an individual who maneuvers within the realm of relationships, circum-

stances, and human qualities to cumulate a set of publicly seen and worldly consequent traits and ties. It is a world—and hence a self—in which people are known by their situated obligations and by the impact their actions have on the entire chain of obligations by which they and their society are known. Human beings do not create themselves, but they do place themselves in those contexts—with teachers, partners, kinsmen, and strangers—through which their bargained-for relationships will yield an identity of their own. (1984, 178–179, emphasis added)

Rosen's concept of self seems to deny the self-as-individual and to focus on the self created by interaction with others, a self that varies with context and has no stable character. However, the fact that the Moroccans he describes "place themselves in those contexts" through which he says they form an identity implies the existence of both: self-as-agent, and self-as-product in social interactions.[23]

We do not claim that an "individual self" is uninfluenced by the wider society, but that one can carry norms and values from one context to the next rather than constantly shifting them to fit the situation. The youth of Zawiya describe a self-awareness ('aql) that recognizes the importance of context, as well as a self-awareness that some contexts are to be avoided if one is not to compromised. Immoral companions might lead one astray; light-headed companions might provoke one into a fight which would exhibit a lack of 'aql.

Adolescence has been as much invented as discovered by Western philosophers and social scientists in the last two centuries. The picture of youthful idealism and romantic passion suggested by Rousseau, the "storm-and-stress"-full period described by Hall, the renegotiated "Oedipal" crisis adduced by Freud, the reflective cognitive style defined by Piaget—all these are theoretical constructions by writers responding both to the effects of cultural changes in Western societies and to the demands of their own theoretical premises. While each of these theoretical stances can be applied to some of the data presented in this volume, none can be fully corroborated in Zawiya. We lack the detailed personal histories and the locally validated tests to adequately apply theories produced in other social climates. We know enough of Zawiya to conclude that some Western theoretical claims will never make much sense there, and the Moroccan social science that would write an eclectic theory is still developing.

Despite our interest in theories of adolescence based on psychoanalysis and the work of Freud and Erikson, we can on the basis of our data only sketch the outlines of adolescent psychodynamics in Zawiya. At an individual level, for example, doubt about one's own capacities can reflect blurred lines of respect and responsibility in parenting (see chap. 7). Boys especially need to redirect their childhood dependence on mother and older siblings to male companions as they enter the adult world of male-centered job and political hierarchy.

Erikson's account of an adolescent identity beleaguered by contradictory role expectations (1950, 1968) sounds like it should work well in the rapidly changing Moroccan setting, but in fact we have not seen much of the "role confusion" of which Erikson writes. Zawiya youth seem to us surprisingly good at negotiating the twists and turns of daily life. The most striking resonance to Erikson's concepts is perhaps in the repeated return to issues of trust/mistrust in friendships and relationships among these young Moroccans, but the concern with how one is both judged and shaped by the company one keeps seems adaptive and sensible rather than regressive or defensive for the youth of Zawiya.

For today's young Moroccans as well as for the young Americans who concerned Sullivan (1953), it is most helpful in dealing with the joys and frustrations of the teen years to have a best friend, with whom fantasies and hopes can be shared. The transition from same-sex friendships to unlike-sex loves seems less clear-cut or absolute in Zawiya than in Sullivan's portrayal of adolescence—although more detailed clinical data are needed to show how these two domains of life relate.

Carol Gilligan's concepts of adolescent connectedness and caring have been useful in understanding Zawiya. Since the people we are describing have experienced conditions of rearing and culture different from those Gilligan portrays in *In a Different Voice* (1982), and since male as well as female Zawiya youth value reciprocity and mutual respect over abstractions of ethics, we are moved to agree with her that it is time to revise theories that see autonomy and independence as the mark of maturity.

Hall's (1904) work contains an impassioned plea for the adaptive significance of adolescent struggle—an argument that adolescence represents a necessary shaking-up of the status quo as individual youths struggle against social expectations. We have repeatedly noted that the young people of Zawiya do not seem to be in rebellion, and we have suggested that being part of familial, cultural, and religious value systems that still command respect is an important source of strength.

Increasing numbers of Zawiya youth are becoming convinced that broad change is afoot in a world where youth (*shabab*) do not fear to challenge oppression and inequity. They now see and read about the activist youth of the Middle East and Europe, and some have begun to compare this activism with their own political powerlessness. Perhaps their society, and ours, will find ways to benefit from this youthful energy—to become more equitable and humane, more reflective of ʿaql.

On the whole, youth in Zawiya seem to us to be coping with the problematic aspects of their lives better than the American literature on adolescent problems would lead us to expect. Although they are aware that their parents have a limited view of the world beyond Zawiya and Morocco, the educated youth of this community generally respect their parents' values and trust in the correctness of their religion. The years ahead will be difficult, perhaps crisis-ridden, but for many they still seem to hold the promise of better material circumstances without the loss of traditional strengths. The traditional value of ʿaql or social sense has made Moroccans sensitive to varied social contexts, and the skills required are useful in adapting to new conditions.

The young people of Zawiya are not alone in dealing gracefully with changing Muslim communities. Fernea notes that while rapid alteration in the conditions of women and the family throughout the Middle East has produced disappointment and anxiety, "an immense creativity is also present, a resourcefulness in grappling with difficult economic, social, and emotional pressures" (1985, 2). Moroccan sociologist Fatima Mernissi presents a vivid picture of today's situation: "The wonder about the Muslim world is that people still manage in these apocalyptic, revolutionary times to make sense out of absurd, despotic forces scavenging their lives, that they still have an unshakable belief in a powerful future" (1987, ix).

Despite their often impoverished circumstances, the youth of Zawiya aspire to a much more affluent life, often one taking them far beyond the scope of their semirural community and family ties. While more educated males at least may view the traditional practices of their parents with skepticism, they recognize the possibility of hidden influences on their dreams and behavior, and they have seen the efficacy of popular religious means to explain and control such influences even as they deplore folk belief as old-fashioned. On the other hand, Islam provides a sense of identity in which they take pride. They remain rooted in tradition, even as they prepare for a future beyond the dreams of their grandparents.

■ Appendix
Interview Protocols

These questions were asked of over one hundred young people individually, in Moroccan Arabic, by Susan, Douglas, or a research assistant. The answers were recorded in English.

FORM A2 ACCULTURATIVE POTENTIALS

Ego's name_____Age____Sex____ID No_____Household No____
Interviewer_____Date_____Field Station_____Page____

I. TRAVEL
Relative or other person frequently visited who resides where acculturative potential exists:

Name and relationship
Place
Distance (approx. mi.)_____Time to travel_____Means_____
Frequency of visits_____Usual length of stay_____
When did ego last visit this person_____
Who usually accompanies ego on visits_____
Reason for visits_____
Does this person visit ego_____
Usual length of stay_____
How often does ego use other means of communication with this person_____
Other comments:

II. LANGUAGES
a. _____spoken_____written_____
b. _____spoken_____written_____
c. _____spoken_____written_____
d. _____spoken_____written_____

III. MEDIA

For each of the following, ask if they own, frequency of use, and types of program preferred.

	Own?	Days/week?	Type of program?

Do you watch television?
Do you listen to radio?
Do you listen to cassettes?
Do you read outside school?_____What?_____
Do you ever go to the cinema?_____

IV. RESIDENTIAL HISTORY

Have you always lived with your parents? Yes_____ No_____

V. ASPIRATIONS AND FRIENDSHIP

What do you hope for in your future?
Want to marry?
Ideal husband/wife?
Who chooses spouse—parents or couple?
Where would you like to live after marriage and why?
How do you know you're a man/woman [grown up]?
Did you fast this Ramadan?
How many Ramadans before it?
What would you do if you were given 100,000 *reals* [$1,000]?
Everyone is dear to you at home, but who do you prefer?
Whose advice do you seek at home?
Did you ever refuse or disagree with your mother?
If yes to the above, why and what happened?
Do you have friends? Close? How many close?
How/why did you choose the close ones as best?
Are they neighbors or relatives?
What do you do with these friends?
Do kids your age, or your friends, have problems? What?
Do you have any problem(s)? What?
What do you do in your free time?

■ Glossary

'adl   notary
'a'ila   family
'amm   paternal uncle
'aql   reason, social sense
awlad   children, offspring
'azri, 'azba   unmarried male, female (also virgin)
baccalaureate   (Fr.) the high school examination diploma
baraka   blessedness, holy power
bint   girl, virgin
bughatat   nightmare creature
bulugh   physical puberty
collège   (Fr.) secondary school, junior high school
douar   village
faTar   eating rather than fasting during Ramadan
fsad   sexual immorality
fuqaha   religious scholars
ghshwa   corruption
Hadith   authenticated saying of the Prophet
haik   large rectangular cloth, used as woman's outer garment or as a cover
Hammam   public steam bath
Haram   forbidden by Islam
Hashak   colloquially "excuse me," for impolite language
Hasham   shame, modesty
Hawwa'i   active participant in sexual intercourse
Hmar   donkey
Hulum   puberty
'iyyr   to insult
insha'llah   if God wills
jama'   mosque
jellaba   long robe worn as outer garment
jnun   spirit beings (sing. *jinn*)
khall   maternal uncle

khaSm   to scold
khayal   imagination
khesser   to break
khfif   light, quick (applied to thinking)
kilma   word, truthfulness
makruh   religiously reprehensible
manay   semen
moussem   annual festival for a saint
mra   woman, nonvirgin
mTuwwr   clever, subtle in understanding
muaddin   one who calls believers to prayer
mukallaf   to be responsible (for something)
murahaqa   adolescence, puberty
nafs   desire, appetite
nefkha   pride, conceit
nisba   a characteristic, used in a name (farmer, Mexican)
niya   faith, intent
nSara   Nazarenes, Christians; refers to French in Morocco
qadiya   event, problem, affair, situation
qHb   prostitute, slut
ruH   soul, spirit
rushd   legal maturity, rationality
Sadiq   friend
SaHeb   friend, boyfriend (*SaHeba,* girlfriend)
sbu'   week, naming ceremony for seven-day-old child
shabb   people
shabab   young people, youth
shikhat   professional female dancers
sinn   age, life stage
siyyed   shrine for a saint, polite term for a male adult
suiqa   little market, shopping street
sunna   orthodox Muslim practice
suq   market area
tajine   stewlike main dish
Taysh   flighty, youthful exhuberance
tfella   to play around with (someone), to lead on
tqaf   magical spell
tqil   heavy, weighty, slow of arousal
usra   family; usually used for nuclear family
wa'iya   sophisticated
zamel   passive homosexual
zawiya   site of a saintly lineage, religious brotherhood
zenka   street

■ Notes

CHAPTER 1. INTRODUCTION

1. Like the rest of the proper names we use for residents of Zawiya, Rashid is a pseudonym, in this case for a young man who was a high school student at the time he told of his preadolescent reveries on the hillside. We have known him since he was a small boy.

2. "Zawiya" and "Kabar" are terms used locally for the two communities referred to throughout this volume; we have adopted them rather than the official names of the towns.

3. Other ethnographic descriptions of adolescence include Whiting's *Becoming a Kwoma* (1941) and Mead's *Growing up in New Guinea* (1930).

4. In spite of this limitation, Schlegel (pers. comm.) and Barry are pulling together available holocultural information in a work in progress examining adolescent socialization across cultures.

5. Paige and Paige's *The Politics of Reproductive Ritual* (1981) utilizes the holocultural method in explaining why some cultures have reproductive rituals, including initiation rites, and others do not. Briefly, they say that stateless societies use such rites to emphasize the kin group's control of the females' reproductive capacity. In state societies, this control is less tenuous and these ceremonies are not necessary. All the cultures in the Harvard Adolescence Project were currently under the domain of a state, which may explain why we found no initiation rites being practiced.

6. Using psychoanalytic concepts, Devereux (1967) develops and illustrates the thesis that the researcher's personal needs and defenses affect all aspects of social research. In the introduction to *Writing Culture*, Clifford (1986) argues that our understanding of other cultures is strongly influenced by the fact that our accounts of them are written. Maybury-Lewis (1965) and Briggs (1970) openly discuss the fieldworker's experience in the culture—a treatment that has been described as a "reflexive ethnography," one that "encounters others in relation to itself, while seeing itself as other" (Clifford 1986, 23). Recent writing on Morocco has been strikingly concerned with reports of relationships and dialogues between Western ethnographer and Moroccan subject (Rabinow 1977; Crapanzano 1980b; Dwyer 1982; Munson 1984). Kevin Dwyer's *Moroccan Dialogues* includes a detailed critical discussion of the ways field-workers have handled their relationship to the informants and communities

studied (Dwyer 1982). Some work in this genre attempts to present the voice of the informant as well by presenting dialogues (Mernissi 1984). We use excerpts from interviews on many topics since, although we have structured the questions, the adolescents may be heard speaking to a large extent in their own words.

CHAPTER 2. DAILY LIFE IN ZAWIYA

1. The day described below is not a literal account of a single day; rather it is a composite based on the routines of two girls we knew. If a girl is much older or much younger than Hakima, or if she is not attending school, her day will differ in some ways, which we describe later.

2. This account is based closely on several daily activity accounts supplied in interviews with this nineteen-year-old from a family of about average economic level.

3. It may surprise the reader to learn that, at the age of nineteen, Abdelaziz still had several years of school ahead of him. Although he was a serious student, he had repeated two years after failing the difficult year-end examinations.

4. In the quotations we present, we translate the literal meaning of the Arabic as much as possible. The interested reader can find a more complete account of this woman's life in S. Davis 1977.

5. A junior high school opened in 1987, and running water began in 1988.

6. The term *tribe (tribu)* was widely used by the French in their ethnographic portrayals of Morocco and is now in need of revision. Tribes have much less significance than formerly, and as is the case with other Moroccan social labels, tribal ties have varied import depending on the situation (see Rosen 1984).

7. During 1982, the town post office processed about $45,500 in money orders from abroad and $53,500 in money orders from inside Morocco.

8. The number and technical quality of programs in colloquial Arabic had increased dramatically by 1987.

CHAPTER 3. DEFINING ADOLESCENCE IN ZAWIYA

1. Morocco has no clear initiation ceremonies during the teen years. A few girls had heard of a small ceremony at menarche when the mother gives the girl milk and dates, but none knew anyone who had had such a ceremony; Zawiya girls were more likely to hide the onset of menstruation from their mothers. A Casablanca sample told Naamane-Guessous (1987) of menarche ceremonies in the past in which girls were made up and then went to visit neighbors. The girls of this sample also discussed menarche with their mothers. In fact, there are no specifically adolescent ceremonies at all unless one counts school graduation for the lucky few who achieve it. Ammar (1954, 183) states that no ceremonies or other social recognition marked adolescence in the Egyptian village he studied in the 1950s.

2. Male circumcision, with its several days of extensive celebration, gift-giving, and treatment of the boy in a manner somewhat analogous to that of bridegroom, could be seen as a kind of transitional ceremony from one phase of childhood to another (see Crapanzano 1980a). Circumcision is typically performed between the ages of five and seven, however, while the male is clearly still seen as a small boy, and is followed by no clear change in the status of the one so honored. Thus, unlike a few Muslim countries in which circumcision occurs closer to puberty, in Zawiya it would be more accurate to describe it as a precondition for than as a transition to adolescence.

Male circumcision is a strongly recommended practice (a *sunna*) rather than a requirement in Islam. In a discussion based primarily on Tunisian practices Bouhdiba describes the importance of circumcision as "a passage to the world of adults and a preparation, carried out in blood and pain, and therefore unforgettable, into an age of responsibilities" (1975, 182).

3. While there may indeed be less literal adherence to this and other tenets of Islam among some of today's young men, we reiterate that Zawiya residents today are proud of being Muslims and believe they ought to follow religious prescriptions.

4. Ammar notes that, in the Egyptian village he studied, villagers recognized *bulugh* at age thirteen or fourteen, when the child's sexual organs matured (Ammar 1954, 183).

5. The niece is Fatima Mernissi, today a feminist scholar of Moroccan society.

6. In another work Eickelman provides an excellent elaboration of this concept:

Since the pattern of events of any given moment is divinely ordained, the "reasonable" man sets about perceiving the multiple empirical ties between persons and adapting them to his interests as best he can. All formal roles—kinship, political, religious, and economic—are open to a wide range of negotiation as to their exact parameters and contents.

Reason (*'qal*) is the capacity to discern the meaning of social action and, on the basis of this perception, to engage in effective social action. It signifies adroitness or cleverness, without the pejorative English connotations of the latter word, more than a capacity for dealing with abstract rational phenomena. Its possession assumes an empirical knowledge of and ability to manipulate the shared code of conduct called the *qa'ida*, "the way things are done." (Eickelman 1976, 130)

7. The content of this interview was reconstructed from notes made while talking too Sa'id, rather than translated from a tape recording.

8. *Shab* can be used in literary Arabic to refer to the exhuberance of a pony or to rhapsodize about a beloved person (Wehr 1966, 451).

9. Thirty-seven girls answered the question. Most gave a single short response, but a few ran to several sentences. These were tabulated and grouped according to the frame of reference or characteristics cited by the girl.

10. Three of these mentioned the onset of menstruation as a criterion, and 2 referred specifically to *bulugh* (physical puberty). One girl mentioned pregnancy as a factor.

11. Ammar (1954, 186) quotes from the Egyptian village he studied a lyric sung by adolescent boys in which both 'aql and Taysh occur:

> O thou girl with bracelets,
> thou hast rendered my mind ['aql] crazy [Taysh],
> and hast made me neglect my work.

12. School materials come from French and also from Arabic sources, so it is difficult to say how much the school-derived concepts of adolescence are related to the literate culture of the Middle East.

13. This extended period in which one has attained nearly adult physical and cognitive capacities but has not yet assumed the social roles constituting adult status

has been referred to as a "psychosocial moratorium" by Erikson (1968), who argues that such a "liminal" period is part and parcel of psychological adolescence.

14. A number of these parents had attended the *jama*ᶜ or religious school, in which children acquired basic literacy in Arabic and learned portions of the Qur'an, but usually briefly and without retaining literacy.

15. Spratt (1987) provides Moroccan national rates of school promotion, repetition, and dropout.

CHAPTER 4. THE FAMILY

1. Offer and Offer (1975) found fewer problems and less conflict than is commonly expected for American adolescents; their research was on males and used questionnaires.

2. Barakat (1985, 32, 45) notes the general importance of hierarchy in Arab society and families.

3. Among many works discussing family relations, Fernea (1985) and Barakat (1985) are especially relevant because they focus on the relationship of the family to the individual, using Arabic reports from Middle Easterners as the basis of their work.

4. Geertz (1983) and Rosen (1984) argue that one's *nisba*, one's varied social connections or attributed qualities, is a key factor in Morocco. While *nisba* may be based on family, it may also come from one's occupation, geographic or ethnic origin, or other characteristics.

5. This change in terminology may also be a result of the increasing use of classical Arabic by the general population.

6. The verse allowing polygyny reads, "And if ye fear that ye will not deal fairly by the orphans, marry of the women, who seem good to you, two or three or four; and if ye fear that ye cannot do justice (to so many) then one (only) or (the captives) that your right hands possess. Thus it is more likely that ye will not do injustice" (Qur'an 4, 3; Pickthall 1953, 79). However, a later verse appears to agree with feminist claims that equal treatment is impossible: "Ye will not be able to deal equally between (your) wives, however much ye wish (to do so). But turn not altogether away (from one), leaving her as in suspense. If ye do good and keep from evil, lo! Allah is ever Forgiving, Merciful" (Qur'an 4, 129; Pickthall 1953, 91). Yet Muslim jurists have not forbidden polygyny, seeing the latter verse as open to interpretation.

7. It is important to remember that we are describing a fairly small, rural community. Major cities in Morocco do have some teenage delinquency, and parents there have complained to us about their children's attitudes in terms very much like those used in the United States.

8. Abu-Lughod (1986, 109) notes that male wilfulness may be encouraged as a valued characteristic in the Arab family, because it provides men with a sense of personal power in dealing with others.

9. Physical punishment is not unusual for younger boys and girls. Parents and sometimes older siblings and teachers strike them with a hand, a stick, or a belt. Young people are not usually upset about this, and in fact feel corporal punishment is necessary at times; both generations would heartily agree with "Spare the rod and spoil the child." Physical punishment ends around the time of the growth spurt for both sexes, at about twelve and a half years of age for girls and fifteen for boys. While

it would be grossly disrespectful, and highly unlikely, for a child to strike back, it may be partly the increase in size that deters parents at this age.

10. Barakat notes that most contact in the Arab family is with the mother, and "both sons and daughters are consequently much closer to their mother than to their father" (1985, 32).

11. Little girls seldom have tantrums: we only observed one, in an only child of two. In boys between two and five, however, tantrums are frequent and rarely punished, even if older siblings or adults are struck.

12. This is not however to deny that conflicts occur, either in extended families when two women are working in the same house all day, and sometimes competing for the same resources to sustain their children, or between female in-laws living separately.

13. Male relatives were more often called *khalli* (mother's brother) than *'ammi* (father's brother), probably because the former relationship is more relaxed. A father's brother is more likely to fill in for the father in his authoritarian role.

CHAPTER 5. FRIENDSHIP

1. Leis and Hollos (1989) note that adolescent friendship in Nigeria is less important than in the United States because large households contain several peers about the same age. Moroccan youth fall between these two cases: they have friends outside the family, but are not as intensely dependent on them as Americans tend to be. Whiting and Edwards (1988) provide a theoretical discussion of the influence of family members and peers in socialization.

2. In addition to our ethnographic sense of the issues associated with friendship in Zawiya, the data to be reported are of several sorts. First, we report generalizations from questions included in the structured interview conducted with all adolescents in the neighborhood. Forty-four males and fifty-two females responded to this portion of the interview, providing data concerning the bases of friendship for Zawiya youth and reports of the number of friends and the activities engaged in with them. The topic of friendship was pursued in longer and less-structured interviews conducted with the clinical subsample of fourteen girls and eight boys during the latter part of the 1982 field trip; these included the previous data as well as information on sources of conflict and means of its resolution. Finally, during a subsequent visit Susan expanded this information in tape-recorded interviews with five male and fifteen female adolescents and young adults from our neighborhood sample.

3. Freud's treatment of adolescence ([1905] 1953) is in the context of the "transformations of puberty," the period during which emerging secondary sexual characteristics and strengthened drives challenge the ego development and style of interacting with others laid down in the "Oedipal" phase of childhood. Psychoanalytic writers have generally portrayed the period of adolescence as a testing ground for new images of oneself, reflected in close friends (usually of the same sex), and as a time of intensified and increasingly physical search for a love object (typically of the opposite sex). The coexistence of these two tendencies in the teen years plays a central role in Erikson's influential theory of adolescent identity formation (1950). The separation of the "identity" and the "intimacy" aspects of adolescence in Erikson's writing has been

criticized by Gilligan (1982), who suggests that for girls these issues are likely to be fused.

In the work of Sullivan (1953) the transition from childhood to adolescence is centered on the character of intense like-sex friendships which prepare the individual to experience love (and lust) for nonfamily members and serve as a crucial alternative to the loneliness and anxiety that would otherwise accompany the changes wrought by puberty. Like most Western social science theories, Sullivan's ideas have not been systematically tested in other cultural settings. We hope to illustrate the quality and development of adolescent friendships in Zawiya, so the reader can compare the picture that emerges with what has been written about friendships in the United States and Europe.

Seltzer suggests that "the adolescent peer group might well be counted along with the family, the school, and the church among the social institutions of Western society" (1982, 57). She notes that within the peer group, "adolescents use one another to examine, assess and evaluate—in the service of beginning a framework of self" (1982, 248). Youniss and Smollar note that while popular culture often stresses "peer pressure" as a negative influence that leads youth to experiment with drugs or sexuality, relations with peers are just as important as relations with parents for adolescent development in the U.S. samples they studied (1985, 159). They agree with Piaget that young people learn general moral principles through their interaction with peers (1985, 133–134). Youniss and Smollar also investigated many of the same areas of friendship that we did, including characteristics sought in a friend, shared activities, and sources of conflicts and their resolution.

4. A central point made by Joseph and Joseph (1987) is that Moroccan Berber society in the Rif Mountains is characterized by dual emphases on collective and individual goals, which are often in conflict. This leads to uncertainty about social situations and resultant distrust. The concern with trust and distrust in Zawiya reflects similar characteristics.

5. The questions we asked ninety-six adolescents about friendship were, "Do you have friends? Close ones? How many? Why did you choose the close ones as best? Are they neighbors or relatives? What do you do with these friends?" Most males reported three or fewer friends, with the median at two; the median for females was one.

6. When these figures were calculated, we ignored some reports of large numbers of friends because the reports appeared deviant (e.g., two males and one female over fifteen mentioned 9 or 10 close friends when the highest number their peers gave was four). For females, an average of 2.1 friends was reported by those younger than fifteen, while 1.1 was the average for those fifteen and older. For males, the average number of reported friends was 2.4 for males younger than 16.5 and 1.5 for those older.

7. Twelve of fourteen girls said cross-sex friendship was possible, while one said it was not and the last said it could only happen to girls in school. This is related to the fact that most girls mentioned studying as the activity they would pursue with a platonic male friend, although a few mentioned talking and joking. Girls who were not in school described as male friends companions of their older brothers who would visit their home and with whom they felt comfortable exchanging a few words.

8. Youniss and Smollar mention several similar qualities sought in friends by American teens, including symmetrical reciprocity as "the basis for all friendship" (1985, 132), as well as perceived equality and a desire for self-disclosure only to those who can keep secrets (1985, 4, 111).

CHAPTER 6. SEXUALITY, COURTSHIP, AND MARRIAGE

1. The Moroccan poet, novelist, and psychiatrist Tahar Benjelloun has discussed in detail the significance of sexual activity for Moroccans in general and for North African workers in Europe whom he has seen clinically (Benjelloun 1977). Some of Benjelloun's Moroccan patients compared loss of potency to death and asserted that it would deprive them of both family life and any meaningful relationship with a woman (1977, 84).

2. Miller and Simon distinguish three crucial positions taken by Western theorists and researchers toward adolescent sexuality: the "classic" psychoanalytic theory of Freud ([1905] 1953), in which adolescence follows a period of "latency" during the elementary school years and is the setting for replay and final consolidation of personality in light of the "Oedipal" dynamics of childhood on the one hand and the newly strengthened emotional need for a sexual partner on the other; the "revisionist" position of Erikson (1950) and the Offers (Offer and Offer 1975), in which sexuality is seen as a more or less continuous part of a set of social competencies developed gradually throughout the life cycle and during adolescence brought into the service of "identity" and "intimacy"; and the cognitive-developmental position of Piaget (1972) and Kohlberg (1964), in which the sexual experience of adolescents, like other aspects of their functioning, is constrained by the rate at which reflective "formal operational" thought develops. While none of these characterizations can be simply imposed on the adolescents of Zawiya, the reader will want to consider each as we present our ethnographic data.

3. Frank and accurate data on adolescent sexual behavior and feelings are among the most difficult for the social scientist to collect (see Thompson 1984; Coles and Stokes 1985). Many anthropological and psychological writers have commented on the special difficulties of studying sexual behavior and belief cross-culturally (see Broude 1981; Devereux 1967; Frayser 1985). The discussion of sexual behavior in Zawiya, and its relationship to marriage and the functioning of families, indeed presents difficulties. Moroccan society views any open display of sexual activity with distaste; even a boy and girl holding hands in taboo. Thus almost everything we have to say about actual sexual behavior, as distinct from mores, is based on informants' reports. The accounts often disagree concerning sexual relations between male and female adolescents in the community: males consistently gave higher estimates of the percentage of sexually active females in the neighborhood than did females, and a girl might be described as sexually active by several male informants and yet not be mentioned by knowledgeable local women asked about girls who had had premarital sexual relations. Younger adolescents were in almost every case shy about discussing sexual matters, even in the abstract. The most detailed accounts we have of sexual socialization are thus from older adolescents and young adults reconstructing their own sexual histories or reporting on the general features of local sexual activities (cf. S. Davis 1984).

4. The cultural settings in which Islam is practiced influence which aspects of the religion are emphasized (e.g., most Muslim women veil in Saudi Arabia, most do not in Indonesia).

5. Bouhdiba's *Sexuality in Islam* (1985) explores the ideal Islamic unity of the physical and mental aspects of love, and the typical separation of these in social practice.

6. See the detailed description of a traditional wedding, below.

7. In our survey of marriages, few actually followed this pattern. Of thirty-nine parental marriages, 3 percent were between the children of brothers and 23 percent were between other relatives by blood or marriage, leaving 74 percent between unrelated people (who were often neighbors). The percentages were similar for sixteen more recently married siblings of the adolescents.

8. The term *luwwaT*, from the biblical Lot, more precisely connotes sodomy.

9. By way the comparison, Kinsey's group reported that roughly 21 percent of their rural U.S. male sample in the 1940s acknowledged homosexual experience to orgasm by the age of twenty (Kinsey, Pomeroy, and Martin 1948, 460). The recent *Rolling Stone* survey is especially revealing concerning the reluctance of U.S. teenagers to label themselves homosexual (gay): only one of more than a thousand teenagers did so (Coles and Stokes 1985, 138). Only 5 percent of the males responding to the survey reported homosexual activity during adolescence (20 percent reported same-sex play as children). It seems likely, in view of the much higher incidence found by the Kinsey researchers' fairly insistent interview procedures, that the apparently much lower figures in the *Rolling Stone* survey are attributable mostly to underreporting as a result of U.S. teens' fear of the label "homosexual."

10. For the rural portion of their post–World War II U.S. sample, for example, the Kinsey researchers report a 17 percent incidence of animal contact for male respondents (Kinsey, Pomeroy, and Martin 1948, 459).

11. The donkey (*Hmar*), the essential working companion of the peasant, is the butt of a good deal of rough treatment, as well as a wealth of colloquial humor. The term *donkey* is a moderately severe insult that implies stupidity or vulgarity when applied to a human, although one frequently hears Moroccans use it with an edge of humor to refer to their children. When one must refer to the donkey in polite conversation, one first excuses oneself with the word *Hashak*.

12. While probably attributable in part to our different styles of questioning, this difference suggests the contrasting emphases described by Gilligan (1982) in her work on adolescence in the United States. In the course of interviewing 150 U.S. teenagers about the "teen romance," Thompson (1984, 351) encountered a similar sex difference. The greater reticence of females to report the details of their sexuality has been noted repeatedly in surveys of sexual activities in the United States, although Coles has also drawn attention (Coles and Stokes 1985, 5) to the apparent increase in recent years in the readiness of teenage American girls to describe their sexual activities and feelings.

13. Farida is using the "royal we" to refer to herself, perhaps to distance herself from the topic or perhaps to show respect to the listener.

14. A recent Moroccan bestseller, *L'enfant endormi* (Sbaï 1987), is a novel about a series of such experiences in one young woman's life.

15. These contradictions are of course not unique to Zawiya. Mernissi (1975) suggests that Islam benefits by preventing a strongly bonded heterosexual unit; Abu-Lughod (1986) argues that kinship units are also threatened by the couple's emotional attachment to each other. Bouhdiba argues that a split between sexual and spiritual heterosexual love is a central problem for contemporary Muslim societies.

16. We expect real change in this area: in Moroccan cities, at least upper-class adolescents have mixed-sex dancing parties in their homes, and some couples date.

17. In Berber communities in northern Morocco, young men walk behind girls fetching water in a similar attempt to establish contact. They may carry out an entire conversation from a distance, so the contact is less apparent to observers (Joseph and Joseph 1987, 47).

18. Naamane-Guessous describes a similar range of alternatives for single young women aged sixteen to twenty-four in Casablanca. While she does not quantify the varied practices, she found that 65 percent of 75 young women she interviewed in the early 1980s had had at least one of these types of sexual experience. Of 125 married, widowed, or divorced women, 40 percent admitted to such premarital experiences, although none of the oldest women (married between 1945 and 1954) did so (1987, 44–45).

19. This view was reflected by many of the two hundred male high school students studied by Ouzzi (1986), who found that 60 percent expressed negative attitudes toward females when completing sentences about women or marriage. For example, the sentence fragment "I think that most girls . . ." elicited responses like "are sluts," "are treacherous," "are devilish." Negative responses to "My feeling about married life is . . ." included "that I hate it," "it's mixed with treachery," "it is unbearable hell" (Ouzzi 1986, 210–212).

20. Teenage marriage is now uncommon for females and rare for males in Morocco (Royaume du Maroc 1987). During our work in 1982, there were no young men under twenty who were married in our neighborhood PSU. There were two young women who had married and had children before twenty. There were three others who were engaged, two at nineteen and one at fourteen. Many local people commented that fourteen was too young; the couple would probably not cohabit for at least two years. Finally, three girls had experienced broken engagements, one at about seventeen and the others at nineteen.

21. For both sexes slightly over a quarter of these young people indicated they wanted to choose their own marriage partner; the remainder (16 percent of males and 9 percent of females) said the decision should be made by themselves and the parents together.

22. Cross-cultural work by Rosenblatt and Anderson (1981) indicates that in many societies the desire to choose one's own marriage partner goes with increased education and wage labor.

23. Out of fourteen marriages of older siblings of the adolescents, relatives, including parents, chose the spouse in six cases, the couple chose in six cases, and in two cases the couple and relatives chose together.

24. This practice is less common in cities; a Moroccan woman at an elite wedding in 1987 told Susan it was "barbaric" and certainly not practiced in her circle.

25. In 1987 a Zawiya marriage was annulled and the bride returned to her family

after being found not a virgin [*hajba*]. However, we heard that afterward she was leading a normal life with her family and planned to return to school.

26. Indeed, more affluent Moroccan brides sometimes do have the hymen surgically reconstructed. While Mernissi describes this practice as occurring in Moroccan cities (1982, 183–184), we heard of no cases in Zawiya.

27. Although we observed this first in Zawiya, inquiry revealed it to be common in much of northern Morocco. Recent research shows that while in 1960 the average age for all Moroccan girls at first marriage was 17, in 1982 it was 20.8 in rural areas (Royaume du Maroc 1987, 8). In 1982, 27 percent of urban and 9 percent of rural females under 30 had not yet contracted a first marriage, as compared to 3 percent and 2 percent in 1960 (pp. 7–8). While these statistics confirm the trend, reasons for the sharp increase in marital age are not explained.

28. Naamane-Guessous found a similar trend in survey data on the premarital sexual experience of a sample of women in Casablanca (1987, 45), and Bouhdiba (1985, 236) reports that 41 percent of Tunisian girls responding to a newspaper survey (and hence likely to be above average in education) said they favored "flirtation."

29. Joseph and Joseph (1987, 47) note a similar practice in the Berber community they studied in northern Morocco, and they cite a 1931 account by Coon to the effect that couples met the same way then.

30.

> *Amgron lhajban, arra lkhala waTetu;*
> *itfella 'la lbnat, arra liyam 'aTaytu.*
> *Qobb liya, neshrub men dak lmejri;*
> *had l'am maji, l'azba tekhteb l'azri.*

CHAPTER 7. STRESS AND DEVIANCE

1. In a recent discussion of family life in Egypt, Rugh (1984) argues that Egyptian primary emphasis on the family or corporate group leads to different social principles and behaviors than does American emphasis on the individual.

2. Margaret Mead (1928) believed adolescence was so pleasant in Samoa as contrasted with the United States because adult roles and knowledge were appropriate for the new generation. G. Stanley Hall's (1904) classic work treats adolescent striving for autonomy and rebellion against adult cultural values and norms as both the source of deviance and societal stress and a necessary stimulus to cultural evolution.

3. This was in fact a very quiet girl who lived with her maternal aunt—a woman close to her age whom she respected—as "mother."

4. The draw-a-person test (Machover 1949) is easy to administer and was given by all researchers in the Harvard Adolescence Project, providing comparative data. We hypothesized that the greater the cultural constraint or limitation of freedom placed on adolescents at puberty, especially in the area of premarital sexuality, the more they resent their own gender role and thus prefer, and draw first, the opposite sex. Susan compiled and analyzed the draw-a-person data which the project members generously shared, and Richard Condon independently interviewed the researchers about the degree of constraint on premarital sexuality and ordered the cultures from least to most constrained for females (most males faced little constraint). Combining these two types of information supported the hypothesis to some

degree (S. Davis 1983b). The Moroccan females were rated as the next to most constrained (after Romania) and had the highest percentage (60 percent) of females drawing males first, while 28 percent of males drew females first. If many females drew males first because they felt the male role was preferable, we might expect males to be satisfied with their role and very few to show ambivalence by drawing females first. For example, no Australian males drew females first, and only 5 percent of Romanian males and 11 percent of Inuit males did so.

5. Our data are from detailed interviews with fourteen informants, eleven female and three male.

6. The Morocco Literacy Project, directed by Daniel Wagner at the University of Pennsylvania, has compared children of Berber- and Arabic-speaking families in Morocco in how well they learn to read Arabic in school. Arabic speakers performed better the first year, and a superiority in reading ability persisted over the first three years of testing (Wagner and Spratt 1987b, 352). However, by year five of the study, there were no overall differences between Arabic and Berber speakers in reading achievement (Wagner, Spratt, and Ezzaki, in review). This research also examines the effect of preschool experience (Quranic, "modern," or none) and of urban or rural residence on learning to read (Wagner and Spratt 1987a). In the past, school in Morocco was even more difficult, because students were taught topics in French without first studying the language. Now they do not start French until third grade and begin with language lessons.

7. The atmosphere of Zawiya education is congruent with traditional Muslim education in Morocco as described by Eickelman: "Two features consistently associated with Islamic education are its rigorous discipline and the lack of explicit explanation of memorized material" (1985, 62).

8. The Moroccan high school curriculum is being steadily Arabized, and as of 1987–1988 most instruction in the sciences is in literary Arabic.

9. Ouzzi (1986) suggests that examination pressure is a major stressor for Moroccan students, a "shadow" constantly threatening both youth and parents.

10. We focused on siblings instead of parents because the parental generation had little access to formal education, while many of the siblings did. Of seventy siblings on whom we had information, only 11.4 percent held white-collar jobs of the type their brothers and sisters desire. If we add to this percentage those who are university students and have a reasonable chance of a white-collar job, the total is 20 percent. Another 20 percent hold steady blue-collar jobs that pay reasonably well. The largest percentage (34.3 percent) hold unskilled jobs or those that pay poorly, like apprentice, field laborer, or embroiderer. A few males (8.6 percent) are in the army, and 17.1 percent are partly or mostly unemployed.

11. Some religious authorities (*fuqaha*) have concluded that kif and other drugs, although not mentioned explicitly in the Qur'an, should be absolutely forbidden (*Haram*) by analogy with wine, since Islam forbids the use of substances that cloud judgment.

12. This phenomenon is not limited to Zawiya, nor to Morocco. We heard that some young men around twenty suffered crises in Kabar; the main causes were said to be anxiety about school exams or lack of experience with the opposite sex. Spratt (1985) reports a young woman in another town having to abandon her studies

temporarily because of a crisis, and Graef (pers. comm.) saw the phenomenon more than once as a psychologist working with young women being trained for non-traditional jobs in Casablanca. She said that the young women with a high school ed-ucation were more apt to succumb than those who had only finished junior high, and attributed this to the fact that the former had higher career aspirations which they felt they would not meet. Finally, Bouhdiba (1985, 237) reports Tunisian psychiatric stud-ies of "hysteria" among young women. About 30 percent of cases are due to sexual conflicts, including forced engagement and long separation from husbands working abroad; Bouhdiba suggests that this rate is lower than in the past, when there were greater sexual restrictions. With the rapid change in economic and gender roles in Morocco, this is a fascinating area for further research.

13. We have changed names and some of the circumstances in the interview that follows to protect the privacy of the persons involved.

14. The translator comments that Sa'id consistently fails to answer Susan's ques-tions, as if he were hardly listening.

CHAPTER 8. THE ZAWIYA INDIVIDUAL

1. Anderson and Anderson (1986) describe adolescent self-perceptions in a Thai Muslim community studied as part of the Harvard Adolescence Project.

2. This discussion is based on several kinds of data. In addition to structured in-terviews and tests, we asked some of the teenagers to "Tell me a little about yourself," to describe whether and how they had changed in the last year, and to describe their dreams. We also asked older informants about important issues for adolescents.

3. The first response to "Tell me about yourself" was often "What?" These young people do not typically hear, or think specifically about, such questions; nevertheless, all were able to answer, sometimes after a clarification such as, "What is your nature [Tabi'a] like?"

4. This is an idiosyncratic use of nefkha, which most often means conceit (Wehr 1966, 982). The context makes the meaning here clear.

5. The best strategy for solving such a problem involves opening a shutter posi-tion at which half the still-eligible patterns have a black and half a white dot. Each optimal move reduces uncertainty by half, and an eight-alternative problem can al-ways be solved in three moves. Neimark noted that subjects' calculated strategy score for task performance correlated significantly with the rated quality of their verbal de-scriptions of the strategy used (1975). The Zawiya sample for the Neimark test in-cluded sixty-five young people, thirty-one males and thirty-four females, tested during school vacation.

6. The score was treated as a simultaneous function of sex, age, and schooling, using multiple regression analysis; the effects of age and of sex are statistically signif-icant, and that of years of schooling was marginally so. Since the number of girls who had reached secondary school was so small, the mathematical partialing-out of years of school for girls is suspect. It does not allow us to reject the assumption that girls with more secondary schooling would have performed as well as boys.

7. We expected that females might perform better than males on this test be-cause nearly all girls learn a form of embroidery in which varied geometric patterns are produced by counting threads in the fabric.

8. Mitchell Ratner's findings are described in a forthcoming volume of the series *Adolescents in a Changing World*. We thank him and Ann-Mari Gemmill for help with test formulation and analysis of the Neimark data, and for suggestions concerning the social questionnaire. Results for a different set of cognitive measures are reported for the Nigerian communities in the Harvard Adolescence Project by Hollos, Leis, and Turiel (1986).

9. These questions included hypotheticals ("What would happen if a sheep didn't have feet?"), exhaustion of possibilities ("If a farmer plows with two mules and never uses the same pair twice, how many days can he plow if he has three mules?" "Four mules?" "Five mules?"), and counterfactuals ("People began to use cars in 1900. Moulay Ismail was sultan of Morocco in the seventeenth century. Is it possible that in Meknes there is a museum containing the car Moulay Ismail drove?"). A final set of questions concerned moral contradictions in the social realm, e.g., "Is it possible for a schoolteacher to teach something that is not true?"; "Is it possible for a judge to put an innocent man in jail?"

As a rough way of capturing the expected increase in sophistication we simply noted the number of questions with a clear right answer (e.g., "Yes," to "Is it possible for a house of brick to be heavier than a house of stone?") to which each subject responded correctly.

10. The results of this questioning are discussed in more detail in another publication (D. Davis 1989).

11. We asked, "Can you tell me about a time when you were undecided, when you didn't know whether to do something, whether it was the right or the wrong thing to do? What happened? What did you do? Was it right or wrong? Why?"

12. Kilborne (1981) studied dream interpretation in Morocco by having local interpreters work with three of Freud's reported dreams.

13. Five dreams were happy, one had both happy and sad elements (an eleven-year-old dreamed her mother was in labor and was frightened, but was happy after the baby was born), and ten were frightening.

14. This dream, like others reported in detail, was reconstructed from notes made at the telling.

15. Males often associate an inability to move in dreams with the appearance of a nightmare creature, the *bughatat,* but no females mentioned this.

16. This girl had only attended four years of primary school and was totally unexposed to Freud's ideas. Her older brother was one of those who said that to dream of a snake signifies something having to do with Ramadan. He had never heard of the association of snakes with the male genitals, and this connection was not mentioned by others from Zawiya.

17. In Zawiya, Aisha Quandisha is the most frequently mentioned of the jnun and seen as the most powerful; this is significant in an apparently male-dominated society.

18. Youniss and Smollar cite reciprocity both as a positive aspect sought in American friends and as the basis for all friendship (1985, 131–132).

19. Youniss and Smollar report for the American sample that while most adolescents desired mutual caring and trust in a friend, about one-third of males did not; those males wanted to share activities, but not feelings, with their friends (1985, 132).

These findings support the suggestions of Gilligan (1982) that it is more difficult for males than for females to achieve intimacy in relationships. Some males, however, do achieve intimacy in both settings, so the gender difference is hardly absolute.

20. Around the turn of this century, William James (1892) laid the groundwork for this view when he stated that the self was composed of two united aspects. The first was the one discussed above, the self as active agent or knower. The second aspect of the self was as known, as experiencing images and sensations coming in from the environment. Two sociologists, Cooley (1922) and G. H. Mead (1934), stressed the importance of environment by focusing attention on the fact that much of one's self is based on feelings experienced in relationships with others. Their writings are the basis of the symbolic interactionist approach in sociology, and their definition of self as having both internal and external, socially defined components serves as a link between psychology and sociology.

21. Goffman notes (1959, 239) that his analysis is focused on Anglo-American society.

22. Caton argues that in North Yemen, "the self of the honorable tribesman emerges in the compositional process" (1985, 142) as men publicly compose and deliver oral poems at wedding ceremonies. He uses G. H. Mead's model of symbolic interaction in his analysis. In his work on Afghanistan, Anderson warns against using terms like *self* or *individual* which emphasize differentiation and separation. He suggests instead the term *persona*, which designates a "culturally constructed presence" which is useful to draw "attention to how terms of a native analysis are related to each other within frames which unite experience to capacities in which persons are socially present" (1985, 204). His analysis unites the two aspects of self "by speaking of personae or the terms in which persons are socially present" (p. 205). Thus his framework, like Goffman's, includes the individual as both a unique repository of experience and as a social character.

23. Such a view, that internal and situational factors interact to produce the behavior traditionally attributed to "personality," is now widely accepted in academic psychology (see Magnusson and Endler 1977).

■ References

Abu-Lughod, L. 1985. "Honor and the Sentiments of Loss in a Bedouin Society." *American Ethnologist* 12: 245–261.

———. 1986. *Veiled Sentiments: Honor and Loss in a Bedouin Society*. Berkeley: University of California Press.

Alahyane, M., N. E. Arrif, A. Belarbi, M. El Harras, T. Hadraoui, A. Khamlichi, F. Mernissi, A. Moulay Rchid, M. Salahdine, and F. Z. Zryouil. 1987. *Portraits de femmes*. Casablanca: Editions le Fennec.

Ammar, H. [1954] 1973. *Growing Up in an Egyptian Village*. Reprint. New York: Octagon Books.

Anderson, J. 1985. "Sentimental Ambivalence and the Exegesis of 'Self' in Afghanistan." *Anthropological Quarterly* 58: 203–211.

Anderson, W. W., and D. D. Anderson. 1986. "Thai Muslim Adolescents' Self, Sexuality, and Autonomy." *Ethos* 14: 368–394.

Barakat, H. 1985. "The Arab Family and the Challenge of Social Transformation." In E. W. Fernea, ed., *Women and the Family in the Middle East: New Voices of Change*, pp. 27–48. Austin: University of Texas Press.

Benjelloun, T. 1977. *La plus haute des solitudes: Misère affective et sexuelle d'émigrés nord-africaines*. Paris: Editions du Seuil.

Bouhdiba, A. 1985. *Sexuality in Islam*. Boston: Routledge and Kegan Paul.

Briggs, J. 1970. *Never in Anger*. Cambridge, Mass.: Harvard University Press.

Broude, G. J. 1981. "The Cultural Management of Sexuality." In R. H. Munroe, R. L. Munroe, and B. Whiting, eds., *Handbook of Cross-cultural Human Development*. New York: Garland.

Bullough, V. L. 1976. *Sexual Variance in Society and History*. Chicago: University of Chicago Press.

Burbank, V. 1988. *Three Young Girls*. New Brunswick, N.J.: Rutgers University Press.

Burton, R.F., trans. [1886a] 1963. *The Perfumed Garden of the Shaykh Nefzawi*. Reprint. London: Neville Spearman.

———. 1886b. "Terminal Essay." In R. F. Burton, ed. and trans., *The Book of the Thousand Nights and a Night: A Plain and Literal Translation of the Arabian Nights Entertainments*. Vol. 10. London: Burton Club.

Caton, S. 1985. "The Poetic Construction of Self." *Anthropological Quarterly* 58: 141–151.

Clifford, J. 1986. "Introduction: Partial Truths." In J. Clifford, J. Marcus, and G. Marcus, eds., *Writing Culture: The Poetics and Politics of Ethnography*, pp. 1–26. Berkeley: University of California Press.

Coles, R., and G. Stokes. 1985. *Sex and the American Teenager*. New York: Harper and Row.

Condon, R. G. 1987. *Inuit Youth: Growth and Change in the Canadian Arctic*. New Brunswick, N.J.: Rutgers University Press.

Cooley, C. H. [1922] 1983. *Human Nature and the Social Order*. Reprint. New Brunswick, N.J.: Transaction Books.

Crapanzano, V. 1973. *The Hamadsha: A Study in Moroccan Ethnopsychiatry*. Berkeley: University of California Press.

———. 1980a. "Rite of Return: Circumcision in Morocco." In W. Muensterberger and L. B. Boyer, eds., *The Psychoanalytic Study of Society*. Vol. 9. New York: Library of Psychological Anthropology.

———. 1980b. *Tuhami: Portrait of a Moroccan*. Chicago: University of Chicago Press.

Csikszentmihalyi, M., and R. Larson. 1984. *Being Adolescent: Conflict and Growth in the Teenage Years*. New York: Basic Books.

Davis, D. A. 1974. "Temporal Judgment and Memory for Events." Ph.D. dissertation, University of Michigan. *Dissertation Abstracts International* 35 (1975): 5613A. University Microfilms No. 75-10, 156.

———. 1989. "Formal Thought in a Moroccan Town." In J. Valsiner, ed., *Cultural Context and Child Development: Towards a Culture-Inclusive Developmental Psychology*. Toronto: Hofgrefe and Huber.

Davis, S. S. 1977. "Zahrah Muhammad: A Rural Woman of Morocco." In E. Fernea and B. Bezirgan, eds., *Middle Eastern Muslim Women Speak*. Austin: University of Texas Press.

———. 1978. "Formal and Nonformal Roles of Moroccan Village Women." Ph.D. dissertation, Department of Anthropology, University of Michigan, Ann Arbor.

———. 1983a. *Patience and Power: Women's Lives in a Moroccan Village*. Cambridge, Mass.: Schenkman.

———. 1983b. "Sexual Maturation, Cultural Constraint, and the Concept of the Self." Paper presented at the annual meeting of the American Anthropological Association, Chicago.

———. 1984. "Sexual Politics and Change in a Moroccan Town." Paper presented at the annual meeting of the Middle East Studies Association, San Francisco.

Devereux, G. 1967. *From Anxiety to Method in the Behavioral Sciences*. Leiden: Mouton.

Dwyer, K. 1982. *Moroccan Dialogues: Anthropology in Question*. Baltimore: Johns Hopkins University Press.

Eickelman, D. F. 1976. *Moroccan Islam*. Austin: University of Texas Press.

———. 1985. *Knowledge and Power in Morocco: The Education of a Twentieth-Century Notable*. Princeton: Princeton University Press.

Erikson, E. H. 1950. *Childhood and Society*. New York: Norton.

————. 1968. *Identity: Youth and Crisis*. New York: Norton.

Farah, M., trans. 1984. *Marriage and Sexality in Islam: A Translation of al-Ghazali's Book on the Etiquette of Marriage from the Ihya'*. Salt Lake City: University of Utah Press.

Fernea, E. W. 1985. *Women and the Family in the Middle East*. Austin: University of Texas Press.

Foucault, M. 1976. *The History of Sexuality*, vol. 1: *An Introduction*. New York: Random House.

Frayser, S. G. 1985. *Varieties of Sexual Experience: An Anthropological Perspective on Human Sexuality*. New Haven: HRAF Press.

Freeman, D. 1983. *Margaret Mead and Samoa: The Making and Unmaking of an Anthropological Myth*. Cambridge, Mass.: Harvard University Press.

Freud, A. 1958. "Adolescence." *Psychoanalytic Study of the Child* 13: 255–278.

Freud, S. 1900. *The Interpretation of Dreams*. In *The Standard Edition of the Complete Psychological Works of Sigmund Freud*, trans. J. Strachey. London: Hogarth Press.

————. [1905] 1953. "Three Essays on the Theory of Sexuality." In *The Standard Edition of the Complete Psychological Works of Sigmund Freud*, trans. J. Strachey, vol. 7. Reprint. London: Hogarth Press.

Geertz, C. 1968. *Islam Observed: Religious Development in Morocco and Indonesia*. Chicago: University of Chicago Press.

————. 1983. "From the Native's Point of View: On the Nature of Anthropological Understanding." In C. Geertz, *Local Knowledge: Further Essays in Interpretive Anthropology*. New York: Basic Books.

Gellner, E., and C. Micaud, eds. 1972. *Arabs and Berbers*. London: D. C. Heath.

al-Ghazali, A. [1106] 1984. "Book on the Etiquette of Marriage: Being the Second Book of the Section on Customs in the Book *The Revival of the Religious Sciences*." In M. Farah, trans., *Marriage and Sexuality in Islam*. Salt Lake City: University of Utah Press.

Gilligan, C. 1982. *In a Different Voice*. Cambridge: Harvard University Press.

————. 1986. "Adolescent Development Reconsidered." Typescript.

Goffman, E. 1959. *The Presentation of Self in Everyday Life*. Garden City, N.Y.: Anchor Doubleday Books.

Goody, J. 1958. *The Reproductive Cycle in Domestic Groups*. Cambridge: Cambridge University Press.

Granqvist, H. 1950. *Child Problems among the Arabs*. Helsingfors, Finland: Soderstrom.

Group for the Advancement of Psychiatry. 1966. *Sex and the College Student*. New York: Atheneum.

Hall, G. S. 1904. *Adolescence: Its Psychology and Its Relations to Physiology, Anthropology, Sociology, Sex, Crime, Religion and Education*. New York: D. Appleton.

Hallowell, A. I. 1955. "The Self and Its Behavioral Environment." In A. I. Hallowell, ed., *Culture and Experience*, pp. 75–110. Philadelphia: University of Pennsylvania Press.

al-Hibri, A. 1982. "A Study of Islamic Herstory: Or How Did We Ever Get into This Mess?" In A. al-Hibri, ed., *Women and Islam*. Oxford: Pergamon Press.

Hollos, M., P. E. Leis, and E. Turiel, 1986. "Social Reasoning in Ijo Children and Adolescents in Nigerian Communities." *Journal of Cross-Cultural Psychology* 17: 352–374.

Inhelder, B., and J. Piaget. 1958. *The Growth of Logical Thinking from Childhood to Adolescence*. New York: Basic Books.

James, W. 1892. *Principles of Psychology*. New York: Henry Holt.

Joseph, R., and T. Joseph, 1987. *The Rose and the Thorn: Semiotic Structures in Morocco*. Tucson: University of Arizona Press.

Kagan, J. 1972. "A Conception of Early Adolescence." In J. Kagan and R. Coles, eds., *Twelve to Sixteen: Early Adolescence*. New York: Norton.

Kilborne, B. J. 1981. "Moroccan Dream Interpretation and Culturally Constituted Defense Mechanisms." *Ethos* 9: 294–312.

Kinsey, A. C., W. B. Pomeroy, and C. E. Martin. 1948. *Sexual Behavior in the Human Male*. Philadelphia: W. B. Saunders.

Kinsey, A. C., W. B. Pomeroy, C. E. Martin, and P. H. Gebhard. 1953. *Sexual Behavior in the Human Female*. Philadelphia: W. B. Saunders.

Kohlberg, L. 1964. "Development of Moral Character and Moral Ideology." In M. L. Hoffman and L. W. Hoffman, eds., *Review of Child Development Research*. vol. 1. New York: Russell Sage Foundation.

———. 1971. "From Is to Ought: How to Commit the Naturalistic Fallacy and Get Away with It in the Study of Moral Development." In T. Mischel, ed., *Cognitive Development and Epistomology*. New York: Academic Press.

Kohlberg, L., and C. Gilligan. 1971. "The Adolescent as a Philosopher: The Discovery of the Self in a Post-Conventional World." *Daedelus* 100: 1051–1086.

Lane, E. W. 1865. *An Arabic-English Lexicon*. London: Williams and Norgate.

Le Coz, J. 1964. *Le Rharb: Fellahs et colons: Étude de géographie régionale*. 2 vols. Rabat, Morocco: Centre Universitaire de la Recherche Scientifique.

Leis, P., and M. Hollos. 1989. *Betwixt and Between: Ijo Youth in Nigeria*. New Brunswick, N.J.: Rutgers University Press.

Machover, K. 1949. *Personality Projection in the Drawing of the Human Figure*. Springfield, Ill.: Thomas.

Magnusson, D., and N. S. Endler. 1977. *Personality at the Crossroads: Current Issues in Interactional Psychology*. Hillsdale, N. J.: Erlbaum.

Maher, V. 1974. *Women and Property in Morocco*. New York: Cambridge University Press.

Marshall, W. A., and J. M. Tanner. 1970. "Variations in the Pattern of Pubertal Changes in Boys." *Archives of Disease in Childhood* 45: 13–23.

Maybury-Lewis, D. 1965. *The Savage and the Innocent*. Cleveland, Ohio: World Publishing.

Mead, G. H. 1934. *Mind, Self and Society*. Chicago: University of Chicago Press.

Mead, M. 1928. *Coming of Age in Samoa*. New York: William Morrow.

———. 1930. *Growing Up in New Guinea*. New York: William Morrow.

Mernissi, F. 1975. *Beyond the Veil: Male-Female Dynamics in a Modern Muslim Society*. Cambridge, Mass.: Schenkman.

———. 1982. "Virginity and Patriarchy." In A. al-Hibri, ed., *Women and Islam*. Oxford: Pergamon.

————. 1984. *Le Maroc raconte par ses femmes.* Rabat: Société marocaine des editeurs réunis (SMER).

————. 1987. *Beyond the Veil: Male-Female Dynamics in a Modern Muslim Society.* 2d ed. Bloomington: University of Indiana Press.

Miller, P. Y., and W. Simon. 1980. "The Development of Sexuality in Adolescence." In J. Adelson, ed., *Handbook of Adolescent Psychology.* New York: Wiley Interscience.

Munson, H. 1984. *The House of Si Abd Allah.* New Haven: Yale University Press.

Musallam, B. 1983. *Sex and Society in Islam: Birth Control before the Nineteeth Century.* Cambridge: Cambridge University Press.

Naamane-Guessous, S. 1987. *Au-delà de toute pudeur: La sexualité féminine au Maroc* (Beyond all shame: Female sexuality in Morocco). Casablanca: Soden.

Neimark, E. D. 1975. "Longitudinal Development of Formal Operations Thought." *Genetic Psychology Monographs* 91: 171–225.

Neimark, E. D., and N. Lewis. 1967. "The Development of Logical Problem-Solving Strategies." *Child Development* 38: 107–113.

Neimark, E. D., and H. Wagner. 1964. "Information Gathering in Diagnostic Problem Solving as a Function of Number of Alternative Solutions." *Psychonomic Science* 1: 329–330.

Offer, D., and J. Offer. 1975. *From Teenage to Young Manhood: A Psychological Study.* New York: Basic Books.

Ouzzi, A. 1986. *Saykolojiyat al-murahiq: Dirasa maydaniya lil-ittijahat an-nafsiya al-ijtima'iya lil-murahiq al-maghribi* (The psychology of adolescence: A field study of the psycho-sociological attitudes of the Moroccan adolescent). Rabat, Morocco: Manshurat majallat ad-dirasat an-nafsiya wa-terbawiya.

Paige, K. E., and J. M. Paige. 1981. *The Politics of Reproductive Ritual.* Berkeley: University of California Press.

Piaget, J. 1932. *The Moral Judgment of the Child.* Trans. Marjorie Gabain. Glencoe, Ill.: Free Press.

————. 1972. "Intellectual Evolution from Adolescence to Adulthood." *Human Development* 15:1–12.

Pickthall, M. M. 1953. *The Meaning of the Glorious Koran.* New York: New American Library.

Porch, D. 1983. *The Conquest of Morocco.* New York: Knopf.

Rabinow, P. 1977. *Reflections on Fieldwork in Morocco.* Berkeley: University of California Press.

Ratner, M. Forthcoming. *Adolescent Life in a Romanian Village.* New Brunswick, N.J.: Rutgers University Press.

Rosen, L. 1978. "The Negotiation of Reality: Male-female Relations in Sefrou, Morocco." In L. Beck and N. Keddie, eds., *Women in the Muslim World,* pp. 561–584. Cambridge, Mass.: Harvard University Press.

————. 1984. *Bargaining for Reality: The Construction of Social Relations in a Muslim Community.* Chicago: University of Chicago Press.

Rosenblatt, P. C., and R. M. Anderson. 1981. In M. Cook, ed., *Human Sexuality in Cross-Cultural Perspective.* New York: Academic Press.

Royaume du Maroc. 1962. *Characteristiques de la population, d'après le recensement general de la population et de l'habitat de 1960.* Rabat: Ministère du Plan, Direction de la Statistique.

———. 1984. *Characteristiques socio-economiques de la population, d'après le recensement general de la population et de l'habitat de 1982: Niveau national, sondage 1/20.* Rabat: Ministère du Plan, Direction de la Statistique.

———. 1987. *La nuptialitie féminine au Maroc: Variations dans le temps et dans l'espace.* Rabat: Ministère du Plan, Direction de la Statistique, Centre d'études et de Recherches Demographiques.

———. Division du Plan et des Statistiques. N.d. *Résultats de l'enquête à objectifs multiples* (1961–1963). Rabat: Service Central des Statistiques.

Rugh, A. 1984. *Family in Contemporary Egypt.* Syracuse, N.Y.: Syracuse University Press.

Sabbah, F. 1984. *Woman in the Muslim Unconscious.* New York: Pergamon Press.

Said, E. W. 1978. *Orientalism.* New York: Random House.

Sbaï, N. 1987. *L'enfant endormi* (The sleeping child). Rabat: Edino.

Schneider, J. 1971. "Of Vigilance and Virgins." *Ethnology* 10: 1–24.

Seltzer, V. 1982. *Adolescent Social Development: Dynamic Functional Interaction.* Lexington, Mass.: Lexington Books, D.C. Heath.

Snarey, J. R. 1984. "Cross-Cultural Universality of Social-Moral Development: A Critical Review of Kohlbergian Research." *Psychological Bulletin* 97: 202–232.

Spratt, J. 1985. "A New Generation: Young Rural Women in a Modernizing Morocco." Paper presented at the annual meeting of the American Anthropological Association, Washington, D.C.

———. 1987. "Generalization and Selection in Moroccan Education: Conflicting Policy Objectives?" Paper presented at the twenty-first annual meeting of the Middle East Studies Association, Baltimore.

Suggs, R. C., and D. S. Marshall. 1971. "Anthropological Perspectives on Human Sexual Behavior." In D. S. Marshall and R. C. Suggs, eds., *Human Sexual Behavior: Variations in the Ethnographic Spectrum.* New York: Basic Books.

Sullivan, H. S. 1953. *The Interpersonal Theory of Psychiatry.* New York: Norton.

Tanner, J. M. 1960. *Human Growth.* New York: Pergamon Press.

Thompson, S. 1984. "Search for Tomorrow: On Feminism and the Reconstruction of the Teen Romance." In C. S. Vance, ed., *Pleasure and Danger: Exploring Female Sexuality.* Boston: Routledge and Kegan Paul.

United Nations. 1983. *World Statistics in Brief.* Department of International Economic and Social Affairs, Statistical Office, Statistical Papers, series 5, no. 8. New York: United Nations.

Wagner, D. A. 1978. "The Effects of Formal Schooling on Cognitive Style." *Journal of Social Psychology* 106: 145–151.

Wagner, D. A., and J. E. Spratt. 1987a. "Cognitive Consequences of Contrasting Pedagogies: The Effect of Quranic Preschooling in Morocco." *Child Development* 58: 1207–1209.

———. 1987b. "Reading Acquisition in Morocco." In C. Kagitcibasi, ed., *Education, Growth and Progress in Cross-Cultural Psychology.* Lisse: Swets and Zeitlinger, B. V.

Wagner, D. A., J. E. Spratt, and A. Ezzaki. In review. "Does Learning to Read in a

Second Language Always Put a Child at a Disadvantage? Some Counter-Evidence from Morocco." *Applied Psycholinguistics.*

Waterbury, John. 1972. *North for the Trade: The Life and Times of a Berber Merchant.* Berkeley: University of California Press.

Wehr, H. 1966. *A Dictionary of Modern Literary Arabic.* Ed. J. Milton Cohen. Ithaca, N.Y.: Cornell University Press.

Westermarck, E. 1914. *Marriage Ceremonies in Morocco.* London: Curzon Press.

———. 1926. *Ritual and Belief in Morocco.* Vol. 1. London: Macmillan.

———. 1931. *Wit and Wisdom in Morocco.* New York: Horace Liveright.

Whiting, B. B., and C. P. Edwards. 1988. *Children of Different Worlds: The Formation of Social Behavior.* Cambridge: Harvard University Press.

Whiting, J. W. M. 1941. *Becoming a Kwoma.* New Haven: Yale University Press.

Whiting, J. W. M., V. Burbank, and M. Ratner. 1986. "The Duration of Maidenhood across Cultures." In J. B. Lancaster and B. A. Hamburg, eds., *School-age Pregnancy and Parenthood.* New York: Academic Press.

Whiting, J. W. M., and I. Child. 1953. *Child Training and Personality.* New Haven, Conn.: Yale University Press.

Williams, J. 1968. *The Youth of Haouch El Harimi, a Lebanese Village.* Middle East Monograph Series. Cambridge, Mass.: Harvard University Press.

Worthman, C. 1987. "Interactions of Physical Maturation and Cultural Practice in Ontogeny: Kikuyu Adolesence." *Cultural Anthropology* 45: 13–23.

Youniss, J., and J. Smollar. 1985. *Adolescent Relations with Mothers, Fathers, and Friends.* Chicago: University of Chicago Press.

■ Index